ECONOMICS IN THE LONG VIEW

Volume 3 Applications and Cases, Part II

Other volumes of this work

Volume 1 Models and Methodology
Volume 2 Applications and Cases, Part I

ECONOMICS IN THE LONG VIEW

Essays in Honour of W. W. Rostow

Volume 3 APPLICATIONS AND CASES, PART II

Edited by
Charles P. Kindleberger
and
Guido di Tella

First published 1982 by
THE MACMILLAN PRESS LTD
London and Basingstoke
Companies and representatives throughout the world

ISBN 0 333 32832 9 (volume 3)

ISBN 0 333 32830 2 (volume 1)
ISBN 0 333 32831 0 (volume 2)
ISBN 0 333 33033 1 (the set)

Printed in Hong Kong

Contents

VOLUME 2 APPLICATIONS AND CASES, PART I

VOLUME 3 APPLICATIONS AND CASES, PART II

Note on the Editors

Charles P. Kindleberger taught at the Massachusetts Institute of Technology from 1948 to 1980, retiring as Ford International Professor of Economics Emeritus; Fellow at the Center for Advanced Study in Behavioral Sciences at Stanford, California. His latest book is *International Money*.

Guido di Tella, Associate Fellow, St Antony's College, Oxford; Professor of Economics, Catholic University, Buenos Aires. Author of, among other books, *Etapas del Desarrollo Económico Argentino* and *Argentina under Perón, 1973–76*.

List of the Contributors

T. C. Barker, Professor of Economic History, University of London.

Sir Alec Cairncross, formerly Master of St Peter's College, University of Oxford.

R. Cameron, William Rand Kenan University Professor of Economics, Emory University.

S. G. Checkland, Professor of Economic History, University of Glasgow; Visiting Fellow, Australian National University, Canberra.

R. Cortés Conde, Senior Research Fellow, Centre for Economic Research, and President of the Instituto Torcuato di Tella, Buenos Aires.

F. Crouzet, Professor of History, University of Paris–Sorbonne.

E. Dahmén, Professor of Economics and Economic and Social History, Stockholm School of Economics.

C. H. Feinstein, Professor of Economic and Social History, University of York.

R. Findlay, Ragnar Nurkse Professor of Economics, Columbia University, New York.

W. P. Glade, Director, Institute of Latin American Studies and Professor of Economics, University of Texas at Austin.

R. Hall (Lord Roberthall), formerly Economic Adviser to HM Government, United Kingdom.

R. M. Hartwell, Fellow of Nuffield College, University of Oxford.

D. Kendrick, Professor of Economics, University of Texas at Austin.

D. S. Landes, Robert Walton Goelet Professor of French History, Harvard University.

W. A. Lewis, James Madison Professor of Political Economy, Princeton University.

J. Marczewski, Honorary Professor, University of Paris I Panthéon-Sorbonne.

R. M. Marshall, Professor of Economics, University of Texas at Austin, and Secretary of Labour, US Government, 1976–81.
E. S. Mason, University Professor, Emeritus, Harvard University.
R. C. O. Matthews, Master of Clare College and Professor of Political Economy, University of Cambridge.
D. C. North, Professor of Economics, University of Washington.
J. C. Odling-Smee, Senior Economist, International Monetary Fund.
R. de Oliveira Campos, Ambassador of Brazil in the United Kingdom.
W. N. Parker, Professor of Economics, Yale University.
Sir Michael Postan, sometime Professor of Economic History, University of Cambridge.
C. W. Reynolds, Professor of Economics, Food Research Institute, Stanford University.
Sir Austin Robinson, Professor of Economics, Emeritus, University of Cambridge.
S. B. Saul, Vice-Chancellor, University of York.
P. Temin, Professor of Economics, Massachusetts Institute of Technology.
G. N. von Tunzelmann, Lecturer in Economic History, University of Cambridge and Fellow of St John's College, Cambridge.

Preface

This collection of essays in economic history is intended to honour W. W. Rostow for his outstanding contribution to this discipline over more than forty years. The editors are a former colleague in the Office of Strategic Services, the Department of State, the Massachusetts Institute of Technology and, for one term, at the University of Texas at Austin: Charles P. Kindleberger; and Guido di Tella, a former student of Rostow's at MIT who wrote his first book under his aegis.

Most leading economic historians have come across Rostow's imaginative ideas and opinions, and quite significantly have considered it necessary to come into the discussion, either to support, complement or contradict them. Few have been able to ignore them. As the chapters in the three volumes will show, the contributors from all over the world do not necessarily agree with Professor Rostow's views on economic history, or for that matter on anything else, as they pay tribute to his originality, significance and productivity which have stimulated enormously the historiography on business cycles, economic growth and long-term trends.

This compilation is divided, roughly and arbitrarily, into a first volume on Models and Methodology, and another two on Applications and Cases. A chronological order has been attempted in dividing Volume 2 (pre-First World War) and Volume 3 (post-First World War).

The editors were distressed to learn of Sir Michael Postan's death in December 1981 as the proofs of Volume 1 were being read; they feel a special debt of gratitude to him for his contribution of an appreciation of Rostow's intellectual background and personal development, as well as an evaluation of his main and most important production as an economic historian. From this essay we get a clear picture of Rostow the man and of Rostow the economic historian and social scientist: a personal and indeed welcome introduction to this *Festschrift*, based on information supplied by Dean Elspeth Rostow.

The next three chapters in Volume 1 are by D. C. North,

R. Cameron and S. G. Checkland. They point out the need for economic historians to make use of a broader set of theoretical tools beyond those provided by neo-classical economics. D. C. North stresses the significance of current research in demography, ideology, technological and institutional change, and the way it is transforming economic history, shifting it away from the biases built in the previously narrower approach. This new approach carries over from cliometrics the quantitative method and the rigorous use and testing of hypothesis: by broadening the framework it makes economic history more congenial to the traditional historian, and offers the potential of explaining a vast range of historical observations that could not be accounted for within the compass of neo-classical theory.

In the same vein R. Cameron emphasises the need to expand the scope of our analysis if we are to understand the inter-relationship of population, resources and technology in the process of economic growth, stressing the fact that the economy is conditioned by social institutions, embodying values and attitudes. In the past institutional innovation has been at least as responsible as technological change for the economic transformation of Europe, and can still – hopefully – face the challenges posed by the present demographic upsurge in the world and by the energy shortage.

S. G. Checkland's essay is an attempt to analyse the role of the state in the long-term theory of growth, a subject that brings him to delve in the intimate but not necessarily direct relationship between the state and the stage of growth attained. Three different levels of analysis are explored: universalism based upon the nation-state, an insistence on the degree of national uniqueness, and finally a view rising above the nation-states to some kind of structure of world interaction. If brought together in a new synthesis these can throw light on the intricate problem of the role of the state in the process of growth.

While economic historians may benefit from an extended approach, P. Temin underlines the changes that have taken place within the realm of economic analysis. The economic depression in the first place, the post-World War expansion in the second instance and, more recently, the worldwide inflationary process (accounting for the revival of the more orthodox monetary theories) have had a tremendous bearing on economic theory. While this is generally acknowledged, a different strand is pointed out, of a less orthodox flavour, stemming from some of Keynes's psychological insights and from the behaviourist assumptions of Duesenberry and Simon which throw light on some peculiar but relevant aspects of human conduct. The *homo economicus*, free of restrictions, may not, after all, be the best and most relevant paradigm.

R. M. Hartwell, W. A. Lewis, E. S. Mason and R. de Oliveira Campos move on to the problem that has concerned many economic historians, W. W. Rostow in particular, i.e. the nature, constraints and characteristics of the long-term process of growth. R. M. Hartwell discusses parallelism and divergence in 'historical perspective', by which he means the very long run. For some economic historians the long run is the twenty years of the Kuznets cycle, for others the fifty years of the Kondratieff cycle. Hartwell seeks to push beyond these limits to explore the rise, fall, and occasional failures to move of civilisation, which give the result progress and dissimilarity.

W. A. Lewis in turn analyses the major constraints to growth in mature economies, questioning some of the standard answers (the low savings ratio, the inelasticities in the supply of labour, the lack of natural resources or the scarcity of foreign exchange, entrepreneurship and technology) forcefully arguing that the ultimate constraint is the ability of the institutional system to absorb change in an orderly fashion.

Most fittingly, E. S. Mason and R. de Oliveira Campos deal with the stages approach. Mason stresses the insights into the process of growth contributed by Rostow, both in his *Stages of Economic Growth* and in *The World Economy*, but questions whether the historical examples in the latter provide enough evidence to support the sharp demarcations suggested in the first book, and reveals a more continuous, persistent and cumulative process of growth than the stages theory would lead us to believe.

R. de Oliveira Campos's essay appraises the take-off approach from the point of view of the developing countries, for which purpose he deems it necessary to study the interaction between economics and politics. Rapid growth increases social mobilisation, increasing political demands, thus putting strains on the political system. Instead of being rectilinear, the process appears as an adventure threatened by deadlocks. This author's views are a remarkable example of the new wave of scepticism about growth promoting in a straightforward manner democracy and political stability, at least during the course of the crucial transformation from a developing to a fully developed society.

The chapter by Sir Austin Robinson reflects in turn the increasing scepticism regarding the benefits of rapid industrialisation programmes for new countries, while it puts forward the alternative of an agriculture-led strategy. This alternative is not problem-free, mainly because of the danger of accumulating food surpluses, the risk of benefits failing to filter down and a possible increase in the rate of population growth. Such a strategy, being the more decentralised, is prone to greater administrative problems than the more centralised industrial alternative. Still, in Robinson's view it is an appealing path that many new countries may find worth while exploring.

The first volume is closed by chapters by R. Findlay, C. W. Reynolds, and Guido di Tella, all former students of Rostow. They deal with the connection between trade, rents and growth. Findlay's analysis of the trade – growth nexus in the formative period of the Industrial Revolution points out that the causal arrow must run from growth – in the form of technological change in the manufacturing sector – to trade, rather than the other way round assumed by most of the literature on the subject. But even if the 'manna from heaven' nature of technological progress has to be supplemented, the least that can be said is that trade and growth are inextricably intertwined during the first take-off process known to the world.

Reynolds recalls the Prebisch–Singer terms of trade argument of the 1950s, and remarks the drastic change brought about by the post-1973 rises in the price of oil which resulted in an equally drastic change in the pattern and allocation of the world's economic rent. An attempt is made to measure not only the natural resources-based rent but the other two as well, i.e. the one emerging from market imperfections, source of 'protection' rents, and the one stemming from entrepreneurship, source of the so-called 'innovation' rent. Di Tella ends the first volume with an analysis of the impact of the discovery of new resources on the expansion of the world economy, particularly in the nineteenth century. He distinguishes two different kinds of economic frontier expansions, a less dynamic, equilibrium version, and a more dynamic, more equilibrium version, allegedly more relevant to the cases in question. As in the previous contributions, these resources-based rents are put into a more ample perspective, where accumulation and growth are consequences of the strive for non-normal profits by Schumpeterian-styled entrepreneurs.

The second volume deals mainly with specific cases and applications, embracing several centuries and diverse countries in different continents, mostly ordered in a chronological sequence up to the First World War. The volume is relevantly opened by W. N. Parker's views on the European process of development from the standpoint of what he calls a millennial perspective. He selects three different, stylised relationships: the traditional, near subsistence, Malthusian society; the commercial, trade-oriented, expansive Smithian society, free from the limits imposed by the national market on the division of labour; and the capitalist, Schumpeterian society, engaged in a process of creative destruction. The three dominate four particular stages, but are present throughout, their interaction throwing light on the process of growth.

W. P. Glade digs into the roots of the industrialisation process in Latin America, going back to colonial times. Despite the emphasis placed on trade, there is no doubt that the bulk of the goods consumed in the American colonies were produced on the west of the Atlantic. He traces the spread and original organisation of colonial industry, analysing the various reasons which impeded their becoming the springboard to nineteenth-century industrialisation, i.e. the effective insulation from competition and foreign technical knowledge, an insulation that took them further and further away from the European type of evolution.

F. Crouzet's essay explores some aspects of the triangular relationship between the United States, Britain and France between 1793 and 1814, pointing out how, as a consequence of the European War, the United States, a relatively small and new country – by European standards – found itself propelled as a sea-trading power to be reckoned with. This new role was reversed after 1814 when the United States turned away from high-sea ventures and towards 'internal improvements', something not too different from what took place in some European cases: France, Prussia and Belgium. Its power was still to be reckoned with, but its international role receded at least until the middle of the century.

D. S. Landes's detailed account of the French liberation loan of 1871 illuminates the financial conditions prevailing in Europe at the time, showing the limitations that even triumphant powers have in exacting compensation from the vanquished, an experience repeated to some extent the other way round after the First World War. It also shows how the business and financial sectors of both countries vied to take advantage of the loan that had to be issued, with a substantially independent attitude from their respective governments.

S. B. Saul explores in his chapter the peculiarities of a group of small European countries in the nineteenth century. Some special traits are found among such apparently diverse countries as Belgium, Denmark, the Netherlands, Norway, Sweden and Switzerland. They exhibited a greater homogeneity which allowed them to make more easily the necessary social adjustments to take advantage of the new technologies and the changing patterns of trade. Fewer interests had to be reconciled and a more rational economic policy resulted out of this. They were forced, because of their small home markets, to specialise and explore the foreign ones, where they did not find much resistance because of their small significance. These countries had indeed many limitations which are the ones usually pointed out, but in being small they had as well many advantages: as Saul says, 'the importance of being unimportant'.

R. Cortés Conde's analysis of Italian migration from 1880 to 1913 notes the economic determinants of this very intense process and finds a high correlation between the higher level of income in the new American countries, north and south, the result of their higher productivity. The lagged total and average level of remittances are taken as an effective measure of the immigrant's capacity to earn, save and remit. Economic reasons were not the only ones behind these human waves, but they certainly played a crucial and quantifiable role.

T. C. Barker deals with a subject quite in line with Rostow's chief preoccupations, i.e. the role of the new methods of transportation during the nineteenth and early twentieth centuries. While many historians have written extensively about railways, surprisingly few have done so on the spread of motor vehicles, arguably a process which has had an even greater impact not only in transportation, but also in the way of living. The chapter by Barker fills this void, focusing especially on the situation attained before the First World War, more significant than at times is conceded.

The chapter by C. H. Feinstein, R. C. O. Matthews and J. C. Odling-Smee, which closes the second volume, deals with a subject already studied by Rostow in *The British Economy in the Nineteenth Century*. The authors make a new and up-to-date appraisal of the available figures for the 1873–1914 period, both in global and in sectoral terms, which tend to indicate that the alleged retardation of the British economy did not start around 1873, but that it took place only after 1899. An analysis of the productivities of the various factors and sectors is made, where labour and capital productivity can be seen to move in such a way as not to affect total factor productivity, while agriculture and mining can be seen as the main factors influencing the fall in total productivity, joined by manufacturing after 1899.

G. N. von Tunzelmann opens the third volume, which deals with applications and cases for the post-First World War period, with an analysis of the structural change and the role of leading sectors in British manufacturing from 1907 to 1968, questioning the reasons given for the sluggishness of the British inter-war performance, attributed by Rostow to the delay to move from steel, chemicals, and electricity to the typical mass consumption industries: automobiles, plastics, electronics and aeronautics. Von Tunzelmann concludes that the 'shift effect' of resource allocation among sectors was much less important in explaining productivity growth than the internal effect within sectors. Moreover the belief that a structural shift towards the new industries explains the coexistence of high, economy-wide growth rates and high unemployment in the 1930s does not seem to be substantiated.

E. Dahmén's analysis of Sweden's recent industrial development crisis endeavours to merge the conventional macro approach with historical research, utilising a conceptual frame of reference of a neo-Schumpeterian and Austrian type. A sketch of the general economic developments is made, including an account of what most analysts made of macromodelling with broad aggregates, and what this leads them to believe. This kind of analysis disguised some of the major changes that took place particularly in the mid-1960s, a crucial break in the development process, something which would have been detected through a more detailed and disaggregated analysis and a more adequate and broader frame of reference.

D. Kendrick studies the shift in emphasis which is occurring in the macroeconomic paradigm in the US: a shift from the demand to the supply side. This shift is causing a change from aggregative economics, to analysis of the problems in certain sectors and certain regions. This shift calls for a new organisation of the data for the US economy as the ones presently available are organised in aggregative terms for similarly organised econometric models. Insufficient attention is paid to sectors, to the location of economic activity, and to the relationships between economic data. The main purpose of the paper is to explore a new method of organising US economic data, the so-called 'relational database approach'.

R. M. Marshall's concerns refer to the slowing down in productivity growth already detected in the US economy during the 1970s. While recent studies have attempted to find the reasons for this evolution – the shift towards a service economy, the demographic changes in the labour force, the slower growth of investment, the sharp rise in energy prices, the increase in government regulations, and the reduced spending on research – much remains unexplained. One reason is that conventional quantitative techniques fail to capture important behavioural and dynamic forces underlying the productivity process, i.e. individual and national values, relations between workers and management, systems within which workers and enterprises function, and institutional and governmental behaviour. An understanding of these factors must be integrated with traditional resource availability analysis to explain changes in productivity, a statement quite in line with some of the statements made in the first chapters of Volume 1.

We have made one exception in our chronological ordering with Charles P. Kindleberger's contribution, since his subject is very much akin to the one studied by Sir Alec Cairncross. Kindleberger's paper comparing the resumption of gold payments in Britain in 1819 with the restoration of the pound to par in 1925 follows in his tradition of comparative economic history, and is addressed especially to Professor Rostow's expressed view that monetary questions, and the level of sophistication in dealing with them, were less significant before the First World War than after it.

The last three contributions by Sir Alec Cairncross, Lord Roberthall and J. Marczewski deal with shorter-term problems in relatively recent times. Cairncross analyses the traumatic devaluation of sterling in 1949, indeed a turning-point in British economic policy. A detailed narrative of events is made, so as to help the understanding of the conditions and expectations prevailing at the time. This squarely leads to the issue of whether the pressures that led to devaluation were ephemeral, reversible and resistible, or how far they were enduring and likely to be cumulative. An appraisal of the effects of devaluation is obscured by the outbreak of the Korean war, which set the world economy out of balance. However, the wisdom of the decision has to be measured not just in terms of its effectiveness, but also in terms of its appropriateness given the circumstances, and how correctly these were appreciated.

In his chapter Lord Roberthall analyses the British economic performance since the Second World War. The high hopes of overcoming the depression and unemployment in the pre-war years were reasonably successful until the early 1970s, despite an increasing and ominous pressure on the price level. Since 1973, developments in the world and in the UK have been quite different: the outside world has been less benign and the ability of the British economy to adapt has indeed been diminished, while the power and the willingness of the trades unions to exercise it has augmented. The consequences have been felt in increases in the rate of inflation and in the rate of unemployment, reaching figures comparable to all but the worst years of the Depression.

J. Marczewski's paper closes Volume 3, making a comparative analysis of stagflation in France and Germany over the last decade: 1971–9. The analysis is made in quantitative terms starting with the inflationary gap in total resources, followed by that of the structure and evolution of the inflationary gap of costs in France and Germany, which shows a striking similarity. Labour costs, income from property and entrepreneurship, taxes on production (less subsidies), and imports are assessed as contributing to the inflationary gap in costs. A similar analysis is made of the inflationary gap on expenditures, household's consumption and capital formation, enterprises' capital formation, public expenditures and exports. These analyses allow an evaluation of the causes which lie behind the stagflation of these countries and of the world at large.

Volume 3 ends with a bibliography of W. W. Rostow's major works, which unfortunately had to leave aside the long list of articles and addresses, some of them extracurricular, extremely indicative of the evolution of Rostow's thinking.

The editors would like to thank the contributors for their warm response and for their patience in face of the insistence in meeting deadlines. They would also like to thank Lois Nivens for her help in the compilation of the bibliography, and Celia Szusterman for her help in the editing of the three volumes.

1981

C. P. K.
G. di T.

1 Structural Change and Leading Sectors in British Manufacturing, 1907–68

G. N. VON TUNZELMANN

I believe we shall increasingly interpret a significant element in the interwar sluggishness of Western Europe as due to the process of disengagement from the old leading sectors of the pre-1914 and wartime years and to the rather slow preparation for the age of high mass-consumption which, in the 1950s, at last fully seized Western Europe, as the lessons of income analysis were learned and the old men of steel and electricity and heavy chemicals were superseded by the bright young men of automobiles and plastics, electronics, and aeronautics. (*The Stages of Economic Growth*)[1]

Professor Rostow's concept of 'leading sectors' has attracted most favourable notice in the case of the United Kingdom in applications to the classical Industrial Revolution period, that is, Rostow's 'take-off'. Nevertheless it is obvious from repeated utterances throughout his major works on economic growth (*The Stages of Economic Growth* and *The World Economy: History and Prospect* being the two most extensively considered here) that the concept is intended to apply at each stage of modern economic growth, and that technical change within industries and structural transformations among various industries constitute the essence of the 'analytical bone-structure'. It is, however, the case that his work fits readily (and often explicitly) into a substantial corpus of work by economic historians and economists both for Western Europe as a whole (pioneered by Schumpeter and Svennilson[2]) and for Britain in particular. On the latter score, the rise of the so-called 'new industries' in the interwar years (especially) has been a popular theme since the time itself. Its popularity was accentuated in the 1960s through an extensive body of writings by H. W. Richardson and D. H. Aldcroft.[3]

As makes intuitive sense, the study of twentieth-century growth both by Rostow and by Richardson and Aldcroft comprehends demand as well as supply elements – in Rostow's case, suggested by the reference to the 'lessons of income analysis' in the opening quotation here and of course by the whole terminology of an 'age of high mass-consumption'. In my view the fusing of demand and supply sides by British writers, although carried out in the best interests of depicting economic growth and history 'in the round', has had the undesirable effect of confusing the nature of the argument(s); for example, in delineating the hypotheses to be tested and more simply in defining what exactly were the 'new industries'. In this critique I shall be concentrating on the supply side, trusting that the neglect of a richer dimension will be partially offset by a sharper focus on the particular aspects studied. However, problems of simultaneity remain, so that demand-side influences on the variables measured are included.

It has already been noted that at various points Professor Rostow alludes to both intra-sectoral technical change and inter-sectoral structural shifts. For their part, Aldcroft and Richardson originally stressed both the shifts in resource allocation towards new industries and what they considered to be a high rate of technical improvement within the new industries. Subsequent 'arithmetic' by J. A. Dowie (1968) severely mauled the latter of these hypotheses. In the wake of Dowie's article they wrote:

> Thus the improvement in the residual [i.e. total factor productivity] in the interwar years was in large part due to shifts in resource allocation within the industrial sector and a fairly rapid rate of technical improvement which affected both old and new industries alike. (Aldcroft and Richardson, 1969, p. 22).

Despite Dowie's attack on the notion of innovations clustering predominantly in the new industries and the apparent acceptance of the criticism by Aldcroft and Richardson themselves, a recent and fairly critical summary of the argument by B. W. E. Alford (1972, p. 14) concluded that the Aldcroft–Richardson view 'has almost developed into a new orthodoxy'.

The only formal attempt that I am aware of to break down the argument further in fact preceded Aldcroft and Richardson – Salter (1966) referred to 'shifts in resource allocation within the industrial sector' as the 'shift effect' and rates of technical improvement within all industries as the 'intensity effect', and those terms will be borrowed here. Especially as Salter's book, *Productivity and Technical Change*, is much better known for its contribution to the theory of the economics of technological change than to British economic history, it is worth considering Salter's findings in a little more detail. Salter began by pointing out (see especially his Appendix A3, pp. 184–5) that the appropriate way to divide movements in output per head into shift and internal components was multiplicatively, not additively. Let O_{it} equal output in the ith industry in year t, E_{it} likewise be employment and P_{it} ($= O_{it}/E_{it}$) output per head in that industry at year t. Then overall productivity change can be decomposed as:

$$\frac{\sum_i P_{it}}{\sum_i P_{iO}} = \frac{\sum_i P_{it}E_{it}}{\sum_i P_{it}E_{iO}} \cdot \frac{\sum_i E_{iO}}{\sum_i E_{it}} \cdot \frac{\sum_i P_{it}E_{iO}}{\sum_i P_{iO}E_{iO}}$$

(a) (b) (c)

In this decomposition, (a) and (b) together measure the increase in output, subject to the restrictions that output per head in each industry does not change and that the total labour force stays constant – in other words, the 'shift' effect. Component (c) is a base-weighted index of output per head, subject to the restriction that employment in each industry does not change, that is, it measures the 'intensity' effect.

Two elaborative points are given special attention by Salter. The first is that output has to be valued at some set of prices that still need to be defined (the actual set chosen can be selected independently of the decomposition above) – if instead current prices are utilised in an inflationary world virtually everything is bound to accrue to the 'intensity' effect through the consequences of $M3$ (or whatever). Secondly, the overall productivity growth can equally well be decomposed using productivity rather than employment for the base weighting:

$$\frac{\sum_i P_{it}}{\sum_i P_{iO}} = \frac{\sum_i P_{iO} E_{it}}{\sum_i P_{iO} E_{iO}} \cdot \frac{\sum_i E_{iO}}{\sum_i E_{it}} \cdot \frac{\sum_i P_{it} E_{it}}{\sum_i P_{iO} E_{it}}$$

The first two components on the right-hand side are now a base-weighted 'shift' effect and the last one a current-weighted 'internal' effect.[4]

On the basis of his sample of industries (28 selected industries), Salter showed that decisions as to these weightings substantially affected the result. The results he published set year O at 1924 and year t at 1948 for employment weightings of O (that is 1924, corresponding to the first decomposition above), of t (that is 1948, corresponding to the second decomposition), and of an intermediate weighting (1935) they were as shown in Table 1.1. Thus using the first formulation of the problem, the shift and internal effects were about equal in their contribution to overall growth in labour productivity; using the second, the internal effect was over $2\frac{1}{2}$ times as powerful as the shift one.

Salter argued that there was little to choose between the weighting schemes; theoretically they were of equal merit. If one is going to argue a case against (or for) a certain cohort of entrepreneurs for their failure (or success) in shifting into new lines of activity it may seem fairest to them to judge them in terms of the

TABLE 1.1 *Salter's break-down between 'internal' and 'shift' effects*

Employment weights		*1924*	*1948*
1924	Internal	100	136
	Shift	100	133
	Total	100	181
1935	Internal	100	150
	Shift	100	121
	Total	100	181
1948	Internal	100	152
	Shift	100	119
	Total	100	181

SOURCE W.E.G. Salter, *Productivity and Technical Change*, 2nd edn (Cambridge University Press, 1966) pp. 150–1.

relative productivities of alternatives they were facing at the time, that is in terms of the second formulation. On the other hand, much of the new industry debate, for the late nineteenth century as much as for the twentieth, has been conducted as if entrepreneurs were blessed with perfect foresight about *future* relative productivities – in which case the former decomposition is appropriate.

It also needs mentioning that the analysis is conducted on *labour* productivities, whereas the Aldcroft–Richardson quote above clearly relates to total factor productivities. Dowie (1968) has comparisons of the two for the industrial divisions he employs. The data are at present hopelessly inadequate to pursue this point much farther in the present paper.

Rostow has always emphasised that leading sectors derive their significance from their backward, forward, and lateral linkages to the rest of the economy. Thus he has been concerned to draw out the repercussions of their growth on a wide range of supporting (and to a large extent, dependent) industries. Appendix C of *The World Economy*, for instance, is a rough computation of the size of the United States 'motor vehicle sectoral complex' for the early 1970s. (Rostow, 1978, pp. 670–5). For Britain, and especially interwar Britain, authors like Richardson and Aldcroft have accepted that the new sectors in themselves were still a fairly small portion of total output, but their significance was magnified partly by their input–output links with so many other industries (for example, because some new industries were considered to be crucial capital-goods industries) and partly by their links with one another. Richardson emphasised the deadweight of overcommitment to nineteenth-century export staples (such as textiles, steel, coal, and shipbuilding) hindering the expansion of the economy in the early years of the present century. The very inter-relationship between the staples (coal being used in steel-making, steel in shipbuilding, and so forth) made recovery all the more difficult and helped obstruct new activities. A wholly new 'development block' (to use a phrase originally devised by E. Dahmén [1955], subsequently borrowed by Richardson), less dependent on those decaying staples and their problems of over-manning and obsolete plant and equipment was ideally required. Thus he was led to emphasise the interdependence of the new industries (for example, 'New industries tend to have closer input–output connections with each other than with other industries in the economy' (Richardson, 1967, p. 95 – see also Rostow (1978, p. 209)).

The final characteristic often asserted for new industries that will be examined in this paper is their greater impact on output than on employment. Again in referring to the interwar period, Rostow (1978, pp. 208–9) states that,

> The three great new leading-sector complexes which had emerged before the First World War continued to move forward in the erratic, distorted environment of the interwar years: the internal combustion engine, electricity, and chemicals. They supplied elements of growth and development to the most advanced part of the world economy; but, except in the United States of the 1920s, they could not by themselves bring about an environment of relatively full employment in any of the major economies.

However a few pages later he qualifies the assumptions on which these statements partially rest, in noting that,

> Although electricity production itself is (like oil refining) a highly capital-intensive industry, the whole sectoral complex, including the building of power stations and lines, generators, radios, vacuum cleaners, refrigerators, irons, and other electric-powered household gadgetry of high mass-consumption, created substantial increases in employment. (ibid., p. 214)

This qualification foreshadows my own discussion of the point below. The main thrust of the argument is preserved in the view of Richardson and Aldcroft for the UK that, whilst the new industries could take much of the credit for a satisfactory growth of manufacturing output, they did less to assist by way of expanding employment opportunities, since their technology was highly labour-saving. Hence, in part, the coexistence of high unemployment and the upsurge of these new industries in the 1930s.

I

The information necessary for a more extended test of the sources of productivity change in industry has come from re-processing the major Censuses of Production from 1907 to 1968. The ultimate objective is to obtain estimates of net output, employment, and labour productivity, all broken down by standard region at as disaggregated a level of industry as possible. At the time of writing, the data are ready on an industrial base back to 1907 and on a regional plus industrial base from 1948 to 1968. Since 1970 the collection of industrial statistics has been restructured and it will not be possible to link my regional results with those published for the 1970s.

The problem all researchers have encountered in using the Censuses of Production is that the classification of regions changes frequently (on every occasion studied here up to 1948, then again between 1958 and 1963), while the industrial classification is always changing. The former problem does not greatly affect us in this paper (except for the Northern/Southern Ireland difficulty for 1907), but the latter is a considerable obstacle. The Business Statistics Office's recent *Historical Record of the Census of Production 1907 to 1970* (1978, p. x) reckons that the scope of only about twenty industries out of the 150-odd it examines remained 'virtually unchanged'.

> More usually the definition of an industry changed, and the difference compared with 1968 tended to be greater the earlier the census was held. Some industries increased in importance over the years, in some cases starting as specialist sub-divisions within industries in earlier censuses and later appearing as separately distinguished industries for which a full range of industrial statistical data was published, such as Soft drinks, Printing ink, Aluminium and aluminium alloys, and Refrigeration machinery industries. Conversely, some industries important in the earlier censuses declined in importance and were relegated to sub-industry status such as Wallpaper, Matches, and Pens, pencils and artist's materials industries. Many activities, once regarded as being within the scope of the census of production, were subsequently transferred to the distribution or service sectors, and there are also instances of the reverse happening (ibid.).

On the (periodically-revised) Standard Industrial Classification (SIC) industry is classified first by order (loosely speaking, the two-digit level), and beyond that by Minimum List Heading (MLH; the three-digit level). Sub-industries frequently were moved from order to order or MLH to MLH (for example ice cream began in the bread and biscuit industry before being transferred to milk and milk products). Not the least contribution of the *Historical Record* (ibid., pp. 80–102) are general footnotes covering twenty-three large and closely-written pages describing changes that have occurred among and within industrial classifications. The compilers (H. Gracie and I. Duncan) have made extensive efforts to realign categories in order to preserve some sort of continuity – and their account of their procedures makes clear that this can only be achieved by considerable guesswork. Even so, the extensive footnoting just mentioned largely comprises classificatory changes that the compilers were *not* able to take into account.

My own compilations began before (and were ignorant of) the appearance of the *Historical Record*, but do not simply duplicate it, as the classificatory connections through time are made in a quite different way. The original census forms are not available for public inspection and unlikely ever to be so unless the law is changed. My procedure began with the observation that in every major census of production there are figures, broken down by region, etc., – not only for the year in question but for the preceding major census. Since in nearly every case (1958–64 is the main exception) these figures in the later census differ substantially from those in the earlier one, my assumption is that they represent a reclassification of the earlier year's data to the later year's system. Roughly speaking, on this basis it was possible to extrapolate backwards from 1968 to each preceding census in turn. As the quotation given above from the *Historical Record* would imply, the probability is that the divergence between my extrapolations and actuality would be greatest for 1907, and this must be borne in mind in what follows. However in the overwhelming majority of cases the results produced by this procedure look sensible. To take an extreme example, figures for employment in the milk and milk products industry (MLH 215) obtained by my procedure can be compared with those published in the *Historical Record* as in Table 1.2.

TABLE 1.2 *Employment in milk and milk products, 1930–68, in thousands*

	1930	*1935*	*1948*	*1951*	*1954*	*1958*	*1963*	*1968*
Historical record	9.6	20.6	52.8	63.5	23.6	30.2	27.1	70.6
Present figures	26.5	40.5	52.8	63.5	64.1	82.1	73.7	70.6

SOURCES: Business Statistics Office, *Historical Record of the Census of Production 1907 to 1970* (London: HMSO, 1978) p. 5; own calculations.

The major disparities in this example arise from the presence or absence of the heat treatment of milk; in most industries the differences are minor.

My data have been prepared only for manufacturing industry so far. This limitation makes the tests of the role of leading sectors, for example, particularly inadequate, with electricity supply being overlooked. The *quid pro quo* of declining sectors like coal mining is also misrepresented. Whether the results for manufacturing alone can be extended to non-manufacturing industry remains to be seen. The level of disaggregation achieved depended on the information available: I took as my guide the derivation of reasonable *regional* data for the postwar (that is 1948–68) period. The 1968 SIC system of 17 industrial 'orders' was preserved throughout, but at the more disaggregated MLH level it would not have been possible to sustain the 1968 format without wild extrapolation. Sub-aggregations therefore had to be undertaken, resulting in a classification more like the 1958 SIC pattern (furthermore, the level of breakdown required of the 1968 system, for example in electronics, was of little relevance for earlier years in many of the cases). I ended up with 103 industries for the years 1948–68; shrinking slightly to 100 for the interwar period and 96 for 1907. The least satisfactory aspect was that in the engineering industries particularly, large residual categories like 'general mechanical engineering' remained. Over shorter periods of time than 1907–68 it would, of course, be possible to do something about this shortcoming.

The final data problem turns out to be more serious, and the solutions offered so far much rougher. This concerns price deflators. As Salter pointed out, price comparisons are the very essence of productivity assessments through time. Other things being equal (that is the demand side and the general price level), technological change will lower costs and prices and hence be understated by the changes of net output relative to employment actually observed. Unlike Salter, I have made no attempt in this paper to redress the balance for individual industries. Any conclusions about relative rates of technical change, etc., therefore must be taken with a grain of salt. For the 'shift' versus 'internal' effect comparisons, I have simply deflated by a general price index. A windfall gain of relative price for one particular industry (occurring, it can be supposed, for demand-side reasons) is here treated as part of the productivity gain of that industry. Since newer industries are the most likely beneficiaries of such windfalls, their contribution is to that degree overstated.

It quickly became apparent that it was insufficient to plug in any readily-available price index for output – weird results emerged for the Korean War period, etc. Instead separate deflators had to be developed for inputs and outputs. For 'gross output', that is including intermediate payments, I used the Board of Trade index for wholesale prices for output of manufactured products for the postwar period, adjusted for prices in the food-processing industries before 1954 (the *Historical Record* 1978, Appendix II, Table (i)) advises using this index; the data are more accurately specified in Mitchell and Jones (1971, pp. 188–9). The link back from 1948 to 1935 was made using an implicit deflator derived from the work of Brown (1954) in comparing the results of the censuses of those two years. For the interwar period I have compared changes in gross output with changes in the volume of production (available for each industry and sub-industry in the 1935 Census), and aggregated. For 1907 the deflator for GDP developed by Feinstein (1972), adjusted for Northern/Southern Ireland, etc., was used. For intermediate inputs I developed separate series for food, fuel, textiles, and machinery, etc. (accorded weights of 15, 10, 20, and 55 respectively). The Board of Trade indices of industrial materials prices (Mitchell and Deane, 1971, pp. 476–7, and Mitchell and Jones, 1971, pp. 188–9) and the censuses of production themselves were again the chief sources. The price index for net output then emerged implicitly from the separate deflations for gross output and for purchased inputs.[5]

Perverse results still occurred. For the period 1924–30, gross output prices fell, but input prices fell much faster (especially of course in 1929–30; see Rostow (1978, p. 206)), with the result that the implicit price index for net output rose markedly between 1924 and 1930. The outcome is a sharp decline in aggregate productivity between 1924 and 1930 (see the second column of Table 1.3), and in general the ensuing calculations that rely on 1930 net output prices in some way are not to be taken too seriously. In similar vein, though less dramatically, the years of the early 1950s, in the aftermath of the Korean War boom, still behave chaotically.

With these reservations in mind, we may turn first to Table 1.3. The change in aggregate productivity in the second column is divided into 'shift' and 'internal' components using either base-weighted employment (that is, the first formulation above – perfect foresight of future relative productivities) in the third and fourth columns, or base-weighted productivity (that is, the second

TABLE 1.3 *Productivity change broken down by 'shift' and 'internal' components, between censal years, 1907/68 (MLH level of disaggregation)*

	Percentage change in aggregate employment	*Percentage change in aggregate productivity*	*'Shift' component base-weight employment*	*'Internal' component base-weight employment*	*'Shift' component base-weight productivity*	*'Internal' component base-weight productivity*
1907/24	9.8	18.5	3.7	14.5	2.4	15.9
1907/30	10.2	0	2.8	−2.4	2.7	−2.3
1907/35	12.8	40.0	6.6	32.0	3.6	35.8
1907/48	40.3	36.6	4.9	30.2	7.8	26.7
1907/51	50.7	84.6	7.4	72.4	7.2	72.7
1907/54	55.2	108.8	10.9	89.0	6.3	97.0
1907/58	57.3	97.3	15.0	72.3	8.3	82.9
1907/63	60.2	127.6	17.6	94.2	10.2	107.2
1907/68	57.7	182.5	16.6	143.1	9.7	158.3
1924/30	0.4	−14.5	2.7	−16.5	1.3	−15.4
1924/35	2.8	18.4	2.9	15.3	2.8	15.5
1024/48	27.8	16.2	2.8	13.1	5.5	10.2
1924/51	37.3	55.0	4.0	49.2	5.4	47.3
1924/54	41.4	75.2	6.4	65.0	5.7	66.0
1924/58	43.3	67.3	10.1	52.2	8.1	55.0
1924/63	46.0	92.9	12.0	72.4	9.7	76.0
1924/68	43.6	139.0	11.6	114.4	9.2	119.0
1930/35	2.4	30.4	1.0	29.2	0.6	29.7
1930/48	27.3	32.9	2.3	29.9	5.8	19.3
1930/51	36.8	65.2	3.6	59.2	5.5	56.3
1930/54	40.8	85.9	5.3	76.3	6.3	74.6
1930/58	42.8	86.4	8.6	71.7	9.4	70.4
1930/63	45.4	115.0	10.2	94.8	11.4	92.7
1930/68	43.1	164.0	10.0	139.7	11.1	137.3
1935/48	24.3	1.0	1.7	−0.7	5.3	−4.1
1935/51	33.6	27.7	2.5	24.3	5.0	21.4
1935/54	37.5	43.8	4.1	37.9	5.4	36.2
1935/58	39.4	42.7	7.2	32.9	8.4	31.4
1935/63	42.0	64.4	8.9	50.7	10.4	48.8
1935/68	39.7	102.4	8.6	86.0	9.8	83.9
1948/51	7.5	27.3	0	27.5	−0.3	27.8
1948/54	10.6	44.0	0.5	43.5	−1.8	46.8
1948/58	12.2	41.5	2.3	38.4	0.8	40.6
1948/63	14.2	63.0	4.2	56.6	1.9	60.2
1948/68	12.4	100.8	4.2	92.9	1.4	98.1
1951/54	3.0	14.0	0.4	13.6	−0.2	14.3
1951/58	4.4	2.8	2.5	0.4	1.1	1.7
1951/63	6.3	18.7	4.2	13.9	2.4	16.0
1951/68	4.6	48.5	4.1	42.7	2.0	45.5

TABLE 1.3 *Continued*

	Percentage change in aggregate employ-ment	Percentage change in aggregate pro-ductivity	'Shift' component base-weight employ-ment	'Internal' component base-weight employ-ment	'Shift' component base-weight pro-ductivity	'Internal' component base-weight pro-ductivity
1954/58	1.4	−8.5	2.1	−10.4	1.8	−10.2
1954/63	3.2	5.6	3.9	1.6	3.4	2.1
1954/68	1.6	31.7	3.7	26.9	3.2	27.6
1958/63	1.8	15.3	1.9	13.1	0.9	14.3
1958/68	0.2	42.6	1.8	40.1	1.8	40.1
1963/68	−1.6	23.3	0.1	23.2	0.1	23.2

NOTE For sources and methods, see text.

formulation) in the fifth and sixth columns. It will be recalled that these two pairs of columns should multiply out to give the second column, aggregate productivity change (in fact there are slight discrepancies in some cases, arising out of rounding of the original data).

The first observation to be made is that by and large it makes little difference whether employment or productivity is base-weighted, in sharp contrast to the conflicting results Salter obtained, as quoted above. It is, however, true that pairs of years involving 1948 (Salter's terminal year) do provide some of the biggest disparities in the Table – for his own pair (1924/48) the shift effect is twice as large using the 1948 weight for employment as using the 1924 weight (oddly enough this is the reverse of his conclusion). Part of the reason for the difference in our findings may be Salter's sample, which as he admits is biased towards industries with high output and employment variances. However the main reason is probably the difference in our procedures for deflation, as discussed above, although for 1935/48 both Salter and I use Brown.

There is some support in the Table for the long-swing pattern enunciated by Rostow (1978 – Rostow's terminal dates are 1920, 1936, 1951, and 1972), though it will be remembered that the figures in the second column are a guide to technical change only with severe reservations.

The more significant result is the eclipse of the shift component by the internal component in accounting for such productivity growth as here measured; particularly in the long term. Whereas Salter's results quoted earlier gave the shift component up to equal importance, here it is outgunned by five to ten and sometimes twenty to one in the longer run. It is, however, always positive, that is the changes were always beneficial to productivity in aggregate, which is more than can be said for some shorter periods of the internal effect. In other words, in those pairs of years it is preventing aggregate productivity from sagging as much as it might otherwise have done.

What can account for this finding? It may be thought that the shift component is being understated through simultaneity, for example as labour shifts (relatively) into higher-productivity industries, that every process will reduce the productivity advantage of the more productive sectors. A moment's further thought, however, will suggest that such an event is likely to expand still further the 'internal' effect, and indeed in a rough calculation partially allowing for diminishing returns below, I show that the outcomes are persistently a further diminution of the 'shift' effect.

It is supposed in the calculation that the kinds of labour released from relatively declining sectors will be as productive as their counterparts in advancing sectors when they move to join them there. There are obvious reasons for doubting this assumption. Take the case of female versus male workers – employers may be supposed, on the basis of the well-known perpetuation of wage differentials, to perceive real or imaginary differences in capabilities between female and male labour. A rough calculation using Census of Population (occupational) data for the postwar period showed a relatively larger decline in female employment in old industries than their absorption into new industries. This, however, was entirely the result of the textiles and clothing industries. If they are omitted from the calculation, the requirements for males (proportionately speaking) in new industries are more than met. Obviously it is extreme ad-hockery to omit textiles and clothing in this way; a justification could be that many of the remaining old industries (like iron and steel, coke ovens, some machinery manufacture, railway vehicles, shipbuilding, timber; but unlike textiles and clothing) could be regarded as inculcating skills and attributes of considerable use for subsequently redeployed labour. Clearly this matter needs much further consideration than it is given here.

Such understanding as can be advanced here is obtained by breaking the shift and internal components for all industries as in

TABLE 1.4 *Contribution of each industry to 'shift' effect, between censal years (MLH level of disaggregation)*

Industry	*Order*	*1907/24*	*1907/30*	*1907/35*	*1907/48*	*1907/51*	*1907/54*	*1907/58*	*1907/63*	*1907/68*
Food, drink, tobacco	III	−.0077	−.0060	−.0109	−.0093	−.0098	−.0128	−.0121	−.0108	−.0149
Coal and petroleum products	IV	.0062	−.0010	−.0006	.0005	.0005	.0027	.0024	.0025	.0024
Chemicals and allied	V	.0047	.0047	.0088	.0091	.0124	.0133	.0166	.0205	.0204
Metal manufacture	VI	.0011	.0016	.0011	.0021	.0033	.0013	.0017	.0015	.0022
Mechanical engineering	VII	.0005	.0026	.0019	.0001	.0014	.0051	.0052	.0005	.0028
Instrument engineering	VIII	−.0003	−.0000	−.0005	−.0011	−.0013	−.0007	−.0005	−.0018	−.0018
Electrical engineering	IX	.0004	.0025	.0008	−.0057	−.0061	−.0045	−.0042	−.0091	−.0068
Shipbuilding	X	.0027	.0010	.0046	.0016	.0048	.0045	.0050	.0089	.0067
Vehicles	XI	.0009	.0033	.0036	−.0013	.0036	.0103	.0103	.150	.0131
Other metal goods	XII	.0003	−.0005	−.0013	−.0024	−.0025	−.0025	−.0026	−.0054	−.0005
Textiles	XIII	.0092	.0275	.0305	.0220	.0182	.0456	.0685	.0750	.0593
Leather and fur	XIV	.0004	.0003	.0004	−.0002	.0006	.0008	.0014	.0013	.0014
Clothing and footwear	XV	.0134	.0118	.0176	.0244	.0320	.0356	.0419	.0478	.0510
Building materials etc.	XVI	.0011	.0012	.0006	.0002	.0006	.0005	.0026	.0032	.0045
Timber and furniture	XVII	.0004	−.0006	−.0014	−.0000	.0007	.0011	.0016	.0014	.0012
Paper and printing	XVIII	.0026	.0053	.0053	.0026	.0054	.0044	.0043	.0040	.0035
Other manufacturing	XIX	−.0001	.0022	.0013	.0013	.0027	.0018	.0009	.0020	.0021
Total		.0358	.0559	.0619	.0439	.0665	.1066	.1430	.1594	.1387

TABLE 1.4 *Continued*

Industry	*Order*	*1924/30*	*1924/35*	*1924/48*	*1924/51*	*1924/54*	*1924/58*	*1924/63*	*1924/68*	*1930/35*
Food, drink, tobacco	III	.0062	−.0001	−.0034	−.0063	−.0089	−.0067	−.0071	−.0098	−.0015
Coal and Petroleum products	IV	−.0002	−.0005	.0001	−.0004	.0023	.0015	.0023	.0024	−.0003
Chemicals and allied	V	.0002	.0027	.0058	.0087	.0096	.0127	.0162	.0160	.0019
Metal manufacture	VI	.0005	−.0006	.0014	.0018	.0001	.0007	.0007	.0011	.0000
Mechanical engineering	VII	.0010	.0014	.0001	.0011	.0040	.0038	.0007	.0023	.0005
Instrument engineering	VIII	−.0000	−.0002	−.0009	−.0010	−.0006	−.0005	−.0015	−.0016	−.0001
Electrical engineering	IX	.0005	.0002	−.0039	−.0043	−.0033	−.0035	−.0069	−.0054	.0002
Shipbuilding	X	.0024	−.0015	−.0000	.0020	.0019	.0023	.0053	.0064	.0021
Vehicles	XI	.0011	.0018	−.0006	.0023	.0065	.0068	.0106	.0117	.0010
Other metal goods	XII	−.0012	−.0012	−.0021	−.0017	−.0019	−.0019	−.0023	−.0041	−.0007
Textiles	XIII	.0161	.0184	.0147	.0121	.0315	.0519	.0571	.0540	.0023
Leather and fur	XIV	.0000	−.0000	−.0003	.0004	.0007	.0013	.0011	.0013	−.0001
Clothing and footwear	XV	−.0012	.0053	.0133	.0176	.0198	.0249	.0291	.0326	.0061
Building materials etc.	XVI	.0005	.0002	.0003	.0007	.0008	.0024	.0028	.0036	−.0001
Timber and furniture	XVII	−.0011	−.0019	−.0005	−.0001	.0001	.0008	.0008	.0008	−.0005
Paper and printing	XVIII	.0029	.0031	.0015	.0034	.0029	.0031	.0029	.0025	.0007
Other manufacturing	XIX	.0005	.0006	.0003	.0019	.0017	.0014	.0018	.0016	.0005
Total		.0286	.0275	.0257	.0380	.0673	.1010	.1134	.1153	.0121

TABLE 1.4 *Continued*

Industry	*Order*	*1930/48*	*1930/51*	*1930/54*	*1930/58*	*1930/63*	*1930/68*	*1935/48*	*1935/51*	*1935/54*
Food, drink, tobacco	III	−.0029	−.0050	−.0076	−.0053	−.0061	−.0086	−.0000	−.0016	−.0044
Coal and petroleum products	IV	.0002	−.0005	.0025	.0016	.0022	.0028	.0003	−.0007	.0027
Chemicals and allied	V	.0052	.0083	.0090	.0124	.0157	.0157	.0043	.0071	.0076
Metal manufacture	VI	.0018	.0032	.0022	.0028	.0014	.0014	.0017	.0033	.0028
Mechanical engineering	VII	−.0003	.0006	.0034	.0033	.0005	.0021	−.0005	.0003	.0029
Instrument engineering	VIII	−.0008	−.0009	−.0005	−.0004	−.0013	−.0015	−.0006	−.0007	−.0005
Electrical engineering	IX	−.0030	−.0037	−.0029	−.0033	−.0059	−.0048	−.0027	−.0027	−.0023
Shipbuilding	X	−.0005	.0012	.0012	.0015	.0043	.0053	−.0024	−.0020	−.0018
Vehicles	XI	−.0007	.0017	.0053	.0056	.0089	.0104	−.0012	.0006	.0036
Other metal goods	XII	−.0016	−.0012	−.0014	−.0014	−.0018	−.0033	−.0012	−.0000	−.0008
Textiles	XIII	.0090	.0065	.0180	.0339	.0377	.0372	.0075	.0059	.0158
Leather and fur	XIV	−.0003	.0003	.0006	.0012	.0010	.0011	−.0002	.0005	.0007
Clothing and footwear	XV	.0144	.0187	.0209	.0259	.0301	.0336	.0089	.0116	.0132
Buidling materials etc.	XVI	.0008	.0012	.0014	.0028	.0028	.0033	.0012	.0017	.0017
Timber and furniture	XVII	.0005	.0013	.0016	.0023	.0023	.0014	.0008	.0018	.0021
Paper and printing	XVIII	.0002	.0015	.0022	.0024	.0022	.0020	−.0007	−.0003	.0013
Other manufacturing	XIX	.0001	.0019	.0018	.0017	.0020	.0017	.0001	.0011	.0009
Total		.0219	.0353	.0575	.0868	.959	.0999	.0152	.0257	.0457

TABLE 1.4 *Continued*

Industry	*Order*	*1935/58*	*1935/63*	*1935/68*	*1948/51*	*1948/54*	*1948/58*	*1948/63*	*1948/68*	*1951/54*
Food, drink, tobacco	III	−.0021	−.0026	−.0045	−.0021	−.0035	−.0018	−.0022	−.0042	−.0014
Coal and petroleum products	IV	.0016	.0023	.0033	−.0004	.0018	.0012	.0016	.0020	.0010
Chemicals and allied	V	.0111	.0142	.0144	.0003	−.0005	.0024	.0042	.0039	−.0008
Metal manufacture	VI	.0034	.0017	.0017	−.0007	−.0007	.0002	.0001	.0005	−.0001
Mechanical engineering	VII	.0027	.0004	.0020	.001	.0007	.0014	.0004	.0012	.0004
Instrument engineering	VIII	−.0004	−.0012	−.0014	−.0001	−.0001	−.0001	−.0005	−.0007	−.0001
Electrical engineering	IX	−.0027	−.0050	−.0041	−.0007	−.0008	−.0017	−.0031	−.0027	−.0004
Shipbuilding	X	−.0015	.0005	.0010	.0019	.0018	.0021	.0050	.0060	.0001
Vehicles	XI	.0039	.0068	.0085	.0007	.0018	.0025	.0062	.0077	.0008
Other metal goods	XII	−.0009	−.0012	−.0025	.0001	.0002	.0001	.0002	−.0002	−.0002
Textiles	XIII	.0310	.0347	.0347	−.0005	.0011	.0088	.0138	.0156	.0021
Leather and fur	XIV	.0013	.0011	.0013	−.0000	.0001	.0005	.0004	.0005	.0000
Clothing and footwear	XV	.0177	.0213	.0248	−.0009	.0002	.0033	.0060	.0091	.0012
Building materials etc.	XVI	.0031	.0030	.0035	.0003	.0005	.0011	.0014	.0016	.0002
Timber and furniture	XVII	.0028	.0028	.0016	.0003	.0007	.0011	.0014	.0008	.0003
Paper and printing	XVIII	.0017	.0017	.0016	.0008	.0010	.0014	.0013	.0013	.0007
Other manufacturing	XIX	.0006	.0008	.0007	.0005	.0006	.0003	.0002	−.0000	.0001
Total		.0734	.0805	.0855	.0000	.0049	.0231	.0362	.0423	.0041

Table 1.4 *Continued*

Industry	*Order*	*1951/58*	*1951/63*	*1951/68*	*1954/58*	*1954/63*	*1954/68*	*1958/63*	*1958/68*	*1963/68*
Food, drink, tobacco	III	.0005	.0003	−.0012	.0025	.0020	.0008	−.0001	−.0011	−.0008
Coal and petroleum products	IV	.0010	.0011	.0010	.0005	.0003	−.0003	−.0003	−.0013	−.0010
Chemicals and allied	V	.0024	.0040	.0035	.0031	.0048	.0046	.0010	.0006	−.0010
Metal manufacture	VI	.0008	.0003	.0004	.0008	.0002	.0003	−.0001	.0000	−.0001
Mechanical engineering	VII	.0011	.0004	.0012	.0006	.0004	.0010	.0002	.0007	.0003
Instrument engineering	VIII	−.0000	−.0004	−.0007	−.0000	−.0003	−.0006	−.0002	−.0006	−.0004
Electrical engineering	IX	−.0011	−.0025	−.0022	−.0006	−.0021	−.0019	−.0012	−.0012	−.0001
Shipbuilding	X	.0004	.0028	.0035	.0003	.0027	.0034	.0023	.0030	.0004
Vehicles	XI	.0015	.0049	.0065	.0008	.0052	.0057	.0044	.0047	.0016
Other metal goods	XII	−.0003	−.0003	−.0007	.0000	−.0003	−.0006	−.0004	−.0005	−.0001
Textiles	XIII	.0103	.0150	.0164	.0070	.0124	.0144	.0055	.0084	.0038
Leather and fur	XIV	.0004	.0004	.0004	.0003	.0003	.0004	.0000	.0000	.0000
Clothing and footwear	XV	.0043	.0071	.0100	.0031	.0057	.0087	.0024	.0052	.0027
Building materials etc.	XVI	.0009	.0013	.0016	.0008	.0010	.0013	.0004	.0007	.0003
Timber and furniture	XVII	.0009	.0010	.0008	.0006	.0007	.0005	.0001	.0001	.0001
Paper and printing	XVIII	.0012	.0012	.0012	.0006	.0006	.0006	−.0000	.0001	.0001
Other manufacturing	XIX	.0000	−.0003	−.0005	−.0000	−.0004	−.0006	−.0005	−.0007	−.0004
Total		.0243	.0363	.0412	.0205	.0332	.0377	.0136	.0183	.0061

Table 1.3 down into contributions from individual industries, as in Table 1.4 and 1.5. Since there is little difference in general between the results of different weighting patterns, I have worked henceforth on the basis of base-weighting employment. Unfortunately the measures for the shift effect used for Table 1.3 do not disaggregate in a way that is both simple and meaningful. Statistically speaking, the reason is the presence of the term $\Sigma E_{it}/\Sigma E_{iO}$ in the relevant equations; all industries are having their labour force deflated by this factor, irrespective of their own performance with regard to employment. Thus if an industry's level of productivity is below average (in year *t* in the first formulation; year *o* in the second) it will tend to add a negative contribution to the overall total, whether it gained or released labour on balance. It seemed more appropriate to devise a measure of industrial contribution which resulted in a positive contribution towards 'shift' if *either* an industry with productivity above average gained labour *or* an industry with productivity below average released labour (the gains and losses being defined relative to the national change, $\Sigma E_{it}/\Sigma E_{iO}$). Conversely if an industry with productivity above average released labour or one with below-average productivity gained it, the contribution would be negative. Several possibilities for such a measure commend themselves; the one adopted here consisted of computing the expression $(P_{it}-\overline{P}_t)\ (E_{it}-E_{iO}\cdot\overline{\Delta E})$, where the terms are as before and $\overline{\Delta E}$ is shorthand for the aforementioned national change in employment ($=\Sigma E_{it}/\Sigma E_{iO}$).

The trouble with this measure, and of others I tried, is that it fails to aggregate simply to the national 'shift' component. The shift factor that emerges from this expression is highly dependent on the level of disaggregation maintained. Suppose one takes an industry like vehicles which has large sub-industries (like motor vehicles and aerospace) with high productivity and growing fast, and equally large sub-industries (like railway carriages and locomotives) of low productivity growing slowly or declining. Calculated at the two-digit level, the expression just discussed will yield a small contribution, positive or negative; however at the three-digit level its contribution will be large and positive. The figures in Table 1.4 are all calculated at the three-digit level (the MLH level) then re-aggregated at the end to the two-digit level. There is no straightforward way of undertaking still further disaggregation to see the consequences, but in the reverse direction it is possible to recalculate the Table directly at the two-digit level. As the example just given implies, the contribution of vehicles then drops sharply away, as do those, to a lesser extent, of coal and petroleum products and of textiles. Most industries, as one would expect, show a mild decline in contribution for most pairs of years. The industry that really loses from being exhibited, as here, on the basis of MLH-disaggregation is food, drink, and tobacco, which at the direct two-digit level shows mainly (small) positive contributions rather than largish negative ones. This results from declining employment in one or two of its particularly high-productivity sub-sectors (brewing and malting in the earlier years, later grain milling).

With that rather quirky exception, the picture is dominated by the positive contributions of two industries normally thought of as 'new' – chemicals and vehicles – and even more two 'old' industries –textiles and clothing. However some new industries (instrument engineering and electrical engineering) yield generally negative contributions, lowering the overall contribution of new industries and giving rise to the possibility that, say, the positive contribution of vehicles may come from its declining as well as its expanding sub-branches. A different classification is required to shed more light on the new industry debate, and this will be done after considering Table 1.5.

Industry-by-industry disaggregation of the 'internal' effect suffers from none of the statistical ambiguities of that for the shift. The contribution of industry i is given as $E_{io}(P_{it}-P_{io}\cdot\overline{\Delta r})$, with $\overline{\Delta r}$ here the implicit price deflator for net output discussed above. This aggregates perfectly simply to the national total for the 'internal' effect as given in Table 1.3. The general pattern in Table 1.5 is not vastly dissimilar to that in Table 1.4, with powerful contributions from chemicals, textiles and clothing. Food, drink and tobacco joins them in importance, while vehicles slip back a little; but by and large the contributions are much more evenly shared around than is the case with the shift effect.

The tables give the lie to the traditional 'over-commitment' view of a deadweight of manpower in the decaying export staples. If anything, their shedding of labour accounted for more of the rise in productivity for the country as a whole than did the rising share of labour in the fast-growing industries (remember that all figures in both Tables 1.4 and 1.5 are a compound of productivity and employment factors). However to trace this in more detail a sharper set of distinctions between old and new is called for.

We come back to Rostow. As the quotation at the beginning of

TABLE 1.5 *Contribution of each industry to 'internal' effect, between censal years*

Industry	*Order*	*1907/24*	*1907/30*	*1907/35*	*1907/48*	*1907/51*	*1907/54*	*1907/58*	*1907/63*	*1907/68*
Food, drink, tobacco	III	.0410	.0168	.0875	.0166	.0534	.0882	.0832	.1110	.1761
Coal and petroleum products	IV	−.0021	−.0009	.0014	−.0040	−.0038	.0051	.0021	.0034	.0121
Chemicals and allied	V	.0052	.0010	.0227	.0049	.0275	.0470	.0445	.0601	.0878
Metal manufacture	VI	−.0033	−.0179	.0191	.0170	.0645	.0873	.0786	.0796	.1039
Mechanical engineering	VII	−.0049	−.0134	.0094	.0071	.0367	.0577	.0464	.0630	.0995
Instrument engineering	VIII	.0003	−.0001	.0011	.0006	.0024	.0045	.0039	.0048	.0069
Electrical engineering	IX	.0020	.0007	.0052	.0027	.0086	.0120	.0113	.0137	.0211
Shipbuilding	X	−.0038	−.0036	.0122	.0112	.0275	.0413	.0359	.0447	.0657
Vehicles	XI	.0028	−.0015	.0091	.0053	.0166	.0253	.0195	.0248	.0311
Other metal goods	XII	−.0028	−.0111	.0078	.0128	.0416	.0497	.0424	.0512	.0806
Textiles	XIII	−.0344	−.0106	.0166	.0979	.2114	.1853	.1133	.1685	.2835
Leather and fur	XIV	.0028	−.0005	.0033	.0079	.0076	.0085	.0063	.0099	.0148
Clothing and footwear	XV	.0259	.0088	.0505	.0598	.0850	.1033	.0866	.0169	.1520
Building materials etc.	XVI	.0120	.0034	.0214	.0179	.0363	.0471	.0390	.0526	.0715
Timber and furniture	XVII	.0082	−.0007	.0124	.0144	.0268	.0355	.0316	.0434	.0694
Paper and printing	XVIII	.0240	.0086	.0342	.0245	.0686	.0717	.0607	.0800	.1158
Other manufacturing	XIX	.0028	−.0026	.0058	.0054	.0138	.0200	.0177	.0243	.0388
Total		.1445	−.0237	.3197	.3022	.7245	.8896	.7230	.9418	1.4309

TABLE 1.5 *Continued*

Industry	*Order*	*1924/30*	*1924/35*	*1924/48*	*1924/51*	*1924/54*	*1924/58*	*1924/63*	*1924/68*	*1930/35*
Food, drink, tobacco	III	−.0205	.0354	−.0177	.0140	.0435	.0398	.0668	.1201	.0521
Coal and petroleum products	IV	−.0003	.0025	−.0014	−.0002	.0066	.0050	.0053	.0128	.0022
Chemicals and allied	V	−.0048	.0172	−.0008	.0198	.0377	.0357	.0507	.0776	.0216
Metal manufacture	VI	−.0117	.0201	.0178	.0581	.0769	.0705	.0714	.0929	.0287
Mechanical engineering	VII	−.0085	.0142	.0118	.0392	.0598	.0510	.0649	.1005	.0189
Instrument engineering	VIII	−.0003	.0011	.0003	.0025	.0052	.0047	.0056	.0085	.0012
Electrical engineering	IX	−.0025	.0066	.0015	.0135	.0210	.0198	.0246	.0403	.0097
Shipbuilding	X	.0007	.0107	.0104	.0205	.0296	.0267	.0325	.0463	.0079
Vehicles	XI	−.0060	.0108	.0048	.0258	.0422	.0347	.0476	.0595	.0165
Other metal goods	XII	−.0069	.0089	.0131	.0361	.0430	.0376	.0457	.0688	.0155
Textiles	XIII	−.0615	−.0146	.0486	.1358	.1213	.0662	.1157	.2072	.0363
Leather and fur	XIV	−.0029	.0005	.0041	.0040	.0048	.0029	.0063	.0105	.0030
Clothing and footwear	XV	−.0108	.0161	.0243	.0397	.0522	.0420	.0564	.0867	.0255
Building materials etc.	XVI	−.0072	.0074	.0043	.0189	.0276	.0220	.0339	.0506	.0149
Timber and furniture	XVII	−.0062	.0031	.0050	.0136	.0201	.0174	.0260	.0455	.0101
Paper and printing	XVIII	−.0127	.0090	.0003	.0381	.0403	.0314	.0484	.0791	.0208
Other manufacturing	XIX	−.0032	.0042	.0045	.0126	.0178	.0147	.0224	.0371	.0064
Total		−.1653	.1531	.1308	.4917	.6497	.5221	.7243	1.1440	.2914

TABLE 1.5 *Continued*

Industry	*Order*	*1930/48*	*1930/51*	*1930/54*	*1930/58*	*1930/63*	*1930/68*	*1935/48*	*1935/51*	*1935/54*
Food, drink, tobacco	III	−.0024	.0213	.0519	.0590	.0907	.1492	−.0433	−.0225	.0021
Coal and petroleum products	IV	−.0016	−.0009	.0056	.0049	.0053	.0120	−.0028	−.0018	.0025
Chemicals and allied	V	.0038	.0224	.0408	.0426	.0597	.0881	−.0155	.0006	.0157
Metal manufacture	VI	.0300	.0628	.0798	.0806	.0822	.1031	.0005	.0273	.0402
Mechanical engineering	VII	.0191	.0420	.0633	.0602	.0750	.1126	−.0007	.0190	.0363
Instrument engineering	VIII	.0006	.0025	.0056	.0057	.0068	.0101	−.0006	.0012	.0040
Electrical engineering	IX	.0048	.0171	.0270	.0289	.0348	.0556	−.0052	.0071	.0164
Shipbuilding	X	.0096	.0159	.0245	.0249	.0308	.0442	.0006	.0042	.0085
Vehicles	XI	.0118	.0317	.0507	.0474	.0636	.0779	−.0046	.0134	.0296
Other metal goods	XII	.0230	.0436	.0511	.0499	.0596	.0849	.0056	.0233	.0295
Textiles	XIII	.1022	.1661	.1562	.1182	.1693	.2522	.0481	.0986	.0925
Leather and fur	XIV	.0124	.0060	.0068	.0057	.0094	.0137	.0036	.0025	.0031
Clothing and footwear	XV	.0389	.0471	.0598	.0556	.0715	.1040	.0084	.0152	.0240
Building materials etc.	XVI	.0127	.0257	.0353	.0334	.0482	.0690	−.0023	.0094	.0176
Timber and furniture	XVII	.0149	.0224	.0306	.0305	.0421	.0686	.0063	.0133	.0202
Paper and printing	XVIII	.0144	.0513	.0527	.0498	.0704	.1065	−.0059	.0262	.0269
Other manufacturing	XIX	.0085	.0145	.0201	.0189	.0280	.0445	.0007	.0060	.0100
Total		.3027	.5916	.7618	.7162	.9474	1.3962	−.0071	.2431	.3791

TABLE 1.5 *Continued*

Industry	*Order*	*1935/58*	*1935/63*	*1935/68*	*1948/51*	*1948/54*	*1948/58*	*1948/63*	*1948/68*	*1951/54*
Food, drink, tobacco	III	.0055	.0301	.0754	.0191	.0407	.0436	.0648	.1053	.0180
Coal and petroleum products	IV	.0021	.0023	.0065	.0005	.0065	.0053	.0060	.0118	.0061
Chemical and allied	V	.0159	.0300	.0529	.0243	.0436	.0438	.0642	.0970	.0161
Metal manufacture	VI	.0395	.0416	.0586	.0337	.0484	.0460	.0487	.0696	.0117
Mechanical engineering	VII	.0328	.0440	.0742	.0298	.0550	.0486	.0650	.1085	.0217
Instrument engineering	XIII	.0039	.0049	.0078	.0033	.0063	.0061	.0076	.0124	.0027
Electrical engineering	IX	.0173	.0231	.0427	.0184	.0320	.0325	.0418	.0701	.0117
Shipbuilding	X	.0083	.0113	.0180	.0064	.0137	.0130	.0180	.0293	.0049
Vehicles	XI	.0261	.0399	.0528	.0261	.0488	.0433	.0610	.0832	.0193
Other metal goods	XII	.0279	.0358	.0562	.0211	.0290	.0266	.0361	.0585	.0065
Textiles	XIII	.0614	.1002	.1628	.0362	.0325	.0104	.0376	.0808	−.0020
Leather and fur	XIV	.0022	.0028	.0084	−.0009	−.0004	−.0013	.0010	−.0038	−.0004
Clothing and footwear	XV	.0200	.0308	.0525	.0054	.0112	.0082	.0157	.0309	.0050
Building materials etc.	XVI	.0153	.0269	.0451	.0108	.0186	.0167	.0269	.0426	.0064
Timber and furniture	XVII	.0194	.0289	.0509	.0060	.0106	.0100	.0183	.0357	.0040
Paper and printing	XVIII	.0229	.0394	.0685	.0281	.0282	.0224	.0370	.0604	.0005
Other manufacturing	XIX	.0089	.0155	.0270	.0066	.0099	.0087	.0165	.0290	.0028
Total		.3293	.5074	.8602	.2749	.4348	.3841	.5661	.9287	.1358

Table 1.5 *Continued*

Industry	*Order*	*1951/58*	*1951/63*	*1951/68*	*1954/58*	*1954/63*	*1954/68*	*1958/63*	*1958/68*	*1963/68*
Food, drink, tobacco	III	.0094	.0250	.0563	−.0066	.0076	.0345	.0166	.0474	.0263
Coal and petroleum products	IV	.0037	.0046	.0100	−.0026	−.0014	.0044	.0017	.0087	.0058
Chemicals and allied	V	.0090	.0242	.0505	−.0052	.0082	.0306	.0162	.0419	.0221
Metal manufacture	VI	.0021	.0040	.0202	−.0072	−.0055	.0085	.0014	.0162	.0127
Mechanical engineering	VII	.0066	.0190	.0543	−.0120	−.0011	.0306	.0120	.0466	.0308
Instrument engineering	VIII	.0013	.0024	.0064	−.0011	−.0000	.0037	.0012	.0053	.0041
Electrical engineering	IX	.0057	.0124	.0348	−.0047	−.0019	.0222	.0079	.0315	.0233
Shipbuilding	X	.0017	.0046	.0118	−.0024	.0002	.0064	.0027	.0089	.0038
Vehicles	XI	.0067	.0203	.0389	−.0110	.0017	.0219	.0143	.0368	.0186
Other metal goods	XII	−.0009	.0056	.0222	−.0058	.0001	.0145	.0064	.0209	.0132
Textiles	XIII	−.0289	−.0078	.0276	−.0206	−.0037	.0249	.0163	.0420	.0190
Leather and fur	XIV	−.0009	.0006	.0026	−.0009	.0003	.0019	.0011	.0024	.0011
Clothing and footwear	XV	−.0015	.0041	.0165	−.0050	−.0002	.0103	.0047	.0146	.0078
Building materials etc.	XVI	.0011	.0084	.0205	−.0041	.0024	.0127	.0065	.0167	.0087
Timber and furniture	XVII	.0005	.0062	.0190	−.0026	.0023	.0131	.0048	.0152	.0086
Paper and printing	XVIII	−.0107	.0007	.0201	−.0089	.0011	.0180	.0118	.0307	.0171
Other manufacturing	XIX	−.0009	.0051	.0149	−.0029	.0025	.0111	.0059	.0151	.0091
Total		.0039	.1394	.4265	−.1036	.0162	.2692	.1315	.4010	.2320

this paper makes clear, it is oversimplifying things to conjecture leading sectors that operated throughout the first two-thirds of this century. Rostow's more recent thoughts, in *The World Economy*, however indicate a rather higher degree of continuity. Chapter 28 on Great Britain notes that steel, which had become a leading sector in the 1870s, had ceased to lead by the 1920s; motor vehicles are estimated to have become a leading sector in the 1920s and ceased to lead in the 1960s; and electricity to have become a leading sector in the first decade of this century and forecast to cease leading in the 1970s. Nitrogen, plastics and resins, and synthetic fibres all achieved their maximum rate of expansion in the first half of this century but were individually too small to act by themselves as leading sectors (all these observations from Rostow (1978, Table V-2, p. 379)). The earlier cross-country comparisons of trend periods and business cycles in *The World Economy* (Chapters 14–17, 22–5) reinforce the argument from an internationalist perspective. As already quoted, 'the internal combustion engine, electricity, and chemicals' lead for the interwar period (ibid., pp. 208–17, 227, 335–6). The next trend period Rostow identifies, 1936–51, is more confused because of the wars, but the same underlying pattern is present.

> Energy consumption increased modestly, on balance, between 1938 and 1948, lifted notably by the U.S. figures; but it then moved forward rapidly, with electricity, petroleum, and natural gas increasing their share of the total, as against coal . . . Like electricity, the other interwar leading sectors (e.g., motor vehicles and chemicals) quickly re-emerged and moved forward at high rates, with the age of plastics coming into its own. (ibid., pp. 231–2, also pp. 235–6)

Finally – so far as my study is concerned – for the trend period 1951–72:

> For Western Europe as a whole, for example, Table III-59 shows the disproportionate rise down to 1963 in the three leading sectors which had begun to emerge before 1914 – motor vehicles, chemicals, and electricity – sectors which cushioned the stagnation of the interwar years, and finally carried Western Europe forward at relatively full employment in the 1950s and 1960s. (ibid., p. 261)

In this period there is especially great emphasis on electric-powered consumer durables and electronics (pp. 260–3).

As already stated, my data for non-manufacturing industry such as electricity supply still remain to be prepared. Within manufacturing itself, I have therefore taken electrical goods and equipment, motor vehicles, aircraft, and chemicals as 'leading sectors' for the period studied here. Since there are other sectors – some of which have already been mentioned – which are individually too small for Rostow to classify them as leading sectors but which nevertheless clearly impart some of the sectoral growth impetus, I have further subsumed the leading sectors into a wider group of 'new industries' – the additions being petroleum refining, non-ferrous metals, constructional and mechanical handling equipment, instrument engineering, man-made fibre production (weaving cannot be separately measured in these data), rubber, and plastics products (plastics manufacture is already included in chemicals). The 'old staples' are probably less contentious to define (see the list at the foot of Table 1.6) – marginal candidates like wood products (based on ibid., p. 260) and steel tubes can be dropped and others included with very little alteration to the results (certainly per capita).

Net output, employment, and labour productivity according to these breakdowns are given in Table 1.6. It will be seen from Part B of the Table that net output in 'new industries' rose from less than 10 per cent of net output in manufacturing as a whole in 1907 to 38 per cent by 1968. Employment in these industries rose from under one-fourteenth of the total for manufacturing in 1907 to about one-third by 1968. Conversely, net output of the 'old staples' as here defined fell from over half the total for manufacturing in 1907 to little more than one-fifth in 1968. In terms of growth rates (Part C of the Table) it will be noted that the fastest rates of growth of *employment* in leading sectors and new industries were probably experienced during the First and Second World Wars (that is in 1907/24 and 1935/48). Fastest rates of growth of *net output* and *productivity* however occurred in 1948/54, consonant with Rostow's reference (1978, pp. 231–2, 235–6) to the end of the period 1936–51 (though it must be remembered that problems with price deflators severely affect this particular conclusion).

For leading sectors and new industries generally, there does seem to be some indication of inversity between rates of growth of employment and those of real net output (these latter being the

TABLE 1.6 *Net output, employment, and labour productivity in 'leading sectors', 'new industries', and 'old staples', censal years, 1907/68*

(A) Levels

	Leading sectors			*New industries*			*Old staples*		
	Net output	*Employ-ment*	*Pro-ductivity*	*Net output*	*Employ-ment*	*Pro-ductivity*	*Net output*	*Employ-ment*	*Pro-ductivity*
	£m	*000s*	*£/man*	*£m*	*000s*	*£/man*	*£m*	*000s*	*£/man*
1907	31.5	235.4	133.7	45.3	340.5	132.9	250.9	3123.9	80.3
1924	136.3	520.8	261.8	188.9	732.0	258.0	527.0	3023.9	174.3
1930	161.8	599.8	269.8	222.7	832.9	267.4	447.1	2815.1	158.8
1935	203.1	710.9	285.7	271.1	965.9	280.7	451.1	2676.9	168.5
1948	758.6	1294.6	586.0	1026.1	1736.4	590.9	1388.0	2784.3	498.5
1951	1062.4	1432.4	741.7	1436.9	1914.8	750.4	1684.2	2908.7	579.0
1954	1475.9	1580.8	933.6	1965.7	2095.0	938.3	1891.1	2856.0	662.1
1958	2021.7	1729.5	1169.0	2606.6	2271.9	1147.3	2159.7	2622.6	823.5
1963	3020.9	1924.4	1569.8	3991.1	2556.5	1561.2	2488.9	2377.7	1046.8
1968	4230.5	1900.0	2226.6	5777.2	2591.1	2229.6	3231.1	2149.8	1503.0

TABLE 1.6 *Continued*

(B) Shares

	Leading sectors			*New industries*			*Old staples*		
	% of all manu-facturing	*% of all manu-facturing*	*% of national average*	*% of all manu-facturing*	*% of all manu-facturing*	*% of national average*	*% of all manu-facturing*	*% of all manu-facturing*	*% of national average*
1907	6.6	4.7	138.3	9.4	6.9	137.4	52.3	62.9	83.0
1924	11.5	9.6	120.8	16.0	13.4	119.1	44.6	55.5	80.4
1930	13.8	11.0	125.9	19.0	15.2	124.8	38.1	51.5	74.1
1935	15.9	12.7	125.1	21.2	17.2	122.9	35.3	47.8	73.8
1948	19.4	18.6	104.4	26.2	24.9	105.2	35.5	40.0	88.8
1951	20.9	19.1	109.2	28.3	25.6	110.5	33.2	38.9	85.3
1954	23.6	20.5	114.9	31.4	27.2	115.5	30.2	37.1	81.5
1958	25.6	22.1	115.7	33.0	29.1	113.5	27.4	33.6	81.5
1963	27.8	24.2	114.7	36.7	32.1	114.1	22.9	29.9	76.5
1968	27.7	24.3	114.0	37.8	33.1	114.1	21.1	27.5	76.9

TABLE 1.6 *Continued*
(C) Growth Rates

	Leading Sectors			*New industries*			*Old staples*		
	% *p.a.*	% *p.a.*	% *p.a.*	% *p.a.*	% *p.a.*	% *p.a.*	% *p.a.*	% *p.a.*	% *p.a.*
1907/24	9.0 (5.0)	4.8	4.0 (0.2)	8.8 (4.8)	4.6	4.0 (0.2)	4.5 (0.6)	−0.2	4.7 (0.8)
1924/30	2.9 (0.5)	2.4	0.5 (−1.9)	2.8 (0.4)	2.2	0.6 (−1.8)	−2.7 (−5.0)	−1.2	−1.5 (−3.9)
1930/35	4.7 (9.0)	3.5	1.2 (5.3)	4.0 (8.3)	3.0	1.0 (5.1)	0.2 (4.3)	−1.0	1.2 (5.4)
1924/35	3.7 (4.8)	2.9	0.8 (1.9)	3.3 (4.5)	2.6	0.8 (1.9)	−1.4 (−0.3)	−1.1	−0.3 (0.8)
1935/48	10.7 (3.3)	4.7	5.7 (−1.3)	10.8 (3.4)	4.6	5.9 (−1.1)	9.0 (1.8)	0.3	8.7 (1.5)
1948/51	11.9 (13.9)	3.4	8.2 (10.1)	11.9 (13.9)	3.3	8.3 (10.2)	6.7 (8.5)	1.5	5.1 (7.0)
1951/54	11.6 (9.8)	3.3	8.0 (6.3)	11.0 (9.2)	3.0	7.7 (6.0)	3.9 (2.3)	−0.6	4.6 (2.9)
1954/58	8.2 (0.2)	2.3	5.8 (−2.0)	7.3 (−0.6)	2.0	5.2 (−2.6)	3.4 (−4.3)	−2.1	5.6 (−2.2)
1948/58	10.3 (7.7)	2.9	7.1 (4.6)	9.8 (7.2)	2.7	6.9 (4.3)	4.5 (2.0)	−0.6	5.1 (2.7)
1958/63	8.4 (4.9)	2.2	6.1 (2.7)	8.9 (5.4)	2.4	6.4 (3.0)	2.9 (−0.4)	−1.9	4.9 (1.6)
1963/68	7.0 (3.9)	−0.3	7.2 (4.1)	7.7 (4.6)	0.3	7.4 (4.3)	5.4 (2.3)	−2.0	7.5 (4.4)

NOTES For sources, see text.

Parenthesised figures in Part C of the table are deflated values, using the net output deflator discussed in text. Composition of each grouping is as follows (MLH numbers in parentheses):

Leading sectors
Chemical and allied (271/9)
Electrical engineering (361/9)
Motor vehicles (380/2)
Aerospace equipment (383)

New industries
Leading sectors plus:
Mineral oil refining (262)
Lubricating oils and greases (263)
Non-ferrous metals (321/3)
Construction equipment (336)
Mechanical handling equip. (337)
Instrument engineering (351/4)
Production of man-made fibres (411)
Rubber (491)
Plastics products (496)

Old staples
Coke ovens and mfd. fuel (261)
Iron and steel (general) (311)
Steel tubes (312)
Iron castings, etc. (313)
Textile machinery etc. (335)
Shipbuilding and marine engineering (370)
Locomotives and railway track equipment (384)
Railway carriage etc. (385)
Textiles except MMF (412/29)
Leather and fur (431/3)
Clothing and footwear (441/50)
Pottery (462)
Timber and furniture (471/9)

parenthesised figures in Part C of Table 1.6) and real productivity (displayed likewise) – a kind of inverse Verdoorn effect. Consistent with the frequently-heard complaints about labour dilution during the World Wars, etc., one might posit that through diminishing returns the rate of growth of labour productivity is ultimately hampered by a fast rate of growth of the workforce. The simple correlation coefficient between real productivity growth rate and employment growth rate for new industries is –0.86; so long as 1948/58 is treated as one period and 1924/35 similarly. Using parameters estimated from this equation, it is possible to recalculate 'shift' and 'intensity' effects akin to those of Table 1.3. Using values for P_{it}, E_{it}, etc., taken from Part A of Table 1.6 – that is a very high level of aggregation – I find that the 'shift' effect would have been reduced by about forty per cent in most pairs of years if employment in the new industries had grown only at the rate of all other industries. Since hypothetical productivity would have risen considerably faster than the actual, the 'intensity' effect would have risen more than commensurately. There are so many improbable assumptions in this computation that it does not bear elaboration, but the direction of effect is probably correct. A final and possibly interesting inference from the Table is that no such inversity is evident for the old staples ($r = -0.11$) but productivity growth in the old staples is quite well correlated ($r = 0.69$), and positively, with productivity growth in the new industries. This may suggest a 'lateral' linkage in Rostow's sense – productivity growth in new industries spinning off to older industries, for example through their provision of cheaper and better capital goods or through demonstration effects. However this linkage does not appear to hold for the interwar period when (cf. Dowie, 1968) productivity grew fastest in old staples at times when their labour shake-out was greatest. Much more work especially on the problem of price deflators is necessary before these propositions can be affirmed more strongly (or indeed rejected).

We can now make more precise the contribution of each group of industries to the shift and internal effects spelled out in Table 1.3. In Table 1.7 it will be noted that in every pair of years but one (1954–8) the old staples account for more than three-quarters of the total shift effect. As before, my conclusion is that collectively they cannot take as much of the blame as is often levelled against them for Britain's slow rate of economic growth. Again also, the internal effect is more evenly divided – indeed the shares over the longer runs are very like the shares of the respective industries in manufacturing

TABLE 1.7 *Contribution of 'leading sectors', 'new industries' and 'old staples' to 'shift' and 'internal' effects, between censal years, 1907/68*

	Leading sectors				*New industries*				*Old staples*			
	% of Total Shift Effect	*Growth Rate, Shift Contri-bution*	*% of Total Internal Effect*	*Growth Rate, Internal Contri-bution*	*% of Total Shift Effect*	*Growth Rate, Shift Contri-bution*	*% of Total Internal Effect*	*Growth Rate, Internal Contri-bution*	*% of Total Shift Effect*	*Growth Rate, Shift Contri-bution*	*% of Total, Internal Effect*	*Growth Rate, Internal Contri-bution*
1907/24	18.5	.03	5.8	.05	22.8	.04	6.3	.05	106.7	.17	45.3	.37
1907/30	19.0	.04	−6.8	.01	17.8	.04	−14.2	.01	79.2	.16	146.8	−.15
1907/35	20.7	.05	9.8	.11	20.5	.05	13.1	.15	88.4	.20	36.9	.40
1907/48	3.8	.00	3.2	.02	8.2	.01	3.9	.03	112.2	.09	71.3	.48
1907/51	13.1	.01	6.0	.10	24.0	.03	7.7	.03	82.7	.09	61.0	.84
1907/54	16.7	.03	7.9	.14	23.7	.04	10.5	.19	81.9	.15	55.3	.85
1907/58	14.3	.03	9.0	.12	16.8	.04	11.2	.15	86.5	.19	52.0	.63
1907/63	13.2	.03	9.2	.15	18.0	.04	11.9	.19	85.8	.18	51.4	.71
1907/68	13.6	.03	8.7	.19	19.8	.04	11.6	.25	90.3	.16	51.5	.91
1924/30	5.4	.01	6.5	−.18	4.6	.01	8.4	−.23	76.8	.22	15.3	−.43
1924/35	14.6	.04	20.0	.27	13.6	.04	27.2	.37	76.1	.21	24.8	.34
1924/48	2.6	.00	2.6	.01	7.9	.01	5.7	.03	110.2	.09	87.8	.45
1924/51	13.8	.02	10.5	.19	14.7	.02	15.6	.27	86.4	.10	56.4	.91
1924/54	16.7	.03	13.7	.28	22.8	.04	26.3	.53	82.8	.15	49.1	.93
1924/58	13.4	.03	15.7	.23	15.1	.04	19.3	.28	85.2	.21	45.3	.63
1924/63	12.4	.03	15.6	.27	14.3	.03	21.9	.38	88.8	.18	43.8	.71
1924/68	12.2	.02	14.3	.34	15.7	.03	20.5	.48	90.9	.17	44.2	.93
1930/35	22.1	.06	14.6	.84	20.1	.06	19.4	1.11	86.1	.25	40.1	2.24
1930/48	4.7	.00	5.3	.09	8.6	.01	8.4	.14	111.8	.10	69.8	1.07
1930/51	14.9	.02	10.7	.29	17.0	.02	16.0	.43	88.7	.12	54.7	1.34

1930/54	17.6	.04	14.0	.42	21.5	.05	19.8	.59	81.7	.17	48.3	1.31
1930/58	14.6	.04	15.2	.37	15.4	.04	20.1	.48	82.7	.22	45.8	1.02
1930/63	14.3	.03	15.5	.42	13.8	.03	21.9	.57	88.6	.20	42.4	1.03
1930/68	14.1	.03	14.8	.50	15.8	.03	21.2	.68	91.0	.17	42.5	1.23
1935/48	4.2	.00	347.8	−.19	9.8	.01	448.9	−.25	101.5	.06	−982.8	.52
1935/51	18.7	.02	7.9	.12	19.5	.02	14.3	.21	80.2	.08	65.0	.92
1935/54	18.6	.04	15.1	.29	24.0	.05	21.9	.42	76.0	.15	50.1	.92
1935/58	15.4	.04	17.0	.24	16.2	.04	22.4	.31	79.0	.21	46.8	.63
1935/63	14.2	.04	17.5	.37	13.6	.04	25.1	.52	79.5	.20	41.5	.83
1935/68	15.3	.03	16.5	.40	17.5	.03	23.6	.56	86.8	.15	40.4	.91
1948/51	−144.0	−.10	24.0	2.15	−295.2	−.20	32.9	2.93	466.1	.31	29.4	2.62
1948/54	−4.1	−.01	27.3	1.89	29.3	.03	35.9	2.45	93.8	.10	26.6	1.84
1948/58	7.8	.02	30.1	1.10	11.7	.02	37.1	1.34	82.8	.17	22.9	.85
1948/63	9.2	.02	28.6	1.01	11.2	.02	37.4	1.29	87.5	.15	23.6	.84
1948/68	6.6	.01	26.1	1.09	11.0	.02	34.8	1.41	93.5	.13	26.5	1.11
1951/54	−16.9	−.02	33.1	1.47	−2.2	−.00	42.1	1.87	116.4	.17	20.7	.93
1951/58	8.0	.02	553.9	.31	10.0	.03	474.7	.26	80.6	.22	−564.6	−.32
1951/63	9.1	.02	40.6	.46	8.4	.02	51.1	.57	86.5	.17	8.0	.09
1951/68	6.4	.01	28.6	.68	7.3	.01	38.0	.89	92.7	.14	22.9	.55
1954/58	14.1	.05	18.4	−.48	15.4	.05	31.1	−.81	66.1	.24	36.4	−.96
1954/63	15.3	.03	81.3	.15	14.8	.03	97.3	.17	76.8	.16	−64.8	−.12
1954/68	9.7	.01	27.7	.52	9.2	.01	37.6	.69	87.1	.13	22.8	.43
1958/63	14.8	.02	39.6	1.02	10.6	.01	42.4	1.09	90.9	.10	14.3	.37
1958/68	.08	.00	27.0	1.03	−5.5	−.01	38.1	1.43	111.7	.10	21.6	.83
1963/68	−2.9	−.00	27.2	1.23	−22.9	−.01	38.4	1.72	137.1	.10	22.1	1.01

NOTES For sources and methods, see text.

The 'Percentage of Total Effect' columns are percentages of the two effects for each pair of years quoted in Table 1.3. The 'Growth Rate of Contribution' columns are annual growth rates of the effects computed for each grouping (growth rates are used here rather than the simple ratios used earlier to abstract from the effect of the passage of time). Both sets of data are quoted since, for example, 100 per cent of a very small or negative number may not be especially impressive (see 1935/48 and 1951/58 for good examples).

employment in the base year (Part B of Table 1.6). In effect, productivity growth has behaved even-handedly.

II

The extension of the 'leading sectors' to comprise a wider range of new industries, as in Tables 1.6 and 1.7 , on one level gives a more adequate representation of the role of leading sectors in sectoral change. On the other hand, it risks going too far afield in search of growth nodes – it is obvious that part of the expansion of the rubber industry, to take just one example, results from that of motor vehicles and aerospace (etc.). Even among the primary leading sectors there could have been powerful interdependencies. As Rostow himself points out,

> The three complexes [internal combustion engine, electricity, and chemicals] were related in significant ways. The automobile (and truck), for example, depended on rapidly evolving chemistries of oil refining and rubber manufacture, as well as on the battery, spark plugs, and other light electrical gear. Electric power played a large role in the production of many of the new chemicals. (Rostow, 1978, p. 209)[6]

Above all, the whole range of Rostovian backward and forward linkages to other industries is overlooked. Finally, the links with non-manufacturing industry need further consideration.

If allowance is made for all the backward and forward linkages and interdependencies, then, how much did the expansion of the new industries contribute to economic growth at large? In this paper I tackle this huge question by looking at just one of the 45 spans of years for which the earlier calculations were undertaken: the years from 1930 to 1935. The 1930s have received particular emphasis from some British economic historians, including H. W. Richardson. He states

> By 1930 this burden of "over-commitment" [to the old export staples] was being cast off. Connected with this was the fact that by 1930 the new industries, after two decades of gradual growth, were just beginning to reach the mass production stage of

development, and this revealed new output potentialities. (Aldcroft and Richardson, 1969, p. 251)

Though both Richardson and Aldcroft, *inter alia*, have had occasion to grant the usefulness of input-output methods for resolving the kinds of issues they pose, neither they nor others have gone so far as, for instance, formal computation using the 'Leontief inverse'. Soon after Leontief's own pioneering work on the interwar American economy, Tibor Barna devised an input–output table for the UK for 1935.[7] Barna divided the economy into 36 sectors; by and large his divisions have been imitated in postwar input – output tables for this country (unsurprisingly, since all relate back to the census of production), and will be used in what follows hereafter. Richardson and Aldcroft both (independently) accept Barna's table and his sub-divisions in their writings; so that the degree of interdependence, which is obviously a function of the precise industrial breakdown, is based on a mutually-agreed framework. The classifications are, however, quite different in many cases from the 1958/68 SIC categories used earlier in this paper, and could scarcely be re-developed in that system without a massive amount of work.

The overall contribution of new industries will be studied here in the manner of much present-day historiography by evaluation of the counterfactual outcomes. The same point has indeed been made implicitly by Richardson himself: 'It is obvious that without the new industries – motor-cars, rayon, household appliances, radio and electrical engineering, for example – the increase in productivity and real income would only have been very small compared with what was actually achieved in the interwar period' (Aldcroft and Richardson, 1969, p. 270). The simplest procedure is to suppose that the output (and therefore the derived demands) of new industries were not to have risen at all since 1930 – how much lower would 1935 output then have been? More moderate and plausible counterfactuals such as permitting the new industries to grow at average industrial rates can be gauged in this light. Thus I retain final demands (consumption, exports, etc.) of all other industries at the levels they actually attained in 1935, and attempt to assess the effect on their aggregate gross output (final plus intermediate demands) of the reduction in inter-industry demand arising out of this hypothetical failure of new industries to improve their sales one iota over 1930 levels.

Before this calculation can be carried out, two statistical obstacles have to be overcome. The first follows from the fact that Barna's input–output table is drawn up in terms of current (1935) prices, as opposed to say physical quantities. As such, this raises complications for the counterfactual comparison with 1930. According to Stone and Rowe (1966, Table 24, p. 58) the average price of motor cars consumed in Britain fell from £279 in 1930 to £213 in 1935. Use of current prices for both years might well bias the inter-industry effects downwards. Unfortunately it is not enough to correct for the 1930 level of purchases by converting their physical amounts into an average sales value for 1935. Not only were cars getting cheaper between 1930 and 1935, they were also getting smaller (see Richardson, 1967, pp. 84, 120). The depression years marked the heyday of the introduction of popular small models, like the Morris Eight and the Ford Eight. What is wanted is to correct the 1935 average price by an allowance for changes in 'quality' (size, etc.) since 1930. This amounts to an analogue of the so-called 'hedonic' price index often used to evaluate hypotheses about consumer demand for automobiles; whereby prices are adjusted for differing power, handling, braking, styling, etc., as the consumer detects them in varying sales mixes. My analogue requires the producer's point of view rather than the consumer's. The nearest approach to this ideal readily obtainable is to take the various categories of, say, vehicle (private cars, commercial passenger vehicles, goods vehicles, motor cycles, tractors, pedal cycles, etc.), subdivide so far as is possible by size (horse-power for private cars, passenger and freight capacity for commercial vehicles), and weight each quantity by 1935 price weights. In fact, the Census of Production gives private cars in six groupings (8 HP and under; 8 to 12 HP; 12 to 16 HP; 16 to 20 HP; over 20 HP; and unclassified including taxicabs), internal-combustion passenger vehicles in four, and internal-combustion goods vehicles in five. The same could be done, at varying levels of disaggregation (greatest for chemicals), for electrical engineering, electricity supply, and chemicals and allied industries. It may be noted in passing that this procedure partially obviated the well-known difficulties about input–output coefficients changing through time.

The second data problem is that some of the new industries – rayon and silk, scientific instruments, and electricity supply are those considered here – constitute sub-sectors of the classifications adopted by Barna. Accordingly I had first to deduct the derived demands for the remainder of the relevant classification (cotton, gas and water supplies, and unspecified metal goods other than precision instruments). This had to be done by trial and error; substituting suitable levels of final demand for all other new industries and sub-industries in each case. In theory this could lead to multiple solutions because of the interdependencies, but in practice the reductions in output of cotton, gas and water, and other unspecified metal goods were so small that the trial and error procedure seems accurate enough up to the level of rounding employed.

Standard input–output procedure of course requires the computation of a matrix of input–output coefficients, $A = [a_{ij}]$ ($i = 1, 2, \ldots, 36; j = 1, 2, \ldots, 36$), where the cell components – the a_{ij} – represent the proportion of industry i's gross output coming as an intermediate input from industry j. In addition the vectors $x = (x_i)$ and $c = (c_i)$ are defined, each of 36 elements, representing gross outputs and final demands respectively, for each industry. Prediction then generally involves substituting in new values for the final demands (a new vector c), and establishing the inter-industry effects through the computation of the 'Leontief inverse', $(I–A)^{-1}$.

The basic counterfactual used here however required a slightly different technique. In general I did not have available 1930 data on final demands. I could, though, acquire 1930 material on gross outputs from the Census of Production. Thus my problem was one of setting the gross outputs of the new industries (or sub-industries) at their 1930 levels (measured in 1935 prices), whilst the final demands of all other industries were maintained at 1935 levels. In this way, the task is reduced to solving 36 equations in 36 unknowns (7 unknown c_i's for the new industries and 29 unknown x_i's for the rest). With appropriate algebraic transformations this could be effected using standard simultaneous-equations methods. The results are summarised in Table 1.8.[8] In column (ii) appears the difference between the levels of gross output actually achieved in 1935, according to Barna, and the levels that would have prevailed if the physical quantities of product of the new industries had stayed at 1930 rather than rising to 1935 levels. For the new industries themselves, these differences are obtained from the census, suitably price-and-quality-adjusted. For the remaining industries, the differences reflect the hypothesised diminution of their gross output when the derived demands of the expansion of new industries are eliminated.

TABLE 1.8 *Actual gross outputs and final demands of all sectors, 1935, compared with two hypothetical solutions (£ million)*

Industry	*(i) Actual gross output*	*(ii) Change 1930/35 method I*	*(iii) Change 1930/35 method II*	*(iv) Actual final demand*	*(v) Change 1930/35 method I*	*(vi) Change 1930/35 method II*
Agriculture, forestry, etc.	293.8	−0.2	−40.7	230.5	–	−38.43
Coal mining	146.5	−7.3	−23.1	64.5	–	−0.02
Other mining	21.9	−0.6	−5.9	3.2	–	−0.06
Building materials	62.2	−0.9	−25.1	15.2	–	−15.18
China and glass	32.4	−1.2	−17.9	13.9	–	−13.87
Coke ovens	17.3	−0.8	−9.2	4.8	–	−4.77
Chemicals, etc.	93.2	−16.4	−16.4	48.3	−13.5	−6.17
Soap, polishes	39.2	−0.1	−0.1	34.7	–	−0.01
Oils, paints	81.8	−1.8	−10.3	26.2	–	−0.06
Iron and steel manufactures	193.2	−11.0	−72.0	39.8	–	−0.07
Non-ferrous metals	57.2	−3.8	−35.8	15.8	–	−15.77
Shipbuilding	46.5	−0.1	−41.4	39.3	–	−39.24
Mechanical engineering	186.9	−3.6	−157.3	128.0	–	−127.96
Electrical engineering	109.6	−43.9	−43.9	70.5	−35.5	−28.20
Motor and cycle	171.5	−49.2	−49.2	120.5	−38.7	−34.60
Aircraft	14.4	−5.2	−5.2	13.3	−4.8	−4.80
Railway rolling stock	44.9	−0.4	−25.0	17.2	–	−17.16
Metal goods n.e.s.	173.4	−6.2	−131.0	104.9	−1.3	−104.81
Cotton and silk	211.4	−20.5	−7.9	83.3	−13.3	−0.07

Woollen and worsted	142.2	−0.4	−3.7	55.0	–	−0.06
Hosiery and lace	48.4	−0.0	−0.1	42.7	–	−0.03
Other textiles	61.1	−0.8	−4.3	26.4	–	−0.08
Textile finishing, etc.	32.1	−2.3	−1.2	0.1	–	−0.08
Leather and fur	47.1	−0.7	−1.7	17.6	–	−0.06
Clothing	222.4	−0.0	−0.5	207.5	–	−0.04
Food processing	406.0	−0.1	−7.1	303.6	–	−0.02
Drink and tobacco	360.8	−0.3	−0.6	306.7	–	−0.07
Manufactures of wood	98.6	−1.3	−9.2	56.5	–	−0.08
Paper	74.8	−1.4	−6.1	20.6	–	−0.04
Printing and publishing	145.7	−2.7	−12.6	70.2	–	−0.07
Rubber	28.4	−2.3	−19.2	15.9	–	−15.85
Miscellaneous manufactures	24.2	−0.1	−0.4	20.4	–	−0.00
Building and civil engineering	470.6	−0.3	−74.2	321.5	–	−61.10
Gas, electricity and water	242.5	−59.5	−59.5	159.6	−48.6	−37.50
Distributive services	1700.6	−14.0	−482.1	1298.4	–	−399.80
Other services	1348.5	−1.0	−8.3	1305.5	–	−0.04
Total	7458.0	−267.8	−1408.3	5302.3	−155.7	−966.17

NOTES For sources see text.
Method I = using simultaneous equations (dashes in col. (v) are zeroes by assumption).
Method II = using linear programming.
All figures rounded to one decimal place for cols. (i)–(v) and two decimal places for col. (vi).
Industrial groupings follow Barna (1952).

The direct effect measured by the net decline in gross output as estimated by simultaneous equations is 3.6 per cent, which can be taken as big or small, depending on the point of view of the observer. It will naturally be larger for a longer period. On the other hand, it is probably greatly overstated through assuming zero substitution, that is through assuming that if (say) electricity supply does not grow, no other form of power supply will be forthcoming to fill the void.

More constructively, perhaps, the indirect effects may be seen by comparing the decline in gross outputs, set out in column (ii), with those of final demands in column (v). If attention is limited to the 33 secondary industries by omitting agriculture and the two service sectors, the decline in final demands is actually greater proportionately (6.3 per cent) than that of gross outputs (6.1 per cent), though by very little. In other words, as it turns out, one would obtain virtually the same impression about the impact of the new industries over the years 1930/5 by means of a rough-and-ready calculation based on final demands (consumption, capital formation, exports, etc.) as with the more sophisticated input–output approach incorporating inter-industry linkages.[9]

This modified input–output approach is tantamount to imposing the heaviest burden of adjustment to a world of stagnant new industries on the final demands for those new industries. For most of the new industries the proportionate fall in final demand therefore comes out greater than that in gross output. This is in keeping with the 'age of high mass-consumption' kind of stress on burgeoning consumption levels for the products of new industries – motor cars, vacuum cleaners, radios, and the like. On the other hand, the method of estimation does lead to a result that seems historically implausible. The hypothesised reduction in, say, electricity supply does little to lower the portion of outputs of all other industries going to satisfy final demands. The gross output of industries other than new industries is reduced primarily by the smaller *input* requirements of new industries, rather than the smaller output consequences. In other words, backward linkages are looked after better than forward linkages. This is clearly doing an injustice to Rostow and to Richardson.

Constraints can be introduced into the problem to help cope with this objection. For a second solution, I chose to impose the constraint that final demands for new industries should not be permitted to fall by a greater proportion than their 'actual' fall in gross outputs. This would prevent the adjustment coming wholly through sacrifices in final consumption of electricity, etc., and thereby require the electricity supply available to other industries to fall. The problem to be solved was set out as:

$$\text{Min} \sum_{i \neq n} \Delta x$$

$$\text{subject to} \quad A\Delta x + \Delta c = \Delta x \quad (\text{all } i)$$

$$\Delta x \leqslant 0$$

$$\Delta c \leqslant 0$$

$$\Delta c \geqslant -c$$

$$\frac{\Delta c_n}{c_n} \geqslant \frac{\Delta x_n}{x_n} \quad (n = 7, 14, 15, 16, 34)$$

$$\Delta x_n \text{ given}$$

From the basic theory of linear programming, it follows that an optimum will lie in a corner of the feasible solution space. In this example, as becomes apparent in comparing columns (iv) and (vi) of Table 1.8 this means that for 31 of the 36 industries, final demands will change by either the minimum or the maximum allowable (I altered the x_i in discrete jumps of £0.1 m, so that zero is only approximated in most cases). Now, this may seem as arbitrary as the first method of solution by simultaneous equations. In part it is; but it does help to indicate what would happen were a more historically plausible set of constraints to be found. The coefficients of the input–output matrix assure that the old staples like iron and steel, shipbuilding, railway vehicles, and coke ovens – together with mechanical engineering, parts of which (at least) are often regarded as nineteenth-century staples – will always figure prominently among the industries most badly affected by a retardation of structural change, no matter what other counterfactuals are attempted with new industries in the interwar economy. On the other side, some of the more dependent new industries, like rubber and non-ferrous metals, are also severely hindered. But the overriding impression is the opposite of a new block of industries with weak links back to the lumbering export staples – the most powerful linkages run backwards and forwards to the selfsame export staples. The linear programming approach does seem to have been successful (whatever its other limitations) in picking up some of the forward linkages, as was asked of it. The case of shipbuilding provides a good example. It was not an industry that acted as an important input to any new industry (or any industry, for that matter); it is completely cut back as in column (vi) of Table 1.8 because of significant forward linkages from iron and steel and especially mechanical engineering.

The other side of the 'development block' concept, of strong interdependencies among the leading sectors themselves, is less straightforward to assess from this information, since any reasonable test is eliminated by assumption. It is noteworthy that if the outputs of the remaining leading sectors are consecutively reduced to 1930 levels, the 1935 gross output of chemicals is reduced by just 2.0 per cent, of electrical engineering by 3.2 per cent, of motors and cycles by only 0.1 per cent, and aircraft not at all. On this evidence it would seem preferable to emphasise

> what Strassmann calls the interrelatedness of innovations effect. To explain this: innovations at one stage of production tend by altering the structure of costs at another stage to facilitate innovations there which would not otherwise have been profitable. The degree of interrelatedness is obviously higher in industries with close input-output connections. (Richardson, 1967, p. 95).

Unlike Richardson, my input – output findings here as well as my earlier results on the spillover of productivity change would lead me to pursue much of this effect, too, straight back to the old export staples.

Whether the degree of feed-back (and forward) to the older industries persists into more modern periods remains for future testing. All I am able to do here is collate the input–output coefficients from tables for subsequent years, as in Table 1.9. Transactions between firms but within the industry have been suppressed from this comparative Table, since the basis for collecting such data appears to have altered substantially from year to year. Otherwise the Barna division of industries has been my guide, inasmuch as it produced the kind of results already discussed.

Unsurprisingly, in view of the rapid growth rates of new industries, there was a rise in the proportion of inputs into leading sectors coming from those other new industries, with all of the rise occurring in the period 1935–48. The proportional input from old

TABLE 1.9 *Input coefficients for leading sectors, 1935–68*

	From other leading sectors	*From other new industries*	*From the old staples*	*From old staples plus mechanical engineering*
1935	.0344	.0801	.1102	.1267
1948	.0509	.1397	.1470	.1601
1954	.0466	.1159	.1433	.1721
1963	.0467	.1060	.1318	.1618
1968	.0429	.1232	.1049	.1282

NOTES So far as the columns are concerned (the *j*'s), the leading sectors are as for Table 1.6 plus gas, electricity and water supply. For rows (the *i*'s) they are Table 1.6 leading sectors plus electricity supply. With these additions new industries are as in Table 1.6. Old staples are also as for Table 1.6 with the addition of coal mining. These plus mechanical engineering (less constructional and mechanical handling equipment and textile machinery and accessories) are shown in a further column because of the significance of mechanical engineering in the linear programming solution for 1935.

SOURCES 1935–based on T. Barna 'The Interdependence of the British Economy', *Journal of the Royal Statistical Society* (Series A) (1952), revised upwards to exclude inter-firm intra-industry transactions.

1948–I. G. Stewart's table, republished with amendments in Ghosh (1954), Supplementary Tables B.

1954, 1963, 1968–Central Statistical Office input-output tables.

staples did not, however, fall notably over the period 1935–68, and was much higher between 1948 and 1963 than in 1935. It is thus not obvious that repetitions of the calculations undertaken in Table 1.8 would yield vastly different results for later years.

III

Aldcroft and Richardson have attempted to reconcile the sustained growth of output of the interwar period with its notoriously poor record for unemployment by hinting that the new industries had much more to offer the former than the latter. As Aldcroft stated in 1967, '. . . one has to remember that, apart from building, most of the new and rapidly expanding sectors were less labour intensive than the old staples and so their impact on the labour market was less than might be expected' (Aldcroft and Fearon, 1969, p. 53). Richardson agrees with this relative capital intensity of the new industries, for example pointing out that their contribution to the growth of employment 'is likely to be the least impressive consequence of their expansion' (Richardson, 1967, p. 90). There are many difficulties with defining labour or capital intensity, and it is compounded here by having to marry differing sources. For what it is worth, in Table 1.10 I have tried to combine C. H. Feinstein's figures for capital in manufacturing industry with employment and net output figures from the 1935 census of production. It may be noted that, with the outstanding exception of chemicals, most new industries assessable on this classification (the classification is

TABLE 1.10 *Capital–labour ratios and labour productivity by industry (S.I.T.C./Feinstein classification) 1935*

Industry	*Fixed capital: labour*		*Total capital: labour*		*Net output per employee*	
	£000/man	*rank*	*£000/man*	*rank*	*£*	*rank*
Cotton	0.73	6	0.80	8	116.4	22
Woollen and worsted	0.55	11	0.74	10	179.8	16
Silk and rayon	0.71	7	0.82	7	172.3	18
Linen and jute	1.07	3	1.50	2	143.6	21
Other textiles	0.36	18	0.38	20	170.8	19
Iron and steel	0.66	10	0.71	11	216.0	13
Mechanical engineering	0.54	12	0.65	14	220.2	12
Electrical engineering	0.41	17	0.54	16	231.3	11
Motor and cycle	0.21	21	0.28	21	231.4	10
Nonferrous metals	0.45	15	0.60	15	245.3	8
Drink	1.18	2	1.39	3	658.2	2
Tobacco	0.42	16	1.21	4	662.2	1
Food	0.66	9	0.78	9	283.1	5
Chemicals and allied	1.40	1	1.58	1	456.1	3
Rubber and leather	0.35	19	0.48	18	249.1	7
Textile finishing	0.21	22	0.25	22	151.1	20
Paper	0.78	5	0.92	6	239.8	9
Printing and publishing	0.46	14	0.54	17	284.9	4
Wood and wood products	0.52	13	0.66	13	201.2	14
Brick and cement	0.67	8	0.70	12	251.1	6
China and glass	0.34	20	0.39	19	173.7	17
Miscellaneous n.e.s.	0.82	4	1.12	5	197.8	15

SOURCES Capital – (C. H. Feinstein, *Domestic Capital Formation in the United Kingdom 1920–38* (Cambridge University Press, 1965, Table 8, pp. 102–42). Labour and productivity – Census of Production for 1935. The capital figures are first-cost estimates. If depreciated values are used instead, motor vehicles fall to lowest place for capital: labour ratios, and none of the new industries changes its rank by more than one place.

Feinstein's, based on the 1948 SIC) come well down the list of rankings of capital intensity, with motor vehicles particularly low on the scale. Conversely, many of the old staples – including most of the branches of the textile industry – come quite high up the list. An alternative way of expressing capital intensity would be a relative one, that is relative to manufacturing or the economy as a whole. Figures borrowed from Dowie and aggregated can illuminate this formulation as in Table 1.11.

TABLE 1.11 *Percentage shares in UK employment and capital stock, 1929–37*

	Employment		*Capital*		*Relative capital intensity*	
	1929	*1937*	*1929*	*1937*	*1929*	*1937*
4 New industries	5·8	6.6	2·9	3·1	0.50	0·47
3 Old staples	9·9	8.5	6.7	5·4	0.67	0.64
Total manufacturing	35·7	35·2	17·2	15·4	0·48	0·44

NOTE The four new industries are chemicals, electrical engineering, vehicles, and rayon and silk. The three old staples are iron and steel, shipbuilding, and other textiles.
SOURCE A. Dowie, 'Growth in the Inter-War Period: Some More Arithmetic', *Economic History Review* 1968, Table 4. Dowie's capital figures are based on Feinstein (1965).

The categories differ again from those utilised earlier, but the general impression is probably not misleading. The new industries have about the same shares in the national cake of capital relative to employment as manufacturing as a whole, whereas the old staples have a relative capital intensity half as high again as the new industries (or manufacturing generally). Even textiles, packed with female labour and operating at particularly low levels of output per employee (Table 1.10), have a higher capital intensity in 1929 and 1937 than the mean of these new industries.

Leontief himself was first to demonstrate how input–output techniques could throw further light on employment generated. One begins with a vector of labour requirements per unit of output, $l = (l_j)$, representing the number of employees needed per thousand pounds of gross output. Vector l is rewritten as a diagonal matrix L (with zeroes off the diagonal) and post-multiplied by the matrix of input–output coefficients, A^*.[10] The column sums of the resultant matrix represent the coefficient of direct and indirect labour requirements.

The overall employment effect of the new industries is then calculated in the same way as was output and consumption in Method I of Table 1.8 relying on the usual Leontief assumption of zero elasticities of substitution. The decline in employment between actual-1935 and hypothetical-1935 is 2.9 per cent, the same as in final demand. For secondary industry alone, the decline (5.8 per cent) is only a fraction lower than either final demand or gross output. These results suggest that the new industries were about as good at creating jobs as at increasing output. One or two, like chemicals, are indeed relatively labour-saving with respect to the economy as a whole; but once the indirect employment effects are taken into account, the others more or less compensate for them. As noted in the introduction to this paper, this result is in line with the reservations of Rostow concerning the supposed capital-intensity of electricity supply – his precise point is this very one about the possibilities for indirect employment creation.

The impact on employment may be brought out in another way by considering the magnitudes involved. Employment in the seven new industries considered in Table 1.8 grew by some 170 000 between 1930 and 1935 – a goodly proportion of the 205 000 added to employment in all secondary industry over that quinquennium. So powerful are the labour coefficients, however, that if the gross output of these new industries in 1935 were cut back to 1930 levels, as was done in Table 1.8 then total employment would fall by as much as 513 000. There are grounds for arguing that the benefits conferred by the rise of new industries on the economy lay as much in putting to work factors that would otherwise have been unemployed (at least in the 1930s) as in windfall productivity gains.

IV

The major conclusions are as follows. Over the long run, the 'shift' effect of resource allocation and reallocation among sectors has been much less important in explaining productivity growth in the UK than the 'internal' effect of productivity growth within all sectors. Such shift effect as there was owed most to the relative or absolute displacement of labour from a comparative handful of low-productivity 'old staples', though the recruitment of labour into one or two new industries, especially chemicals, also helped. The internal effect was more evenly shared around among industries, old and new alike (the reasons why productivity growth affected most industries more or less commensurately deserve further attention). With a few obvious exceptions, like rubber and non-ferrous metals, the backward and forward linkages of the leading sectors run consistently to the export staples – it does not seem valid to view the new industries as a 'development block' largely independent of the staple trades. Finally, the belief that a structural shift towards new industries explains the coexistence of high economy-wide growth rates and high unemployment in the 1930s is not supported. The advantage of new industries to the economy emerges not so much as exceptionally rapid technical progress (unless through leading innovation elsewhere) nor as once-for-all productivity gains while they are growing rapidly, but equally as the simple Keynesian effect of employing primary resources in sufficiently large quantities.

NOTES

1. Rostow (1971), pp. 175–6. I am grateful to the Houblon–Norman fund of the Bank of England for financial assistance towards compiling the data herein.
2. Schumpeter (1961) and Svennilson (1954). For an alternative perspective to Rostow's that also anchors itself on these authors see Cornwall (1977).
3. The general tenor of their contributions is perhaps most readily conveyed in the essays published in Aldcroft and Richardson (1969), also Richardson (1967).
4. It should be noted that there is a misprint in this equation in Salter – at least in the edition referred to here (1966).
5. It should be noted that 'net output' is not identical with value-added 'since it contains payments for services rendered by firms, e.g. payments made for repairs, hire of plant, advertising, research work, etc.' (*Historical Record*, 1978, p. xiv). Any corrections on these scores would involve greater errors than the gain in precision.
6. This point will be touched on in what follows but is taken up in more detail in my paper to the Cliometrics Conference at the University of Warwick in 1978 (see the brief summary in the *Journal of European Economic History*, vol. 9:1 (1980), 229–31 from which most of this section derives). My thanks again to the individuals and participants at seminars for their help with that paper.
7. Barna (1952). In using Barna's table hereafter, the one change I have made is in row 34, column 26 – inputs of gas, electricity and water into food processing industries – where Barna has evidently been misled by a misprint in the 1935 census. The figure has been adjusted down from £8.7 to £2.1 millions, and final demands adjusted upwards accordingly.
8. The list of new industries adopted here is that given for the contribution of new industries to output given by Aldcroft in 1967 (see Aldcroft and Fearon, 1969, p. 47). On the following page he gives a quite different list, when discussing their contribution to investment; and then a drastically different list – comprising no less than 71 out of 100 industries! – when talking about

employment. The list given in Aldcroft (1970, p. 177) is similar to that here.

9. The multiplier is accounted for rather perversely, in that the result of the counterfactual is to give most industries other than new industries a higher *share* of 1935 final demand than they actually held in that year. T. C. Thomas' estimate (see Floud and McCloskey, 1981, p. 346) for the public-expenditure multiplier with a cumulative five-year lag is 1.44; which does not indicate a drastic need to amend the results to allow for the multiplier. However, Thomas' figure may be biased downward by ignoring the feedback from British imports (treated as a straight leakage) to British exports (see next footnote).
10. A* is the previous matrix A adjusted by taking account of imports, so that employment generated abroad is excluded; if employment is generated in British exports through Britain accepting a higher level of imports then one can work straightforwardly with the matrix A.

REFERENCES

Aldcroft, D. H., *The Inter-War Economy: Britain, 1919–1939* (London: Batsford, 1970).

Aldcroft D. H., and Fearon, P. (eds), *Economic Growth in 20th-Century Britain* (London: Macmillan, 1969).

Aldcroft, D. H., and Richardson, H. W., *The British Economy, 1870–1939* (London: Macmillan, 1969).

Alford, B. W. E., *Depression and Recovery? British Economic Growth 1919–1939* (London: Macmillan (Studies in Economic History Series), 1972).

Barna, T., 'The Interdependence of the British Economy', *Journal of the Royal Statistical Society* (Series A), 1952.

Brown, B. C., 'Industrial Production in 1935 and 1948', *Bulletin of the London and Cambridge Economic Service*, December 1954.

Business Statistics Office, *Historical Record of the Census of Production 1907 to 1970* (London: HMSO, 1978).

Cornwall, J., *Modern Capitalism: Its Growth and Transformation* (Oxford: Martin Robertson, 1977).

Dahmén, E., 'Technology, Innovations and International Industrial Transformation', in L. H. Dupriez (ed.), *Economic Progress*, Institut de Recherches Economiques et Sociales (Louvain, 1955) pp. 293–306.

Dowie, J. A., 'Growth in the Inter-War Period: Some More Arithmetic', *Economic History Review*, 1968 (reprinted in Aldcroft and Fearon, *supra*).

Feinstein, C. H., *Domestic Capital Formation in the United Kingdom, 1920–38* (Cambridge University Press, 1965).

Feinstein, C. H., *National Income, Expenditure and Output of the United Kingdom, 1855–1965* (Cambridge University Press, 1972).

Floud, R. C., and McCloskey, D. N. (eds), *The Economic History of Britain since 1700*, vol. 2 (Cambridge University Press, 1981).

Ghosh, A., *Experiments with Input–Output Models: an Application to the Economy of the U.K., 1948–55* (Cambridge University Press, 1954).

Mitchell, B. R. with Deane, P., *Abstract of British Historical Statistics* (Cambridge University Press, 1971).

Mitchell B. R. and Jones, H. G., *Second Abstract of British Historical Statistics* (Cambridge University Press, 1971).
Richardson, H. W., *Economic Recovery in Britain, 1932–9* (London: Weidenfeld & Nicolson, 1967).
Rostow, W. W., *The Stages of Economic Growth*, 2nd edn (Cambridge University Press, 1971).
Rostow, W. W., *The World Economy: History and Prospect* (London: Macmillan, 1978).
Salter, W. E. G., *Productivity and Technical Change*, 2nd edn (Cambridge University Press, 1966).
Schumpeter, J. A., *The Theory of Economic Development*, 2nd edn (New York: Oxford University Press, 1961).
Stone R. and Rowe, D. A., *The Measurement of Consumers' Expenditure and Behaviour in the United Kingdom, 1920–1938*, vol. II (Cambridge University Press, 1966).
Svennilson, I., *Growth and Stagnation in the European Economy* (Geneva: Economic Commission for Europe, 1954).

2 A Neo-Schumpeterian Analysis of the Recent Industrial Development Crisis in Sweden*

E. DAHMÉN

METHODOLOGICAL SUGGESTIONS AND SOME MAIN RESULTS

> Most of the fundamental errors currently committed in economic analysis are due to lack of historical experience more often than to any other shortcoming of the economist's equipment.
>
> J. Schumpeter

> In fact, neither aggregates nor averages do act upon one another.
>
> F. A. Hayek

The following paper presents some main results of recent research on post-war industrial development in Sweden. Although some international readers may be interested in the substantial findings as such, the account is given mainly in order to articulate a methodological point. The primary objective is to illustrate advantages of complementing the conventional macro-approach by historical research, partly on the corporate decision making level, utilising a conceptual frame of reference of a Neo-Schumpeterian and 'Austrian' type.[1] What more exactly is meant by this will hopefully become clear to the reader from what follows.

* I am greatly indebted to Rolf Henriksson at the Stockholm University who commented on early drafts of this paper and offered valuable criticism and constructive suggestions.

The paper starts out by sketching a picture of general economic developments in recent decades. It includes an account of what modern macro-modelling with broad aggregates made most analysts, as well as those relying on them, believe was going on. It then proceeds by reporting on what, according to recent findings, was actually happening. A final section pinpoints and illustrates some of the deficiencies in the traditional macro-modelling approach.

HOW IT SEEMED TO BE

In the post-war period the year 1975 is generally marked out as a dramatic break-off point. Until that year the economy seemed to have progressed without any major and lasting setbacks. Quite unexpectedly the second half of the 1970s showed very slow growth in GNP. Policy makers were unprepared to cope with this new situation. The sustained upward trend before 1975 had created confidence in the strength of the economy. Variations in the rate of expansion were taken as a normal pattern but the possibility of a long lasting stagnation was not seriously considered.

A basic thesis in the following is that the way things were generally looked upon can to no small degree be ascribed to interpretations characterised by a one-sided reliance on macro-economic models of a too highly aggregative kind. The 'search-lights' had not been properly focused on the factors crucial for the severity and length of the stagnation following the 1975 downturn. What was it, then, that had instead been in focus?

A fairly steady upward trend in industrial production had been observed throughout the post-war period up to the middle of the 1970s. Particularly rapid growth occurred in the early 1960s but there was a strong expansion also in 1973–4. It had also been recorded that productivity had increased satisfactorily and that despite inflation unit labour costs had not, until 1975, increased more than in competing industries abroad. There had been little concern about inflation as such though much lip-service had been paid to the need to fight against it. A certain upward pressure on the general price level had been regarded as beneficial for industry not only as a sign of, but also a cause of, predominant sellers' markets. It was also supposed to ease burdens of indebtedness. Increasing nominal interest rates had been registered but the real rates were thought to be low.

Another record fact was that there had been no lasting trade deficits and that the terms of trade had not deteriorated. Net borrowing abroad had not been necessary. In 1973–4 the export industry had been able to raise its prices, following the rise in import prices, without, on the whole, losing market shares. The 1973–4 boom, looking roughly like the preceding ones, had displayed particularly strong industrial performances. This had made management, employees and, not least, politicians quite optimistic. Demands for exceptionally large wage increases were met with no decisive resistance. Large investments were carried out. A lively investment activity was forecast also for the rest of the 1970s. Central and local government revenue rose quickly largely due to the inflationary wage rise combined with high marginal tax rates. This generated a strong rise in public expenditure. The expanding public sector did not, in the eyes of most people, seem to overburden the economy.

The setback in 1975 was triggered by the international recession and by the oil crisis. As no clear warning signals had been observed in the preceding long period of time, the downturn was viewed as one not essentially unlike those experienced earlier. It was therefore met by a set of fairly traditional countercyclical steps as well as by subsidies to crisis-ridden firms, *inter alia* for stock-keeping purposes. Such subsidies were paid in an attempt to bridge what was thought to be just a temporary setback for a basically strong industry. The idea was to put industry in a position to take advantage of the international business improvement expected to occur rather soon. The bridging policy as such was successful in the sense that at least employment was maintained on a satisfactory level. However, Swedish industry failed to hook on to the international upturn which, correctly anticipated, came in 1975. The failure was generally attributed to the overvaluation of the Swedish krona that followed from the wage explosion in 1975–6. Business firms and shareholders lost not only a lot of money but also their earlier optimism. Investment plans and investments were sharply cut back and the interest in shares weakened. The non-socialist government having come into office in 1976 after 44 years of social-democratic rule, or governments dominated by the social-democrats, was very anxious to refute the accusation of being against social welfare and full-employment policies. Public expenditure therefore soared, for one thing because of extensive aid to ailing industries. Because of the already very high taxes the steep rise in public expenditure could not altogether be covered by increasing tax incomes. The ensuing very large budget deficits were financed both by 'note-printing' and by borrowing at home and abroad.

When the business situation began to be unbearable due to much red ink having been spread over the income statements, and thus also to cumulating difficulties in maintaining high employment, the krona was devalued in two steps in 1977. Because of the general interpretation of the basic economic trends over the last decades and of the immediate causes of the 1975–6 disaster this step was supposed to restore, by and large, the general competitiveness of most industries, the only exception being those hit by some particular so-called 'structural' difficulties. This presumption proved to be a mistake. Conventional macro-analysis had missed too much of what had happened, particularly since the mid 1960s. The question then is: What was it that actually happened in what appeared to happen?

HOW IT REALLY WAS

What has been revealed by the Neo-Schumpeterian and 'Austrian' approach to the study of industrial development cannot possibly be summed up in a brief space without forsaking many important points. Although the broad lines are clear enough and the main findings sufficiently well documented, the picture presented in the following is bound to be quite schematic. It should also be kept in mind that uncertainties still remain, leaving much to be explored and explained by further research.

The exposition is divided into three main parts: the first dealing with the period before 1960, the second one with the years 1960–5 and the third with the following fifteen years. A comparison between these periods will help bring to light what the macro-analysts and those more or less influenced by their analyses did not see.

The necessarily short presentation is organised around one basic discovery, namely that there was a crucial break in the development in the middle of the 60s.

The period before 1960

A relatively slow industrial expansion in the 1950s was associated with moderate gains in productivity. A considerable part of this gain resulted from a transfer of labour between sectors of industry as well as between plants within sectors. In spite of this, large variations in the degree of modernisation between different plants persisted. Closures were uncommon except in the textile and clothing industry where from the early 1950s onwards weaker firms were forced out of business. The 'Salter-structures' thus stayed rather extended.

High rates of return on capital were obtained by sectors of industry and firms having achieved productivity increases by energetic cost reduction measures. Here profitability and productivity were positively correlated. The highest rates of return, however, were attained by firms creating markets for new products and especially by those being parts of 'development blocks'.[2] These firms generally grew quite fast, sometimes without achieving particularly big gains in productivity. Firms expanding in 'sellers' markets' often made only moderate profits, the reason being that they did not manage adequately to adapt their production equipment and organisation to an increasing capacity.

What happened in the 1950s can be summarised as a result of a considerable advantage enjoyed by the main part of Swedish industry over its foreign competitors. This advantage resulted from the unusually strong demand for Swedish products in countries more or less damaged by the war and from the fact that among the European countries Sweden had in many branches a considerable lead in productivity and product mix. It sometimes made the preparedness for changing future conditions below what later turned out to be highly desirable or necessary. Despite – or sometimes rather due to – the satisfactory profits in many industries, investment activity was not very likely.

Much capital was piling up in some industries without reaching the long-term capital market which, furthermore, was prevented by central bank regulations from performing efficiently in support of the most growth-promoting allocation of resources. In many cases investments were held back also by other particular circumstances. In some regions large investments had to be made to expand and modernise the infrastructure, especially in transportation and urban housing, before manufacturing industry could embark upon extensive investment programmes. Most important, however, was that the prospects for trade policy were clouded by uncertainties about the EEC and EFTA negotiations.

The boom of the early 1960s

In the early 1960s the picture changed. Production and productivity reached unprecedented peaks and industrial investments increased rapidly. The boom was caused first and foremost by the international business upsurge which had much to do with the trade liberalisation, mainly through EEC and EFTA, and US dollar convertibility. At the same time most of the factors retarding investment in the 1950s had become less important or even nonexistent. Many 'development blocks' were initiated and followed up in response to infrastructural improvements or created by more or less new industrial complementarities. In the majority of cases the pioneering innovations originated abroad but there was also much domestic engineering inventiveness and ingenuity put to good use. Mergers began to be common. As a rule they were of the offensive type, that is they were not the result of unprofitable firms selling themselves to more profitable ones. Instead they reflected good profit opportunities that could not always be exploited by one single firm. Some of them were also based on anticipation of stiffer competition in the years ahead. An internationalisation of Swedish industry which in some branches had a long tradition in history made rapid progress and was spread more widely than earlier.

The period after 1965

Many basic preconditions for industrial expansion changed again around the middle of the 1960s but more radically so – and in the opposite direction.

Important changes occurred on the demand side. Competition from other industrialised countries, which had gained much strength in the late 1950s and early 1960s, became much more fierce from now on. Japan, in particular, encroached successfully upon many markets for important Swedish products; somewhat later the so-called NIC countries added further to the difficulties for quite a number of industries.

Strong economic growth in both old and newly industrialised countries also offered many opportunities for Swedish industry. However, in order to seize such opportunities fully a swift resource-reallocation would have been necessary within the Swedish industrial sector and not least regionally. Such an adaptation to the new market conditions actually met with great difficulties because domestic conditions on the supply side had now changed considerably. As a matter of fact, the most decisive difference between the preconditions for industrial expansion before and after 1965 had to do with what took place *within* Sweden.

Behind many more or less new domestic features was the fact that various components of production costs started to develop around the mid 1960s in a very unfavourable way, thus creating much more of a cost push inflation than before. Wage increases now tended to surpass the productivity advance more than before. This was to a great extent a delayed consequence of the boom in the first half of the decade. It was also a result of soaring taxes even on moderate incomes, giving rise to market pressures for compensating wage increases. Such pressures could become very strong because of the strengthened bargaining position enjoyed by employees, reflecting *inter alia* the increasing demand for labour that had characterised the preceding years. Furthermore, white collar workers had become much better organised and had obtained a strong position thanks also to the rapid expansion of the public sector. An additional factor was a new union wage policy, strongly backed by political bodies. In centralised wage agreements special efforts were made to get the earnings of low-wage groups enhanced much more than those of other groups. This was bound to exert a strong upward pressure on the average wage level as it generated partly successful counteractions from these other groups to maintain the distance.

From the middle of the 1960s another fact began to hit industry much more than before. This was the increasing costs of avoiding environmental damages caused by production. This became a burden mainly for industries based on domestic raw materials which had already begun to lose some of their competitive strength. These and other industries with a highly energy-intensive production were later increasingly hurt also by the steep rise in energy prices which had earlier been very low in Sweden. Even capital costs rose to levels not experienced earlier. High interest on loans was caused mainly by three things, namely: an increased awareness among savers of their inflation losses, increased demands on the capital market by industries facing the kind of problem mentioned above and the revival of monetary policy resulting from the fact that fiscal policy appeared increasingly inadequate as a means of stabilising the economy.

It goes without saying that the rather sudden change from

demand-pull inflation to predominantly 'buyers' markets' and cost push inflation around the mid 1960s could not but reduce industry's ability to adapt to the new external circumstances. This was not all, however. Another inhibiting factor was increasing rigidities in the labour market. Much more often than before people refused to move, arguing that it was up to the government to procure, in one way or another, employment opportunities at their place of residence. This new attitude was strongly supported by unions and political parties – in contrast to what had been the case in the first two decades after the war. The increasing domestic rigidities and loss of much of the earlier reallocative capacity could hardly have been more untimely.

How did Swedish industry respond to the changed conditions on the demand side and on the supply side? In general firms took action to invest intensively mainly in order to reduce costs. Unlike previously, the emphasis was on machines in existing plants. In many cases this policy became a question of survival and in these cases there was not much time left for renewing the product and marketing side. Such renewal as a rule would have required a long-term perspective in planning as well as a considerable time to materialise. Cost cuts were achieved not only by modernising the machine park and by reducing the product range but also by means of mergers which were now often of a defensive nature. Strong efforts were devoted to utilising the advantages of economies of scale in order to bring down unit costs. In spite of this, Swedish firms and their plants often proved to be too small since many competitors expanded even more and were therefore often able to make use of even more modern and cheaper techniques. In many cases, the markets proved inadequate for a satisfactory utilisation of increased capacities. In such cases prices came down under the pressure of very strong competition. Under these circumstances cost levels in a great many Swedish firms proved to be still too high in spite of all that had been done successfully to bring them down. This explains why increases in productivity from now on did not always result in improved profitability and sometimes not even in survival. Contrary to what had been the case earlier there were now drastic examples of productivity and profitability developing in exactly opposite directions. Not a few investments appeared as malinvestments and many firms were forced to close down, or alternatively, to sell themselves to another firm or turn to the government for support.

Towards the middle of the 1970s the previously large differences in efficiency between firms and plants in one and the same sector had become much smaller. The 'tails' of the 'Salter-structures' had been very much shortened which explains a considerable part of the productivity increase in many branches of industry. On the other hand, this had made many of them very vulnerable to competition perhaps too powerful even for the most efficient firms. The 'buffers' in the branch structure had been eliminated in the process of restructuring that had been forced upon the branch. The very strong cost-push mainly from the wage side, had in many cases led to rapid productivity increases both by stimulating measures to reduce other costs and by forcing low productivity firms out of business. As this happened in many industries the result was a shrinking industry characterised by impressive productivity gains but also by low profitability.

Another interesting feature is that large differences in productivity appeared between different branches of industry. This, however, did not lead to a rapid rise in the average productivity of Swedish industry because the decreasing mobility of labour made it much more difficult than earlier for the more productive industries to attract labour. There might also have been considerable potential for new firms in some industries but such additions to the 'heads' of the 'Salter-structures' were actually rather few. New firms played a diminishing role in industrial development.

Summarising industry's response to the change of scene around the mid 1960s it can be stated that the sustained rate of increase in production and productivity from 1965 to the mid 1970s was largely due to three main factors: many firms worked off much slack, thus using up an unusually large reserve of cost-cutting opportunities as well as previously accumulated financial means. It was also to a great extent a matter of learning by doing since there was much new capacity that had not yet been fully trimmed. Last, but not least, much restructuring of branches was accomplished. It was in the nature of things that these reactions of industry to the new situation could not remain equally important in the long run. It also seems as if during the years of very pressing conditions too little time had been available for too few people to pay much attention to search activities and strategies for the more distant future. This is likely to have contributed to the difficulties in finding promising investment projects which became characteristic in the second half of the 1970s. Such difficulties, however, were due also to the rapidly increasing costs of acquiring fresh capital. Taking all these factors together it is not surprising that the industrial sector could not grow at the same rate in the 1970s as in the 1960s.

At the end of the 1970s Swedish industry could be proud of high productivity by international standards but it suffered from a profit anaemia. It had become too small, and possibly also insufficiently innovative, to provide for sustained rapid growth of the Swedish economy.

THE METHODOLOGICAL ISSUE: WHAT WAS WRONG WITH SOME PARTICULAR BROAD AGGREGATES?

In the post-war period up to 1975 the trend of total industrial production, as well as many other broad aggregates, disguised the fact that the basic conditions for industry differed in a decisive way between the period before 1965 and the following ten years, and particularly that there were in the latter period a number of underlying characteristics having a very important impact on later developments. The reason why this was disguised should be rather clear from what has already been said. The following hypothetical reasoning may be helpful as further clarification.

Assume that the industrial production curve during the 1950s had pointed more rapidly upwards than it actually did. In that case the first half of the 1960s would not have been marked by such an extraordinary expansion. Neither would there have been a considerable slack to work off in the second half of the 1960s by means of measures which to a high degree were bound to be of a non-recurrent nature. Under these circumstances the profound changes in external conditions for industry that occurred both abroad and domestically around the middle of the 1960s would have led to an easily visible break in the trend of industrial production as an indication of what had been going on below the surface. In the actual case, the most interesting course of events was not at all sufficiently observed. The conventional macro-analysis was to a great extent misled by the broad aggregates.

In order to be somewhat more concrete on this last-mentioned point I would like to finish by commenting on some of the specific developments observed by the conventional macro-analysis which, however, did not reveal the most interesting realities.

The development of unit labour costs in Swedish industry

compared with what happened in other countries, did not give the impression that from the middle of the 1960s Swedish industry suffered from declining competitive power. A fact which unit labour costs did not show, however, was a significant reduction in overseas transport costs which favoured producers of, among other things, iron ore and pulp, located farther away from European markets. Furthermore, unit labour cost series could not indicate the significance of the entry of many new foreign competitor countries which enjoyed a much lower level of costs. This resulted in a rise in the absolute difference in unit labour costs throughout the entire period even though in many cases the rate of increase from the starting point had been the same as in Sweden – or even faster. It should also be observed that the strain naturally got worse over time also in cases where there was no rise in the absolute difference in cost. Thirdly, not even a relatively moderate rate of increase in unit labour costs and technologically advanced position could maintain competitiveness when new sectors and new products were gaining the upper hand among competitors, as began to occur more frequently during the course of the 1960s. In general, comparisons of unit labour cost series through time lose much of their interest in periods of widespread industrial transformation.

Another sometimes misleading component of much macro-analysis is the concept of 'terms of trade'. Although terms of trade did not worsen for Sweden, disaggregation reveals a number of interesting things. From the 1960s onwards the index of import prices was affected more than before by falling prices of goods that Swedish industry itself produced, whereas earlier the fall of prices had been in raw materials, oil and other products which had to be imported. Since there were increasing difficulties to transfer resources within Sweden from industries now experiencing too stiff competition, to industries which still had good competitive ability, the development of terms of trade was not as 'neutral' as it appeared to be.

A third example of what was not at all sufficiently observed in conventional macro-analysis but was revealed by disaggregated analysis concerns the development of the industry's market shares up to 1975 and of the Swedish trade balance. The retention of the former and the balanced trade was based on a state of affairs which was not tenable for any length of time. A considerable number of export and import-competing industries accepted prices too low in relation to costs. The fact that exports kept step with imports and that industries earned foreign currencies for the country did not exclude that the basis for industrial competitive power and a continued rapid development of foreign trade in the long run was being undermined.

A fourth example: The statistical picture of the industry's profitability and equity/debt ratios up to the middle of the 1970s was generally based on aggregated data in a way that was rather misleading. First and foremost, it was easy to disregard the fact that business firms whose profitability deteriorated so much that they were forced to close down, disappeared from the statistics. Since there were many such firms from the middle of the 1960s the picture was misleading as an indicator of what actually happened with respect to economic conditions. Secondly, the deterioration in profitability and equity/debt ratios which was observed should have been understood as a more serious sign of warning than was actually the case, because the new situation made much greater demands on the ability of industry to bridge recessions and to renew itself than before. When the trends of profitability and debt burdens were assessed, one should have taken into account more than the financial aspects of the development as such.

One last example: Few aggregates are more hazardous to deal with carelessly than the concept of 'inflation' and 'the value of money'. As already mentioned the process which lay behind the post-war inflation partly changed character after the middle of the 1960s. It so happened that the course of events which gave rise to fairly moderate inflation before that time was favourable to most firms, while the following one which led to more rapid inflation was unfavourable, although the higher inflation rate did not result in a clearly overvalued currency until 1975. One lesson which should be drawn from this is that business firms have no reason to attach great importance to the value of money. Managers are exposed to less risks if they regard inflation, measured in the usual way, as a 'holistic fiction' than if they see the value of money as a relevant variable for the company. This is because a decline in the purchasing power of money does of course not at all guarantee that the prices of the products sold by the firm will rise, still less that earnings will do so. In times of considerable inflation it is often more likely that most costs will become higher, than that most earnings will rise. From this follows that firms' so-called 'real' assets are far from always representing stable values. Nor is it at all certain that inflation will make their debts less of a burden. 'Inflation pays debts' only on that piece of paper on which one takes the trouble to deflate the amount of debt, using a general price index. In the real world such debts can only be paid for out of earnings. This really trivial but often neglected truth is well illustrated by comparing the different experiences of Swedish industry prior to and after 1965. Many firms having large 'real' assets and/or big debts suffered most when the rate of inflation increased. Those with fewer such assets and relatively lower debts frequently did much better.

CONCLUDING REMARKS

A full demonstration of the advantages of the methodological approach has not been possible in this brief paper. There is need for further theoretical and empirical testing of what can be achieved. A practical consequence is a call for a reunion of economic theory and economic history of a more fruitful type than that achieved by the so-called New economic history of the 1960s. Such a reunion would not mean pushing econometric macro-modelling aside. Rather it would be a way of strengthening the methodology of all kinds of macro-economic modelling by letting historical research and micro-based analysis become a really integral part in the process of modelling. Such research, utilising a Neo-Schumpeterian and 'Austrian' approach, offers a promising possibility to reach a synthesis. It could also help strengthen the basis for forecasting and policy-making.

NOTES

1. This approach is closely related to that applied in my earlier study of Swedish industry, *Entrepreneurial Activity and the Development of Swedish Industry 1919–1939*, originally published in Swedish in 1950, translated for the American Economic Association and published by Richard D. Irwin, Inc., Homewood, in 1970. Some results of the recent research on which this paper is in part based were presented in 1979 in a book published jointly by the Industrial Institute for Economic and Social Research (Industriens Utredningsinstitut) and the Royal Swedish Academy of Engineering Sciences (Ingenjörsvetenskapsakademien) under the title *Technology and Industrial Structure – the Economic Crisis of the 70s in Historical Perspective*. This research was done as a team project at the Institute, in collaboration with the Academy.
2. This analytical concept was introduced in my study mentioned above in order to focus on some specific dynamic aspects of entrepreneurial activities and thus also of important industrial developments.

3 A Relational Database for the US Economy

D. KENDRICK

A shift is occurring in the paradigm for macro-economics in the United States – a shift from the demand side to the supply side. This shift is causing a change in focus from problems in aggregative economics to problems in certain sectors such as energy and autos and in certain states such as Michigan and Ohio. The signs of the shift are widespread. Econometric models are being respecified to include price and output equations for many different sectors. Detailed economic models with activity-analysis structures are being developed for individual sectors. Renewed concern is being voiced about unemployment in regions which are heavily affected by certain industries.

This paper argues that the shift of paradigm calls for a new organisation of the data for the US economy. The data is now organised in a fashion that is suitable for aggregate demand econometric models. It is time-series oriented. It is focused on GNP and other aggregate concepts. Insufficient attention is paid to sectors, to the location of economic activity, and to the relationships among economic data. Therefore, this paper explores a new method of organisation for US economic data – a relational database approach.

This approach arises out of recent developments in large database management. The three main approaches which have been used in computer science are hierarchical, relational, and network (Date, 1977 and Ullman, 1980). It is not the purpose of this paper to compare the three approaches, but rather to adopt the relational approach as the logical one for US economic data and to explore the implications of this choice.

The procedure employed here is (1) to define a number of sets which contain the basic entities for the economy and (2) to show how the relations between these sets provide a powerful way of thinking about economic data and of organising and retrieving those data. Then a simple relational database is presented and examples are given of how it might be used. No attempt is made to be comprehensive, rather only to illustrate the nature of such a database and how it might be constructed and used.

As the examples of uses show, relational databases are not meant to replace econometric models, but rather to provide the ability to answer quickly a wide variety of economic questions that are not routinely posed now because the answers are so difficult to provide. Also, the relational data base provides a structured organisation for the data which will even ease the task of the model builder at a later stage.

Even though there is by now a substantial computer-science literature on relational databases, to the author's knowledge one has not yet been constructed for the United States economy. Therefore a small relational database has been constructed to supply an example for this paper. Parts but not all of this database have been implemented on The University of Texas dual Cyber computers using the GAMS system of Alex Meeraus (Bisschop and Meeraus, 1980).

The intent has been to develop an example database which has the kind of sectoral orientation of much of Walt Rostow's work (see for example Rostow (1960), especially Chapter 11 on leading sectors). Furthermore, geographic and political factors have been added to the database so that it is wide enough in scope to demonstrate that relational databases can be constructed to cover at least a significant part of the wide range of political-economy problems about which Walt Rostow has written (Rostow, 1975 and 1978).

DOMAINS AND RELATIONSHIPS

One way to describe a particular relational database is to display its 'domains' and 'relationships'. The domains are the sets which list the basic elements in the database and the relationships define the connections between these elements. For example, consider a database for production statistics for plants. There are three sets which are the domains for the database, namely

Plants = Inland, ARCO
Cities = Gary, Houston
Production levels = R

There are two plants in the database, namely the Inland steel plant and the ARCO oil refinery. There are also two cities; Gary, Indiana, and Houston, Texas. Finally, there is a set of production levels which can be any real number, R. Next, define a relationship for production as

Production (plant, city, production level)

The elements of this relationship are three-tuples such as

(Inland, Gary, 4)

and

(ARCO, Houston, 73)

That is, the Inland steel works at Gary produced 4 million tons of steel and the ARCO oil refinery at Houston produced 73 million barrels of gasoline products. Thus the relationship is itself a set, but its elements are not single elements but rather n-tuples, that is groups of n names and numbers enclosed in parenthesis. For this example the Production relationship (set) is

Production = (Inland, Gary, 4), (ARCO, Houston, 73)

That is, it is a set with two elements and each element in the set is a three-tuple.

In summary then a relational database may be thought of as a collection of two kinds of sets: (1) domains whose elements are single items and (2) relationships whose elements are n-tuples. In the section to follow first the domains and then the relationships are explicated.

1. Domains

It is useful to separate the domains of the database into two groups: (1) the entities and (2) the statistics. The entities are the basic economic phenomena in the database, namely plants, commodities, corporations, and unions. The statistics are the numbers which are in the database. The reason for the division is that a listing of the elements in the entities conveys substantial information about the database, that is which plants and corporations are in the database. On the other hand the elements in the statistics are usually something so general, such as all real numbers or all integers, that they convey little or no information when listed by themselves apart from their context.

Table 3.1 provides a list of the entities which are used in the example relational database described in this paper. The emphasis is on the supply side of the economy, that is on plants, processes, industries, and sectors; however, there is also attention to geography (cities, states, and regions), to politics (governors and political parties), and time (years). It is small enough to allow one to grasp it as a whole and large enough to permit a rich discussion of how a relational database of the United States economy would be constructed and used.

TABLE 3.1 *Entities*

Entity	*Mnemonic*
Plants	PL
Productive units	PU
Processes	PR
Commodities	CO
Corporations	CR
Unions	UN
Industries	IN
Sectors	SE
Cities	CI
States	ST
Regions	RE
Governors	GO
Political parties	PP
Years	YE

Figure 3.1 provides a diagram of the entities. It is constructed in anticipation of the need to use a similar diagram to explain the relationships in the next section. However, the figure is also useful here to give one a quick view of the structure of the database. It is apparent from Figure 3.1 that the pivotal entities in the model are the plants. The plants contain productive units in which various

processes are used to transform some commoditites into others. The plants are owed by corporations and the workers in the plants belong to unions. Furthermore, the plants belong to industries and the industries are grouped together into sectors. Finally, the plants are located in cities, which are in states, which are in regions. The states have governors who belong to political parties.

One of the entities in Table 3.1 is not in Figure 3.1, namely Years. Its presence would complicate this and subsequent figures without adding much to understanding, so it is omitted.

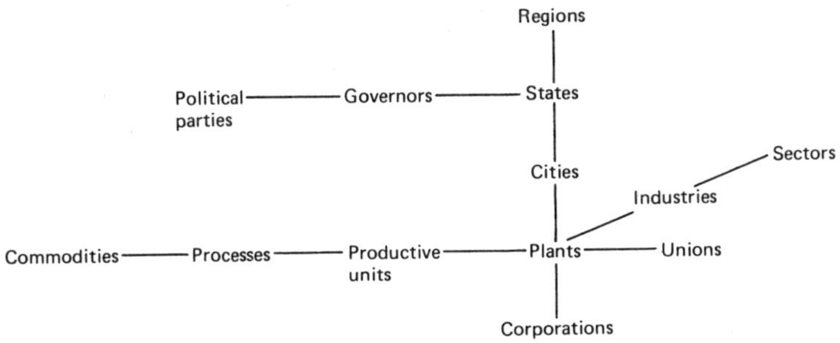

FIGURE 3.1 *Entities*

The statistics are presented in Table 3.2 and in Figure 3.2. The figure includes all the domains, both the entities and the statistics. For example, the inputs to and outputs of commodities by processes are the input–output coefficients. The annual output of commodities by processes are production levels. The use of productive units like blast furnaces and catalytic crackers by processes like pig iron and gasoline production are represented by capital coefficients. The capacity and additions to capacity of productive units in plants are capacity levels and incremental capacities, respectively.

TABLE 3.2 *Statistics*

Statistics	*Mnemonic*
Production levels	PL
Input–output coefficients	IO
Capacity levels	CL
Incremental capacities	IC
Numbers of employees	NE
Capacity coefficients	CC

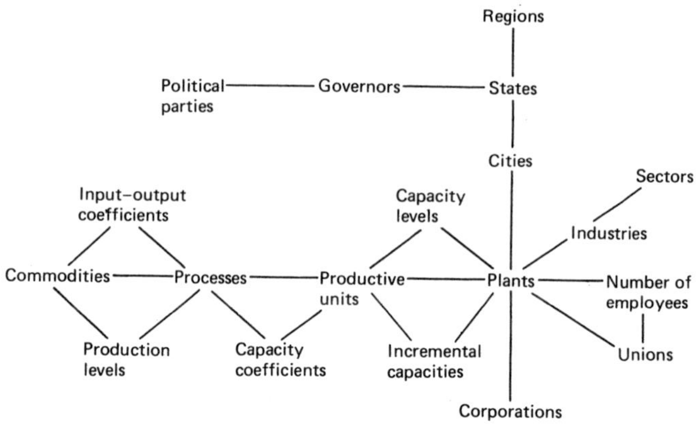

FIGURE 3.2 *Domains*

Finally, numbers of employees are given with a plant and union breakdown.

2. Relationships

As described above, relationships may be thought of as sets whose elements are *n*-tuples. A familiar example of an economic relationship is an input–output table with elements $a(i, j)$ to represent the input or output of the *i*th commodity by the *j*th process. This could be written as a three-tuple

$$(i, j, a)$$

For example, an input of coal to the pig-iron production process of six-tenths of coal per ton of pig iron would be

(coal, pig iron, .6)

In the language of relational databases an input–output table would be described with the relationship

Input–output (commodity, process, input–output coefficient)

This is, a commodity is input to or output from a process in the amount represented by the coefficient.

A list of the relationships used in this paper is given in Table 3.3

and shown graphically in Figure 3.3. Figure 3.3 is the same form as Figure 3.2 which displayed the domains. However, the domains are represented by their mnemonics in Figure 3.3 in order to give emphasis to the relationships. The relationships in Figure 3.3 are represented by lines linking either two or three domains. Thus the Capacity relationship gives the capacity level (CL) of a productive unit (PU) in a plant (PL). Similarly the Capacity use relationship shows via the capacity coefficient (CC) which process (PR) uses which productive unit (PU).

TABLE 3.3 *Relationships*

Input–output (commodity, process, input–output coefficient)
Production (commodity, process, year, production level)
Capacity use (process, productive unit, capacity coefficient)
Capacity (productive unit, plant, year, capacity level)
Increment to capacity (productive unit, plant, year, incremental capacity)
Ownership (plant, corporation)
Plant employees (plant, union, number of employees)
Industry composition (plant, industry)
Sector composition (industry, sector)
Plant location (plant, city)
City location (city, state)
State location (state, region)
State governors (state, governor)
Party affiliation (governor, party)

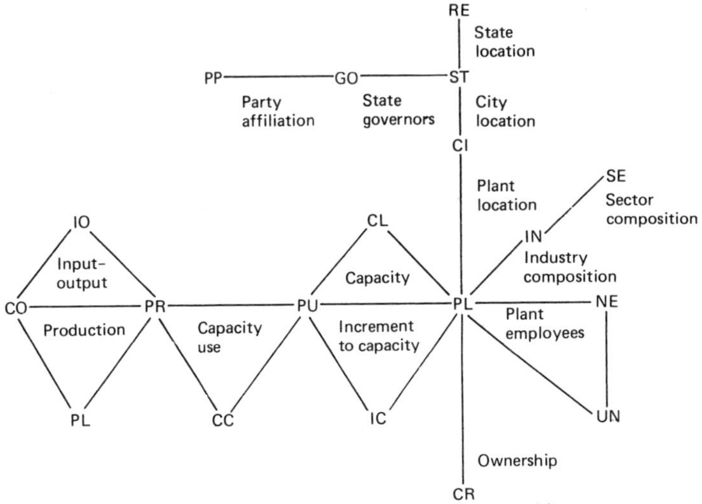

FIGURE 3.3 *Relationships*

Several of the relationships in Table 3.3 have four arguments, but none of those in Figure 3.3 link 4 domains. The reason for this is that the entity 'Years' was omitted in order to simplify the drawings.

In the following section an example relational database is given by presenting the relationships as a series of tables. It would have been useful to present first the domains and then the relationships, but this would have lengthened this article without adding proportionately to understanding. The elements in the domains can be inferred from the relationships.

AN EXAMPLE DATABASE

This section presents fourteen tables which define an example relational database for the US economy. There is one table for each relationship in the database. The tables themselves are to a substantial extent self-explanatory. Therefore, it is suggested that the reader browse through them to gain an impression about the types of data they contain. Several of these tables are cited from the following section on usage of the database. At that time the reader may want to return and study selected tables in more detail.

The general intent has been to use a set of tables which describe an economy from an activity-analysis framework of the sort discussed in Dorfman, Samuelson, and Solow (1958), with an emphasis on industries and sectors as in Rostow (1960), and using the framework developed in Kendrick and Stoutjesdijk (1978). Also, both regional and political phenomena are included.

The input–output table described in Table 3.4 is not so much in the tradition of Leontief (1953) as in that of Dorfman, Samuelson, and Solow (1958). However, aggregation of tables like this to the economy-wide level would produce Leontief-type tables. The processes shown are from the steel, aluminum, oil, and automobile industries. A negative sign indicates an input and a positive sign an output. For example 1.6 tons of iron ore is required to produce a ton of pig iron. One unusual aspect of the table is that two alternative processes are shown for producing steel, one more scrap-iron-intensive than the other. In an activity-analysis model the use of these two processes would depend on the price of scrap iron relative to the cost of pig iron.

TABLE 3.4 *Input–output*

Commodity	*Process*			
	Pig iron production	*Steel production pig iron intensive*	*Steel production scrap intensive*	*Rolling flat steel products*
Iron ore	−1.6			
Pig iron	1.0	−.9	−.7	
Scrap iron		−.2	−.4	
Liquid steel		1.0	1.0	−1.2
Scrap				.2
Flat steel				1.0
	Alumina production	Aluminum production	Primary distillation	Catalytic cracking
Bauxite	−1.4			
Alumina	1.0	−1.2		
Aluminum		1.0		
Crude oil			−1.0	
Distillate			.2	−1.0
Gasoline			.3	.6
Jet fuel			.1	.2
	Auto body stamping	Auto assembly		
Flat steel	−1.2			
Aluminum	−.2			
Auto bodies	1.0	−1.0		
Automobile		1.0		

The production data shown in Table 3.5. is the output level for the year 1979. It is presented in a slightly unusual manner in that output is listed by processes. However, that is the logical way to display the data when one thinks of an economy in an activity-analysis framework. For example 55.5 million tons of liquid steel is produced by the pig-iron-intensive process and 53 million tons is produced by the scrap-iron-intensive process.

Table 3.6. shows which productive unit is used by each process. It should be noted that both of the alternative processes for producing steel use the capacity of the steel shop. Otherwise, the table relates one process to each productive unit. This is the way that capacity

TABLE 3.5 *Production, 1979*

Commodity	*Process*			
	Pig iron production	*Steel production pig iron intensive*	*Steel production scrap intensive*	*Rolling flat steel products*
Pig iron – mty	86.8			
Liquid steel – mty		55·5	53·	
Scrap – mty				18.
Flat steel – mty				90.
	Alumina production	Aluminum production	Primary distillation	Catalytic cracking
Alumina – mty	20.			
Aluminum – mty		16.		
Distillate – tby			1.46	
Gasoline – tby			2.19	2·43
Jet fuel – tby			·73	·73
	Auto body stamping	Auto assembly		
Auto bodies – muy	9·5			
Automobile – muy		9·35		

NOTE mty = million tons per year muy = million units per year
tby = trillion barrels per year

TABLE 3.6 *Capacity use*

Productive unit	*Process*			
	Pig iron production	*Steel production pig iron intensive*	*Steel production scrap intensive*	*Rolling flat steel products*
Blast furnace	1			
Steel shop		1	1	
Rolling mill				1
	Alumina production	Aluminum production	Primary distillation	Catalytic cracking
Alumina plant	1			
Aluminum plant		1		
Primary still			1	
Catalytic cracker				1
	Auto body stamping	Auto assembly		
Auto stamping plant	1			
Auto assembly plant		1		

enters into activity analysis models. Each process may use one or more productive units and each productive unit has a fixed capacity. The capacity of the productive units in 1980 and the expected increase in 1981 is given in Tables 3.7 and 3.8.

TABLE 3.7 *Capacity, 1980*

Productive unit	*Plant*	*Capacity level*	*Units*
Blast furnace	Sparrows Point	2.0	mty
Blast furnace	Inland-Gary	2.5	mty
Steel shop	Sparrows Point	2.35	mty
Steel shop	Inland-Gary	2.8	mty
Rolling mill	Sparrows Point	1.9	mty
Rolling mill	Inland-Gary	2.4	mty
Alumina plant	Point Comfort	.8	mty
Aluminum plant	Point Comfort	.6	mty
Aluminum plant	Rockdale	.5	mty
Primary still	ARCO-Houston	.2	mbd
Catalytic cracker	ARCO-Houston	.23	mbd
Auto stamping plant	Lansing	.6	muy
Auto assembly line	Lansing	.6	muy

NOTE mty = million tons per year muy = million units per year
mbd = million barrels per day

TABLE 3.8 *Increment to Capacity, 1981*

Productive unit	*Plant*	*Incremental Capacity*	*Units*
Blast furnace	Sparrows Point	.5	mty
Blast furnace	Inland-Gary	.0	mty
Steel shop	Sparrows Point	.5	mty
Steel shop	Inland-Gary	.0	mty
Rolling mill	Sparrows Point	.4	mty
Rolling mill	Inland-Gary	.0	mty
Alumina plant	Point Comfort	.5	mty
Aluminum plant	Point Comfort	.4	mty
Aluminum plant	Rockdale	.0	mty
Primary still	ARCO-Houston	.1	mbd
Catalytic cracker	ARCO-Houston	.12	mbd
Auto stamping plant	Lansing	.0	muy
Auto assembly line	Lansing	.0	muy

NOTE mty = million tons per year muy = million units per year
mbd = million barrels per day

TABLE 3.9 *Ownership*

Plant	*Corporation*
Sparrows Point	United States Steel
Rockdale	ALCOA
ARCO-Houston	Atlantic Richfield Co.
Point Comfort	ALCOA
Inland-Gary	Inland Steel
Lansing	General Motors

TABLE 3.10 *Plant employees (per thousand employees)*

Plant	*Union*					
	OCAW	*UAW*	*USA*	*IBEW*	*IBT*	*IAM*
Sparrows Point			1.2		0.3	.05
Rockdale			0.5	.05		
ARCO-Houston	0.4				0.01	
Point Comfort			0.7		0.2	
Inland-Gary			0.4			
Lansing		1.2				

NOTE OCAW = Oil, Chemical and Atomic Workers
UAW = United Auto Workers
USA = United Steel Workers of America
IBEW = International Brotherhood of Electrical Workers
IBT = International Brotherhood of Teamsters
IAM = International Association of Machinists

The next step in the development of the database is to indicate which corporation owns each plant. This is given in Table 3.9. Unions then enter the picture in Table 3.10 which shows the number of employees at each plant who belong to the various unions. These data along with the other data in this example have not been taken from any statistical sources. Rather, they have been chosen to be somewhat realistic and to provide an interesting example.

The next two tables show the industry to which each plant belongs (Table 3.11) and the sector to which each industry belongs (Table 3.12). Following these are three tables which provide the geographic structure for the database. First, Table 3.13 shows the city in which each plant is located. Then Table 3.14 displays the state in which each city is located and Table 3.15 gives the region in which each state is located.

TABLE 3.11 *Industry composition*

Plant	*Industry*
Sparrows Point	Steel
Rockdale	Aluminum
ARCO-Houston	Oil
Point Comfort	Aluminum
Inland-Gary	Steel
Lansing	Automobile

TABLE 3.12 *Sector composition*

Industry	*Sector*
Steel	Primary metal
Aluminum	Primary metal
Oil	Petroleum and coal
Automobile	Transportation equipment

TABLE 3.13 *Plant location*

Plant	*City*
Sparrows Point	Sparrows Point
Rockdale	Rockdale
ARCO-Houston	Houston
Point Comfort	Point Comfort
Inland-Gary	Gary
Lansing	Lansing

TABLE 3.14 *City location*

City	*State*
Sparrows Point	Maryland
Rockdale	Texas
Houston	Texas
Point Comfort	Texas
Gary	Indiana
Lansing	Michigan

TABLE 3.15 *State location*

State	*Region*
Maryland	East Coast
Texas	Gulf Coast
Indiana	Mid-West
Michigan	Mid-West

TABLE 3.16 *State Governors*

State	*Governor*
Maryland	Harry Hughes
Texas	William P. Clements, Jr.
Indiana	Otis R. Bowen
Michigan	William G. Milliken

TABLE 3.17 *Party Affiliation*

Governor	*Party*
Harry Hughes	Democrat
William P. Clements, Jr.	Republican
Otis R. Bowen	Republican
William G. Milliken	Republican

Finally, Tables 3.16 and 3.17 tie geography to politics by giving the governor of each state and the party affiliation of each governor.

This completes the discussion of the relationships used in the database. Next the uses of the database are elaborated.

USES

Computerised databases for economies are traditionally used almost exclusively to provide data for econometric model-building. There is some use of these systems in answering queries about the economy for speech writing and analysis without models, but relatively little. For these purposes economists rely more on the usual published sources. The availability of relational databases for the US economy would change this. Economists would discover that 'back-of-the-envelope' calculations of much greater power and complexity could be made with ease with the aid of this tool. Several illustrations of this 'query' use of relational databases will be given in this section. Also, the latter part of this section will be devoted to ways in which relational databases could be used efficiently in the more traditional modelling activities.

1. Queries

Three examples will be given here. They are of increasing complexity. The first is an application to labour economics, the second to energy economics, and the third to macro-economics. They all make use of the example database which was displayed in the previous section.

Suppose that a corporation executive or a labour union official wanted a table showing the number of employees of each corporation by union affiliation. There are tables in the database which give (1) the number of employees by plant and union affiliation (Table 3.10) and (2) the corporation which owns each plant (Table 3.9). So the desired table can be obtained by the use of these two relationships. The GAMS language (Bisschop and Meeraus, 1980) provides a useful means to illustrate how this can be done. (In the interest of simplicity of exposition the exact syntax of GAMS has not been used.) The desired table can be obtained by creating a new relationship:

Employees of corporations (union, corporation)

That is, a table with union names along the side and corporation names across the top. The desired table (relationship) is created from the two existing relationships with the following command:

Employees of corporations (union, corporation) =

(Sum, plants, ownership (plant, corporation), employees (plant, union))

This states that the new relationship is created by summing over all the plants in the two existing relationships, namely Ownership and Employees. The type of result obtained is shown in Table 3.18.

TABLE 3.18 *Employees of corporations (per thousand employees)*

Union	*Corporation*				
	United States Steel	*ALCOA*	*Atlantic Richfield Co.*	*Inland Steel*	*General Motors*
OCAW	1.2		0.4		
UAW					1.2
USA		1.2		0.4	
IBEW		0.05			
IBT	0.3	0.2	0.01		
IAM	0.05				

A second example employs an application to energy economics. Assume that a government or corporate official wanted to know the capacity of the oil refineries on the Gulf and Atlantic coasts in 1980. A rough measure of this capacity is the capacity of the primary stills in these refineries.

The raw data on refinery capacity (see Table 3.7.) gives the capacity of the primary stills in each plant; however, to answer the query it is necessary to know which plants are located on the Gulf and Atlantic coasts. For the example database this is done with the following four relationships:

Capacity (productive unit, plant, year, capacity level)
Plant location (plant, city)
City location (city, state)
State location (state, region)

From these four one can create the relationship

Regional capacity (productive unit, region, year, capacity level)

This relationship provides a table with productive units as rows and regions as columns (Table3.19.). By inspection of the table the capacity of the primary stills on the Gulf and Atlantic coasts in 1980 is .2 million barrels per day.

This example is useful for illustrating the flexibility of queries with relational database systems. Frequently, data in published

TABLE 3.19 *Regional Capacity, 1980*

Productive unit	*Region* East Coast	Gulf Coast	Mid-West	*Units*
Blast furnace	2.0		2.5	mty
Steel shop	2.35		2.8	mty
Rolling mill	1.9		2.4	mty
Alumina plant		0.8		mty
Aluminum plant		1.1		mty
Primary still		0.2		mbd
Catalytic cracker		0.23		mbd
Auto stamping			0.6	muy
Auto assembly line			0.6	muy

sources is not organised in exactly the way one would like. For example, suppose that in the case above the data was organised with the country divided into six regions. However, the query was for only those states which were at the water's edge and none of the exisiting regions exactly fit that description. Then with a relational database system one could simply replace the existing relationship between states and regions with one having regions defined as desired. Then the query could be answered exactly. Thus the analyst does not have to use the data exactly as it is organised by those who publish it, but rather is free to redesign aggregation schemes to suit his or her own interest.

The third example was mentioned above as being an application to macro-economics. In fact, it is also an illustration of how relational databases may be used for political economy queries. A president is concerned about the impact of imported autos on his or her chances for re-election. A request is made for a list of Democratic governors whose states are likely to suffer the largest increases in unemployment. The query then eventually comes as: 'Provide a list of Democratic governors whose states have more than 10 000 people employed in the automobile and steel industries and rank the list according to the number of people employed.'
To answer the query one uses the following relationships:

Industry composition (plant, industry)
Plant employees (plant, union, number of employees)
Plant location (plant, city).

City location (city, state)
State governors (state, governor)
Party affiliation (governor, party)

to create a new relationship

Employees by governor and party (industry, governor, party, number of employees)

This relationship could then be searched for Democratic governors and checked to see if the number of employees exceed 10 000. Those items which pass this test would then be ranked to give the desired list.

This example illustrates that queries cannot replace models since a more complete answer to the general intent of the question would require an input–output analysis of all the industries whose employment levels might be affected. However, the query could provide a 'straws in the wind' answer with a fraction of the time and expense required for the more refined analysis. Also, for the president's political purposes the degree of accuracy provided by the query may be sufficient; especially so if the answer can be obtained quickly.

The example also illustrates how a relational database can be used to relate economic, geographic, and political entities in ways which could prove to be most useful to applied economists, government officials, and politicians. However, a relational database could also prove to be most helpful to model builders. This is discussed in the following section.

2. Modelling

Most data which are now used in econometric models are stored in libraries of time series. If instead this data were stored in relational databases, some types of pre-processing of the data would be much easier. For example, spatial aggregation and disaggregation would be simpler to do. Spatial models are divided by counties, Standard Metropolitan Statistical Areas (SMSAs), regions, states, water districts, or Congressional districts. The data are rarely available in exactly the spatial disaggregation desired, so computer programmes must be written to read tapes and reorganise the data. As the energy economics query above indicated, this kind of manipulation can be simplified when the data are stored in a relational database.

A second example is size-aggregation of firms. It is sometimes hypothesised that the behaviour of firms depends on their size. With a relational database one can quickly sort the sample data by size and other characteristics. The sorted data can then be used in econometric models.

Sectoral aggregation and disaggregation provide a third group of illustrations. For example, many energy models have been constructed in recent years and some of these require pulling data from various SITC categories and then aggregating the data into the industries or sectors required by the energy model. Another example comes from the field of economic growth. At times the most dynamic industries in an economy are those in which new types of products appear. As these industries develop, they eventually become a disproportionately large part of the existing sectors. Then it becomes necessary to redefine the sectoral composition. With relational databases the economists can easily define his or her own sectors and aggregate the data accordingly.

Finally, the use of relational databases may permit the use of capacity instead of capital-stock data in analysing most supply side problems. Capital-stock data may give misleading evidence about production capabilities. For example, large investments have been made in pollution-control equipment. These investments have increased capital stocks but not capacity. Another example is that automobile plants are being converted to produce smaller cars. This adds to capital stocks but not to capacity. A third example is from oil refineries. The mix of oil received by US oil refineries is slowly changing from light to heavy crudes. This decreases the capacity of the refineries while leaving the capital stocks unchanged.

While models with capacity rather than with capital stocks can be constructed using present database systems, the availability of relational database systems will facilitate the use of capacity data. As the energy economics query above indicated, it is possible with relational databases to go deep into the data in order to retrieve exactly the capacity figures desired.

SUMMARY

Most economic databases are presently organised as unrelated collections of time series which may be appropriate to aggregate demand models but not to disaggregated supply models. A relational database system is more appropriate to current needs both for answering queries and for preprocessing data for economic models.

REFERENCES

Bisschop, J. and Meeraus, A., 'Selected Aspects of a General Algebraic Modelling Language', mimeo, Development Research Center, *World Bank* (Washington, DC, 1980).

Date, C. J., *An Introduction to Database Systems*, 2nd edn (Reading, Massachusetts: Addison-Wesley, 1977).

Dorfman, R., Samuelson, P., and Solow, R., *Linear Programming and Economic Analysis* (New York: McGraw-Hill, 1958).

Kendrick, D. A. and Stoutjesdijk, A. J., *The Planning of Industrial Investment Programs* (Baltimore, Maryland: John Hopkins University Press, 1978).

Leontief W. W. *et al.*, *Studies in the Structure of the American Economy* (New York: Oxford University Press, 1953).

Rostow, W. W., *The Process of Economic Growth*, 2nd edn (New York: W. W. Norton, 1960).

——— *How It All Began: Origins of the Modern Economy* (New York: McGraw-Hill, 1975).

——— *Getting from Here to There: America's Future in the World Economy* (New York: McGraw-Hill, 1978).

Ullman, J. D., *Principles of Database Systems* (Potomac, Maryland: Computer Science Press, 1980).

4 Factors Influencing Changes in Productivity

R. M. MARSHALL*

INTRODUCTION

Productivity measures the use of economic resources and is, therefore, a major index of economic welfare for individuals and the nation. The rate of productivity growth over the long run determines economic growth and makes possible improvements in living conditions and the attainment of national objectives. A slow growth economy will have difficulty reconciling society's desire for general economic progress and resolving domestic and international problems; slow growth will therefore cause internal political and social problems, because improvements for some groups must come at the expense of losses for others. The decomposition of society into competing groups attempting to improve their relative positions when the nation as a whole loses (as with OPEC price increases), can escalate inflationary pressures, further shrinking national wealth. Thus, our national prestige, competitiveness, security, and welfare depend heavily on the level and growth of productivity.

Relatively high US productivity performance in the two decades following the Second World War helped the nation achieve important social objectives. Productivity growth averaging more than 3 per cent annually supported an ever-rising standard of living, created millions of new jobs, and contributed to rising expectations regarding the quality of work, the environment and the reduction of economic and social inequities.

* I gratefully acknowledge Jerry Mark and his colleagues at the Bureau of Labor Statistics and Nancy Barrett and Peggy Connerton of the Office of the Assistant Secretary for Policy, Evaluation and Research for their help with this paper.

In sharp contrast, the growth of productivity slowed dramatically in the United States and other industrialised nations during the 1970s. US productivity growth now averages less than 1 per cent annually. This has meant not only a lower rate of increase in our standard of living, but also higher inflation, reduced competitiveness in international markets, and increased social and political tensions.

As a result of these developments, renewed productivity growth must be high on our national policy agenda. Concern for our long-run economic prospects has intensified pressures on policymakers to develop programmes to reverse lower productivity trends. However, policies for revitalising productivity must be based on a better understanding of the causes of inadequate productivity growth.

Recent studies have attributed the decline in productivity growth to such factors as the shift towards a service economy, demographic changes in the workforce towards younger and less skilled workers, slower growth in investment, the sharp rise in energy prices, increased government regulations and reduced spending for research and development. While analyses of these factors have shed some light on productivity changes, much remains unexplained.

Perhaps one reason why so much remains unexplained is that conventional quantitative techniques fail to capture important behavioural and dynamic forces underlying the productivity process. The efficiency of production depends on complex phenomena such as individual and national values, relations between workers and management, the systems within which workers and enterprises function, and institutional behaviour including the role of the government. An understanding of these factors must be integrated with traditional resource availability analysis to explain changes in productivity.

This paper re-examines some potential causes of the productivity decline with a view towards better understanding the appropriate policy responses. The first section surveys the statistical evidence on factors influencing productivity in the United States. The section entitled 'Sources of the productivity decline' explores some of the difficulties with traditional analytical techniques that look solely at factor inputs. The last section examines the prospects for productivity growth and concludes with some policy prescriptions for enhancing productivity performance during the 1980s.

CAUSES OF THE PRODUCTIVITY DECLINE

In contrast to an over 3 per cent annual growth rate from the late 1940s to the mid-1960s, productivity growth in the United States slowed to a 2.3 per cent annual average rate between 1965 and 1973. The period since 1973 has witnessed a further deceleration in productivity growth to about one per cent annually.

While there is considerable variation among industries, the decline in US productivity has been pervasive. Table 4.1 presents changes in average annual growth rates by major sectors between 1948–65 and 1973–8. This table shows that the bulk of the total productivity decline (nearly 80 per cent) resulted from a slowdown in productivity growth within sectors, rather than from a shift of employment towards less productive sectors. Only communication, finance, insurance, and real estate improved their productivity performance. Further disaggregation would show similar patterns of decline, although naturally there are fast growth industries within each sector. For example, the automobile industry experienced a 3.9 per cent annual gain in productivity during the 1970s.

While manufacturing productivity growth rates dropped by about half, the rate of decline was less than in nonmanufacturing industries. In fact, manufacturing productivity actually raised the economy-wide average. Mining and construction exhibited absolute declines over the 1973–8 period, while gains were virtually nonexistent for utilities. Together, these problem sectors account for almost a third of the total productivity slowdown in recent years.

The reasons for the productivity fall-off in these industries are not completely clear, but some possible explanations can be suggested. The decline in mining productivity undoubtedly was due to worsening labour relations in the coal mining sector before 1977 and to greater difficulties involved in extracting oil from less productive wells where recovery costs are higher. Safety, health and environmental regulation have also played a role in measured productivity declines in mining, but, as will be discussed later, this result must be interpreted with caution. First, most of the decline in the mining sector occurred in the oil industry, which is less affected by these regulations. Secondly, the internalisation of environmental and health costs to firms raises a measurement problem – it is not clear that these costs were lower prior to regulation, since they were borne mainly by workers, their families and society as a whole.

TABLE 4.1 *Productivity growth rates by sector in the private business economy, selected periods*

	Growth rates: average Annual rates of change (per cent)		Contributions to productivity growth slowdown by sectors
	1948–65	1973–8	per cent of total slowdown
Private business	3·2	1.1	
Mining	4·2	−4·3	9·0
Manufacturing	3·1	1.6	20.8
Durable	(2.8)	(1·1)	(14·5)
Nondurable	(3·4)	(2·3)	(6·3)
Transportation	3·3	0.6	6.8
Communication	5·5	7·1	−7·7
Utilities	6.2	0.1	5·9
Trade	2·7	0·5	19·5
Wholesale	(3·1)	−(0·1)	(10.0)
Retail	(2·4)	(0·7)	(9·5)
Government enterprises	−0.8	−0·7	−0·5
Agriculture	5·5	2·9	8.1
Construction	2·9	−1·3	13.6
Finance, insurance, and real estate	1.0	1.1	−0·5
Services	1·5	0·3	5·0
Slowdown within sectors			80.0
Slowdown in shift effect			18.6
Interaction term			1·4
Total slowdown			100.0

NOTE Details may not add to totals due to rounding.
SOURCE US Department of Labor, ASPER

The apparent decline in construction productivity may also rest in part with measurement problems. Since there is no standardised unit of construction output, the usual technique is to measure output by the volume of construction materials used (inputs), a procedure which would understate productivity gains if processes have become more efficient. Construction industry experts also believe that declining productivity is the result of cyclical and seasonal fluctuations in demand, creating uncertainty in the industry, which causes all resources to be used less efficiently. There is general agreement that productivity in this industry could be improved by measures to stabilise demand, leading to more efficient planning, training and resource use.

The poor productivity performance of utilities reflects in part the slow output growth in this industry during the 1973–8 period. Since utilities carry high fixed costs for both labour and plants, slack demand causes both resources to be utilised less efficiently.

An examination of the statistical evidence provides another perspective on the sources of the current productivity slowdown. While productivity is related both to the quantity and quality of factor inputs and to the efficiency with which resources are utilised, those factors most amenable to measurement typically refer to changes in inputs. They are familiar to any long-run analysis of economic growth – structural shifts in employment between sectors, demographic changes in the labour force, capital formation, and resource availability. Less tangible, though also frequently mentioned factors, are government regulation and research and development.

1. Structural shifts

Historically, the transfer of labour from agriculture to the industrial sector has been a major force in economic growth. Since the absolute level of productivity is lower in agriculture than in the rest of the economy, this shift contributes positively to aggregate productivity levels. The reduction in farm employment also leads to increases in agricultural productivity as farm operators mechanise production.

At the end of the Second World War, 20 per cent of the US workforce was employed in agriculture, but by 1965 farm employment accounted for only 5 per cent. This transfer caused much of the extraordinary increase in productivity during the early post-war years. For the 1948 to 1965 period, this shift is estimated to have added as much as 0.4 per cent per year, more than 10 per cent, to total US productivity growth. The shift of labour out of farming was largely completed by the mid-1960s, removing this important contributor to earlier productivity gains.

Another potentially important structural shift is the relative growth of employment in the service sector, where average productivity is lower than in manufacturing. However, the actual impact of this movement on overall productivity has been minimal.

There has been no appreciable shift to service jobs within the nonfarm sector when total hours worked is taken into account. Further, both service and non-service sectors contain mixes of fast and slow productivity growth industries, particularly if we broaden the definition of services to include all noncommodity producing activities – trade, communications, transportation, public utilities, finance, insurance, and real estate, as well as business and personal services.[1] Therefore, although much emphasis has been placed on the shift to services as a source of declining productivity, its contribution to the current slowdown is rather small.

2. Changes in labour force composition

Demographic, skill and educational changes affecting the quality of labour are important sources of productivity growth. As Table 4.2 illustrates, there has been a rapid increase in the labour force, caused by (1) the post-war 'baby boom' cohort reaching working age, and (2) the increased employment of women. During the 1965 to 1973 period, workers between the ages of 16 and 24 increased more than twice as fast as the total labour force; by 1973, this group accounted for nearly 25 per cent of the work force. Although the rate of growth in the number of young workers has since slowed, they continue to represent almost 25 per cent of the labour force.

TABLE 4.2 *US labour force, 1948–78*

	Annual rates of growth			*Per cent of labour force*			
Labour force groups	*1948–65*	*1965–73*	*1973–8*	*1948*	*1965*	*1973*	*1978*
Workers aged 16–19	1.6	4.2	2.2	7.8	8.3	9.7	9.6
Workers aged 20–24	1.0	4.9	2.9	12.6	12.1	15.0	15.3
Women	2.5	3.5	4.0	28.0	34.0	38.0	41.0
Total labour force	1.3	2.1	2.4	—	—	—	—

SOURCE *BLS Employment and Earnings*, various issues.

The employment of women has been increasing for at least 20 years, but the recent growth has been astounding. Since 1972, the participation rate of women has increased 1 per cent per year. In 1948, women accounted for only 28 per cent of the labour force; this increased to 34 per cent in 1965 and 41 per cent in 1978.

These shifts in the composition of employment, it is argued, reduce productivity because the employment of inexperienced workers lowers the average productivity level. However, the net productivity effect of increased numbers of young workers and women is ambiguous. Although younger workers are inexperienced, they also tend to be better educated than older workers. An upswing in the educational distribution of employed persons should act to raise average productivity levels. Moreover, female employment has grown mainly because fewer women now leave the work force, so the average experience of women workers is increasing. We should also consider the occupational and industrial distribution of young workers and women. These workers could increase average productivity if they enter higher skill jobs in high productivity industries.

When these factors are controlled for, there is a significant net positive contribution to productivity from changes in the composition of the labour force for both the 1948–65 and 1965–73 periods.[2] While some of the positive contributions resulted from changes in labour force demographics (age, sex, education, and occupational levels), there were also significant effects from the entrance of young workers and women into more productive industries (changes in inter-industry mix). For 1973–8, the net contribution to productivity from compositional changes declined, but remained marginally positive. However, this factor explains only a fraction of the total slowdown in productivity growth.

Thus, while individual estimates differ, the evidence does not support the conclusion that the changing age and sex composition of the labour force in the late 1960s and 1970s had a substantial adverse impact on productivity. The reversal of these demographic trends in the 1980s, when four million fewer young people are expected to enter the labour force, will, therefore, play only a small role in restoring labour productivity growth.

3. Growth of capital per worker

Growth models using the production function framework have found a significant relationship between increases in capital per worker and productivity growth. This relationship has led researchers to explore impediments to capital formation as a source of the current productivity slowdown.

Although these studies[3] have produced mixed results, the weight of the evidence suggests that a reduction in the growth rate of the capital–labour ratio explains a substantial part of the 1973–8 productivity slowdown. However, this factor does not appear to have been a significant contributor to the 1965–73 slowdown. Indeed, the growth rate of capital per worker actually increased during the latter period. Table 4.3 presents the results of a Bureau of Labor Statistics study on the role played by capital formation in the current slowdown.

TABLE 4.3 *Relationship between productivity and capital; US private business sector average annual rates of change*

Time period	*Labour productivity*	*Capital labour ratio*	*Capital growth*
1948–65	3.3	2.8	3.2
1965–73	2.3	3.2	4.6
1973–78	1.0	.9	2.5

NOTE Excludes government enterprises. Capital is measured as a translog index of equipment and structures.

SOURCE Bureau of Labour Statistics, Office of Productivity and Technology

While shifts in the inter-industry mix and in the composition of employment are direct contributors to the productivity decline, changes in capital intensity are symptomatic of more indirect influences. Researchers have attempted to measure some of the factors contributing to the slowdown in the growth of capital per worker, including slow economic growth, excess capacity, increases in energy prices, declining research and development spending, government regulations, and the general climate of uncertainty in a period of high inflation and rapid structural change.

4. Energy prices, capital formation and productivity

The sharp drop in productivity growth coincided with the sudden increase in OPEC prices. This, together with the pervasiveness of energy effects, lends substantial credence to explanations that attribute the productivity slowdown to increased energy price. Higher energy prices provide firms with strong incentives to become more energy efficient – to consume less energy per unit of labour and capital. This adjustment process affects labour productivity through several mechanisms.

In the short run, firms turn to conservation which requires some combination of labour and capital as a substitute for energy. Some short-run conservation measures include increased maintenance of equipment and modifications of structures to conserve heat and economise energy, often by utilising more labour input in the process. Labour productivity, thus, will decrease with these increases in energy-efficiency. As noted above, the poor productivity performance of public utilities probably is due to the slow growth in the demand for energy as a result of greater conservation and efficiency.

Increased energy prices also will affect investment and the efficiency of capital more directly. Much of the existing capital stock, created in an era of low energy prices, was rendered obsolete by the new constellation of energy prices. Firms may directly substitute labour for capital by using more labour-intensive processes or increasing work shifts to meet expanded capacity needs. Alternatively, they may install more energy-efficient technology. This should operate to increase investment levels, although it will not necessarily increase capital per worker. Moreover, there is evidence that even the newest generation of technology is already obsolete. Thus, firms may simply defer investments until more energy-efficient technologies come on-stream.

Finally, there are reductions in the output of some sectors as price levels rise and a shift in the output mix away from more capital- and energy-intensive industries towards labour-intensive industries. Such output adjustments would also lower labour productivity.

While these general effects are well-understood, the actual magnitude of the energy price impact on labour productivity is highly controversial. Studies using a growth-accounting framework[4] generally conclude that not much of the decline can be attributed to higher energy prices, since energy inputs represent only a small fraction of total costs (the value of energy is between 1 and 5 per cent of output, depending on how output and energy are measured). Other investigators argue that the responsiveness of factor proportions to changes in relative prices can best be studied using industry production functions.[5] Such studies generally find that energy price hikes have exercised a strong effect on such major growth variables as the capital-labour ratio.

Hudson-Jorgenson (1978), for example, using a general equilibrium model of the US economy concluded that energy price increases lowered GNP per unit of labour by 2.57 per cent over the 1973–6 period, or about 0.8 per cent annually. This represents over half of the trend decline in productivity. These studies have also shown that energy price increases shifted the production mix in favour of lower productivity industries. However, highly restrictive assumptions about factor substitution are required to reach these results.[6] In addition, these models have not captured long-run behavioural changes and important feedback effects between relative price changes and other characteristics of the environment (such as uncertainty and high inflation) on capital intensity. The debate over the role of energy prices on the current productivity decline is therefore far from concluded.

5. Regulation, capital formation and productivity

The growth of regulatory requirements is a frequently mentioned source of our productivity ills. Government regulations allegedly lower measured output per unit of input by diverting resources from the basic function of producing goods and services into nonproductive uses. Estimates of this diversion vary widely because there is no commonly accepted method of quantifying the costs or benefits of social regulation. Studies of the impact of regulation on productivity generally use a growth-accounting framework to identify the capital investment costs imposed by government mandated requirements and ignore the benefit calculus entirely.

Even though most studies fail to account for the unmeasured benefits of regulation – cleaner air, a safer work environment and so on, – they nevertheless find that the adverse effects on measured productivity are quite small. One limited study of the costs imposed by programmes for pollution control and worker health and safety estimated that government mandated investments have reduced labour productivity growth by less than 0.1 per cent per year since 1973, and by less than 0.2 per cent in manufacturing, where the costs of these programmes are concentrated.[7]

6. Research and development and productivity

In the larger process of technological innovation – the conversion of ideas into new products and processes – research and development is only the first stage. The forces underlying innovation are not well understood, leading investigators to focus on research and development expenditures as a proxy for the innovation process. A number of researchers have reported significant contributions to productivity growth from research and development spending.[8]

Observers point to the decline in research and development since the 1960s as a major source of the productivity decline. Total R&D expenditures, in constant 1972 dollars, peaked at $29.8 billion in 1968 and spending levels remained essentially flat through 1976. Expressed as a percentage of gross national product, research and development spending has declined from 3 per cent in 1964 to 2.2 per cent currently. Furthermore, basic research which is important to the development of new products and processes fell from about 8 per cent of R & D expenditures to 4 per cent between 1960 and 1974.

Estimates of the role of research and development spending in explaining the recent productivity slowdown suggest that lower R & D spending levels may have reduced productivity growth by only about .1 or .2 percentage points.[9] However, not enough is understood about the mechanisms through which R & D expenditures influence productivity to assess the validity of these estimated percentages.

7. Economic conditions

Looking at the growth of productivity over the business cycle, it is clear that productivity generally increases with movements toward fuller utilisation of plant capacity and low levels of unemployment. Thurow, for example, attributes about 30 per cent of the current decline in productivity to idle plant capacity.[10] This results from high overhead costs, including labour, in modern plants which are designed to operate most efficiently near full capacity. Since overhead labour cannot be reduced proportionately when output declines, more labour must be used per unit output. Similarly as business conditions improve, output can expand faster than labour inputs, causing a growth in productivity.

SOURCES OF THE PRODUCTIVITY DECLINE – NO SIMPLE ANSWER

In examining the traditional factors, we are able to draw only limited conclusions about the sources of the productivity decline during the 1973–9 period. Our analytical tools leave much of the change in productivity unexplained. Where individual factors can be identified, estimates of their relative contribution often vary widely among researchers. The problem rests largely with the data and conceptual approaches that we use to measure productivity growth.

1. Measurement Problems

Our reliance on the single-factor labour productivity measure raises questions about our interpretation of productivity growth. For example, with the increases in energy and capital prices relative to wages, greater efficiency in the use of higher-priced factors may have increased total factor productivity in the economy, even though productivity as measured by labour inputs fell. A productivity index measured solely in terms of labour inputs may offer a similarly misleading impression of productivity performance in particular sectors. For example, in the mining industry where labour productivity fell 4.3 per cent per year between 1973 and 1978, 83 per cent of the total decline stemmed from reductions in the oil and gas extraction industry where higher energy prices made the development of less accessible resources more profitable. Extraction of these reserves requires more labour inputs.

Part of the slowdown in the 1970s may simply be a statistical artifact. Measurement errors in price indices used to obtain real output estimates (particularly in such areas as computers, integrated circuits and construction), may have artificially reduced our productivity measures. Errors in price deflators tend to be especially acute during periods of high inflation.

These measurement problems are compounded when the influences that we wish to examine do not fit neatly into the usual GNP framework employed in analyses of productivity growth. For example, studies of the productivity impact of the increased employment of women exclude output from home activities. Under a broader definition of production that includes the household, the rise in the labour force participation of women would augment total productivity growth as women move from less-productive housework to higher productivity jobs in the market economy.[11]

Regulations to improve the health and safety of workers and the general environment further illustrate the failure of market criteria. In the spectrum of human welfare, production of goods and services is but one element. To the extent that society values other benefits such as a cleaner environment and prevention of occupational diseases and accidents, regulation is needed to internalise these social goods to the firm. Social regulation represents a fundamental re-direction of societal resources towards the production of socially desired goods. Consequently, while these government requirements reduce measured output by increasing the capital and operating expenditures of firms, they also raise social welfare which is not measured in the GNP framework.

Even within the restricted GNP measure, the net impact of regulation on productivity is not necessarily negative because of differences in the inter-temporal distribution of costs and benefits – short-term costs outweighing benefits with a reversal in the long run. For example, occupational diseases and industrial accidents impose current costs on workers and their families which are not measured as costs to the firm, thus overstating true productivity growth. Requiring firms to internalise these costs may lower their measured productivity levels. However, to the extent that preventive programmes reduce long-run health care costs, regulations could actually increase future levels of national productivity, rather than diminish it as is often alleged. A recent study of the Occupational Safety and Health Administration's (OSHA) cotton dust standard finds that the long-run benefits of this regulation, including fewer workdays lost and lower health care costs, will substantially exceed short-run compliance costs.[12]

Productivity levels in firms may benefit even more directly from regulation. There is evidence that regulation often stimulates innovation and the introduction of new technologies, process design and product substitution. Thus, regulation may have significant technology-leveraging effects as evidenced by the US chemical industry's experience with an OSHA standard controlling vinyl chloride emissions. A retrospective analysis of the vinyl chloride standard indicated that significant process innovations in response to the regulation lowered unit costs of production and increased productivity.[13] Measured productivity may also increase in regulated industries from such factors as lower employee absenteeism and turnover and reduced equipment damage and downtime, among others. However, these productivity gains often take some time to be realised.

2. Dynamic factors influencing productivity

A significant hindrance to analysing the productivity decline rests with the conceptual approach underlying growth accounting as a framework for modelling productivity behaviour. These techniques simply attempt to decompose measured productivity change by the increase or decrease in factor inputs. Such partial analyses fail to capture important dynamic attributes of the productivity process. Measuring the impact of energy price increases, for example, in terms of the energy factor share omits important feedback effects that could greatly magnify its estimated impact. Production function techniques suffer from similar problems because they also ignore important dynamic effects. Such techniques cannot capture the potential dynamic and synergistic effects among various productivity variables. For example, changes in relative energy prices, higher inflation and uncertainty all impact on each other and ultimately on capital formation and hence productivity growth.

3. Behavioural and organisational influences

In addition to dynamic and interactive effects, analyses of productivity growth must capture important behavioural and organisational influences on the process. Such behavioural and organisational variables, while difficult to incorporate formally, are critical to our understanding of the productivity process.

For example, traditional analysis might focus on the shortfall of capital investment as an important source of the productivity decline. This conclusion, however, rests on assumptions of full employment of resources and profit-maximising behaviour, even though the conditions required by these assumptions rarely prevail, particularly in recent years. Indeed, perhaps the most significant factor influencing short-term behaviour during the 1970s was slack demand leading to under-utilisation of labour and capital resources. In addition to the direct impact of under-utilised capacity on productivity rates discussed earlier, the failure to fully employ resources drives a wedge in the productivity growth process. With excess capital and surplus labour, entrepreneurs have little incentive to improve production processes. Innovative techniques – making more efficient use of labour and capital resources – give way to short term profit maximisation with current technology. For example, with excess labour, farmers tend to use the piece-rate system of wage payments in order to maximise profits since there is little incentive to develop processes which utilise labour in a more efficient manner. These processes appear to be efficient when viewed from the perspective of the firm, but not when viewed from the perspective of the total labour market.

Similarly, slack demand impacts investment behaviour thereby hindering capital formation, through excess capacity and uncertain economic conditions. Reduced investment, innovation and technological advances in turn lower the rate of productivity growth. Moreover, this innovation-investment-productivity growth framework operates best in a stable, certain environment. Stable prices and demand are conducive to risky investment decisions that require long-term commitments. Conversely, the uncertainty accompanying inflation and recession will bias business decisions towards myopic investments encouraging short-term pay-offs. The irrevocability of capital decisions will cause hurdle rates of return to rise in an uncertain environment, limiting qualified investment projects. The behavioural implications of uncertainty have not been adequately integrated into analyses of changes in productivity.

Attempts to remedy the capital shortfall problem without addressing the problems of slack demand and uncertainty may well prove ineffective. We must understand that full utilisation of labour and capital is a critical productivity-inducing force. Indeed, it is the relative scarcity of workers which prompts investment in processes that more efficiently utilise labour resources. Policies to stimulate capital investment will be similarly inoperative in lowering hurdle rates of return as long as economic uncertainty continues. Failure to recognise these behavioural factors will only lead to inaccurate analyses of the productivity decline and inappropriate policies.

The fundamental complexity of the productivity process becomes clear when we recognise that productivity is the product of all human interactions and not, as is commonly assumed, the simple result of quantitative changes in capital or other physical factors. It results from such 'intangibles' as national will and mood and the nature of relations between different groups in society, as well as through more tangible factors like the quantity and quality of management, labour, capital, and natural resource.

An important example of the influence of these intangible forces upon productivity levels occurs in labour markets, where the efficiency of the workforce depends in large measure on the structure of relationships between employers and employees. The literature provides substantial evidence on the positive influence of good labour-management relations on productivity levels.[14]

These productivity gains are realised through a variety of mechanisms that affect management and worker efficiency and introduce channels of communication and mutual cooperation – increased managerial efficiency and quality of the workforce, lower quit rates, reduced absenteeism, increased training, improved motivation and morale of workers, better labour-management cooperation and industrial stability. Conversely, poor industrial relations environments characterised by a high number of work stoppages, low levels of trust, and agreements that contain outmoded work rules, can and do produce negative effects on productivity.

There is increasing interest in the development of cooperative approaches to improving productivity which involve joint labour-management committees at the plant level. Although these experiences have not been systematically evaluated as a group, the evidence indicates that they have, in many cases, contributed significantly to improved worker motivation, productivity growth and industrial peace. For example, at the Tarrytown, New York General Motors assembly plant, the establishment of a labour-management committee was credited with substantial reductions in absenteeism and in the number of grievances filed and significant improvements in quality control.[15] The 1980 labour agreement negotiated in the steel industry calls for similar plant level experiments. Another promising effort for improving labour-management dialogue involves joint councils of unions and employers at the industry level. The joint councils of construction unions and contractor associations established in six localities have introduced some successful productivity-enhancing measures.

Other experiments have attempted to improve productivity performance through the harnessing of worker information and ideas on production processes and by reducing the 'heavy- handed' approach to supervisory control. Some of these experiments have taken the form of gain sharing plans which establish bonus payments for employee suggestions that reduce costs.[16] Others have set up autonomous work groups emphasising more challenging work, team work with minimum supervision, and more training.[17]

A variety of other labour-management initiatives are in progress. These experiments include programmes in training, work scheduling, changes in organisational structure, supervisory methods, job design, financial incentives, goal setting, and changes in the entire work system. A study of these quality of work life experiments carried out in both union and non-union plants reported favourable results in most cases.[18] Significant improvements in worker performance were reflected through increased quantity or quality of production, lower production costs and reduced labour turnover.

Not all of these experiments raise efficiency, however. The success or failure of individual programmes depends on numerous behavioural variables – employer and employee commitment and involvement, personalities of key committee officials, extent of external pressure, etc. We will not capture the influence of these behavioural forces on productivity outcomes through any aggregate productivity model.

Recent research has shown that the collective bargaining process contributes importantly to economy-wide productivity growth. These studies find that productivity is, on average, 20–30 per cent higher in the union than in the non-union sector.[19] Other evidence focuses on the productivity losses that can result from poor labour-management relations. For example, a study of industrial relations in the US bituminous coal industry finds substantial productivity losses as a result of a deteriorating labour climate in the union sector in the late 1960s and 1970s.[20]

A potentially important avenue for enhancing our productivity outlook may rest with a strategy that focuses on improving labour-management cooperation. These programmes already constitute an important new trend in US industrial relations. Unions are increasingly cooperating with management in problem-solving efforts to improve industrial efficiency. These new developments are crucial at this time, given the increasing evidence of tensions in current bargaining relationships and at the job site due to reductions in real purchasing power.

In summary, it is difficult to explain the decline in US productivity by looking solely at traditional factor inputs. We must be careful in drawing inferences from this evidence, in view of the serious conceptual and measurement errors inherent in our state-of-the-art methodologies. Most importantly, we must recognise the complexities of the productivity process, including the behavioural and dynamic factors that influence long-run productivity growth. We need to understand the fundamental forces affecting productivity change before we embark on efforts to solve the productivity problem.

IMPLICATIONS AND CONCLUSIONS

Traditional growth accounting and production function approaches have been applied to explain the recent slowdown in US productivity growth. These analyses have singled out factors such as reduced investment spending, high energy prices, increased environmental and health and safety regulations and employment shifts to lower productivity service jobs as major causes of the productivity decline. Policymakers have frequently concluded from these analyses that merely reversing these patterns will steer us back on the course of high productivity growth. This paper suggests that such policy solutions may be overly-simplistic because they fail to capture the complex dynamic and behavioural elements that contribute importantly to productivity growth in the economy. The policies that we develop to remedy our productivity ills will be substantially more effective, if they reflect some of these fundamental complexities underlying the growth process.

Our forecasts anticipate annual productivity growth rates of about 1.5 per cent for 1980–5. Further increases in productivity to 2 per cent per year are expected by the late 1980s. This projection points to productivity advances well above those experienced over the past 10 years, but somewhat lower than the post-war average. The expected resumption in productivity growth can be attributed to improvements in exogenous factors and the absence of certain productivity-depressing forces. For example, the longer-term adjustment to higher energy prices through more energy-efficient technology should provide a boost to productivity growth during the 1980s. However, unless we adopt new productivity policies, other negative influences – especially those associated with uncertainty, slow growth and rapid structural change – are not likely to disappear in the next decade and will therefore continue to have a dampening effect on US productivity growth.

Our prospects could be considerably enhanced with a productivity based economic policy that reflects the complexity inherent in productivity growth. An appropriate programme would include incentives for improved management and productive processes, increase the education and training of workers and improve the dialogue and cooperation between labour, management, and government in the resolution of economic problems. Such a policy would provide the framework necessary for high levels of productivity growth and assure fuller utilisation of the economy's productive resources.

I am convinced that improving labour-management cooperation is a potentially important avenue for achieving productivity growth. While capital formation is an important element in the production process, labour has historically accounted for two-thirds of economic growth. It is doubtful whether substantial productivity improvements are possible without efficient utilisation of this resource.

Empirical evidence is mounting that better labour-management cooperation leads to substantial productivity gains. Such productivity-enhancing programmes already constitute an important new trend in US industrial relations. Unions are increasingly cooperating with management at the plant level in problem-solving efforts that augment industrial efficiency. Industry level tripartite committees recently established in the steel, automobile, coal, and construction industries also have shown significant promise. These industry committees provide an important institutional forum for discussing future industry growth prospects, potential sources of productivity gains, alternatives to government regulations, incentives for stimulating investment and technological innovation and improved human resource management. Dialogue at this level is essential if we are to move beyond crisis management and instead rely on the combined efforts and knowledge of management and labour to promote positive adjustment to longer-run structural changes in these industries.

Management must assume an important leadership role in developing the industrial relations climate conducive to increased productivity. Management is, by definition, responsible for planning the efficient use of resources. Thus, productivity is mainly a management responsibility. The economic health of firms and industries depends on the competence of management, as well as the environmental context within which management decisions must be made. Public policy should establish mechanisms for encouraging effective management. To some degree competition will accomplish this, but competition must take place within a policy framework that makes survival depend on greater efficiency and responsibility for management decisions. Government policy must also make it difficult for management to transfer the costs of inadequate private decisionmaking to the workers (in the form of low wages or unemployment) or to society (in the form of environmental or health care costs).

Perhaps the most important element of a productivity-based economic policy would be the assurance of full employment of all resources – labour and capital. In a slow growth economy, labour will be ineffectively utilised and investment incentives for both physical and human capital will remain weak. Commitment of government policies to the maintenance of full employment of such resources would be a major factor in reducing uncertainty and restoring the longer term investment horizon so necessary for innovation and process changes underlying the productivity growth process. Full employment policies are also essential to developing the social consensus necessary for ensuring continued improvements in living standards.

Productivity policy, thus, must begin with full employment policies coupled with renewed leadership by the government in promoting labour-management cooperation at all levels. A higher level of cooperation and consensus building between labour, management and the government will provide the economic and social climate necessary for long-run productivity growth.

NOTES

1. See R. E. Kutscher, J. A. Mark and J. R. Norsworthy, 'The Productivity Slowdown and the Outlook to 1985', *Monthly Labor Review* (May 1977) pp. 3–8.
2. A number of recent articles have tried to capture the effects of these changes: Denison (1979), Gollop and Jorgenson (1979), Norsworthy, Harper and Kunze (1979), and Chinloy (1980).
3. For example, Norsworthy, Harper, and Kunze (NHK) of the Bureau of Labour Statistics (BLS) (1979) find that the capital–labour ratio explains a large portion of the current slowdown, while Denison (1979) finds only a relatively small impact. The results of most other investigators support the NHK findings.
4. See, for example, Perry (1977) and Denison (1979).
5. For an example of this approach, see E. A. Hudson and D. W. Jorgenson, 'Energy Prices and the U. S. Economy, 1972–1976', *Data Resources U. S. Review* (September 1978) pp. 1.24–1.37.
6. For example, in their model Hudson–Jorgenson assume low elasticities of substitution between energy and capital which are treated as complements and a high elasticity of substitution between energy and capital and labour.
7. E. F. Denison, 'Effects of Selected Changes in the Institutional and Human Environment upon Output Per Unit of Input', *Survey of Current Business* (January 1978) pp. 21–43.
8. For example, Griliches (1973) and Terleckyj (1974) reported that R & D was significantly related to productivity growth in manufacturing, contributing about 0.3 percentage points. Kendrick (1977) estimated a somewhat higher contribution (0.85 percentage points) for the 1948–66 period.

9. See, for example, Griliches (1980) and Kendrick (1979).
10. L. C. Thurow, *The Zero-Sum Society* (New York: Basic Books, 1980) p. 86.
11. N. S. Barrett, 'Productivity Impact of the Housework Shift', US Department of Labor, *ASPER* (May 1980).
12. US Department of Labor, *Cotton Dust: Review of Alternative Technical Standards and Control Technologies*, Report to the US Congress (May 1979) pp. 98–101.
13. S. Dirks-Mason, 'The Effects of the OSHA Vinyl Chloride Standard on the Vinyl Chloride Industry', US Department of Labor, OSHA Policy Office, (August 1979).
14. See, for example, Bok and Dunlop (1970), Brown and Medoff (1978), Clark (1978) and Slichter, Healy, and Livernash (1960).
15. I. Bluestone, 'How to Put QWL to Work', speech to Work in America Institute, 6 December 1979.
16. E. Lawler III, 'Rewards Systems in Improving Life at Work', in J. R. Hackman and J. L. Suttle (eds) *Goodyear Publication Company* (1977) pp. 204–5. Lawler studied 44 gain sharing plans and found that 33 improved organisational effectiveness and productivity.
17. For an example of an autonomous work group, see T. Mills, 'Altering the Social Structure in Coal Mining: A Case Study', *Monthly Labor Review* (October 1976) pp. 3–10.
18. R. E. Walton, 'How to Counter Alienation in the Plant', *Harvard Business Review* (November–December 1972) pp. 70–81.
19. See, for example, C. Brown and J. Medoff, 'Trade Unions in the Production Process', *Journal of Political Economy* (January 1978) pp. 355–78.
20. M. Connerton *et al.*, 'Productivity and Industrial Relations: The Case of U.S. Bituminous Coal', National Bureau of Economic Research Working Paper (December 1979).

REFERENCES

Barrett, N. S., 'Productivity Impact of the Housework Shift', US Department of Labor, *ASPER* (May 1980).

Bluestone, Irving, 'How to Put QWL to Work', speech to Work in America Institute (6 December 1979).

Bok, D. and Dunlop, J. T., *Labor and the American Community* (Harvard University, 1970).

Brown C. and Medoff, J., 'Trade Unions in the Production Process', *Journal of Political Economy* (January 1978) pp. 355–78.

Chinloy, R., 'Sources of Quality Change in Labor Input', *American Economic Review* (March 1980) pp. 108–19.

Clark, K., 'Unions and Productivity in the Cement Industry', Harvard University, unpublished dissertation (1978).

Connerton, M., Freeman, R., and Medoff, J., 'Productivity and Industrial Relations: The Case of U. S. Bituminous Coal', National Bureau of Economic Research Working Paper (December 1979).

Denison, E. F., *Accounting for Slower Economic Growth: The United States in the 1970s* (Brookings Institution, 1979).

Denison, E. F., 'Effects of Selected Changes in the Institutional and Human

Environment Upon Output per Unit Input', *Survey of Current Business* (January 1978) pp. 21–43.

Denison, E. F., 'Explanations of Declining Productivity Growth', *The Survey of Current Business* (August 1979) pp. 1–24.

Dirks-Mason, S., 'The Effects of the OHSA Vinyl Chloride Standard on the Vinyl Chloride Industry', US Department of Labor, OSHA Policy Office (August 1979).

Gollop, F. M., and Jorgenson, D. W., *U. S. Economic Growth: 1948–1973*. Draft of forthcoming book, Economics Department, Harvard University (October 1979).

Griliches, Z., 'R and D and the Productivity Slowdown', National Bureau of Economic Research Working Paper no. 434 (January 1980).

Griliches, Z., 'Research Expenditures and Growth Accounting', in Williams, B. R. (ed.), *Science and Technology in Economic Growth* (London: International Economic Association, 1973) pp. 55–95.

Hudson, E. A. and Jorgenson, D. W., 'Energy Prices and the U. S. Economy, 1972–1976', *Data Resources U. S. Review* (September 1978) pp. 1.24–1.37.

Kendrick, J. W., 'Total Investment and Productivity Developments', paper prepared for the Joint Session of the American Finance Association and the American Economic Association, New York (30 December 1977).

Kendrick, J. W., 'Productivity Trends and the Recent Slowdown', in W. Fellner (ed.), *Contemporary Economic Problems* (American Enterprise Institute, 1979) pp. 12–69.

Kutscher, R. E., Mark, J. A. and Norsworthy, J. R., 'The Productivity Slowdown and the Outlook to 1985', *Monthly Labor Review* (May 1977) pp. 3–8.

Lawler, E. III, 'Rewards Systems in Improving Life at Work', in Hackman, J. R., and Suttle, J. L. (eds), *Goodyear Publication Company* (1977) pp. 204–5.

McLennan, K., 'Productivity Improvement: The Role of R and D and Capital Investment Policies', Committee for Economic Development (1980).

Mills, T., 'Altering the Social Structure in Coal Mining: A Case Study', *Monthly Labor Review* (October 1976) pp. 3–10.

Norsworthy, J. R., Harper, M. J. and Kunze, K., 'The Slowdown in Productivity Growth: Analysis of Some Contributing Factors', *Brookings Papers on Economic Activity* (1979) pp. 2–14.

Perry, G. L., 'Potential Output: Recent Issues and Present Trends', in Center for the Study of American Business, *U. S. Productive Capacity: Estimating the Utilization Gap*, Working Paper 23 (1977) pp. 6–13.

Slichter, S., Healy, J. and Livernash, R. E., *The Impact of Collective Bargaining on Management* (Washington: Brookings Institution, 1960).

Terleckyj, N. E., *Effects of R and D on the Productivity Growth of Industries: An Exploratory Study* (Washington: National Planning Association, 1974).

Thurow, L. C., *The Zero-Sum Society* (New York Basic Books, 1980).

US Department of Labor, *Cotton Dust: Review of Alternative Technical Standards and Control Technologies*, Report to the US Congress (May 1979).

Walton, 'How to Counter Alienation in the Plant', *Harvard Business Review* (November–December 1972) pp. 70–81.

5 British Financial Reconstruction, 1815–22 and 1918–25

CHARLES P. KINDLEBERGER

It may be regarded by some as ill-mannered to argue with Walt Rostow in honouring him. A superficial defence can be found in the modern statement that it doesn't make any difference what you say about a person as long as you mention him frequently and spell his name correctly. More fundamentally, Professor Rostow has posed an interesting and profound interpretation of a classic issue that is worth illuminating.

In the first place, in *The World Economy* (1978, pp. xlii, xliii), he states:

> For some, at least, monetary affairs will appear to have been slighted. In the analysis of the pre-1914 era monetary affairs appear only when I believe they left a significant impact on the course of events, e.g. transmitting the effects of bad harvests in the eighteenth and nineteenth centuries; in helping create the settings for cyclical crises and then (in Britain at least), cushioning their impact; in stimulating, under the gold standard, the inflationary diversion of resources to gold mining. In the post-1918 world of more conscious monetary policies, they emerge on a stage in the 1920s with the French devaluation and the British return at the old rate, as well as the failure of the United States to accept its responsibilities for the trade and monetary structure of the world economy. After 1945, the rise and fall of the Bretton Woods system forms (*sic*), of course, part of the narrative.
>
> Nevertheless it should be underlined that the view taken here of the course of production and prices – in cycles, trend periods,

> and in the process of growth itself – would regard the non-monetary factors as paramount . . . Men and societies have devised and evolved monetary systems which more or less met their deeper needs and purposes as they conceived them. Different monetary policies, at different times and places, might have yielded somewhat different results than history now records. The same could be said with equal or greater strength about fiscal policies. But down to 1914 modern concepts of monetary and fiscal policy did not exist, except perhaps in a few unorthodox minds; and prevailing notions reordered the monetary system substantially passive and responsive.

In a subsequent essay reviewing the new monetarism, he defends this position at length, insists that pre-1914 monetary systems were passive and flexible, and sides once more with the Thomas Tooke position, against David Ricardo, that price changes emanate from the supply side through costs and output changes (1980).

I have a difficult time with these propositions, and especially with the notions: (1) That there was a major discontinuity in 1914; and (2) the pre-1918 world was less conscious of monetary problems than the post-1918 and that the modern concepts of monetary and fiscal policy did not exist theretofore. The more usual view is that monetary orthodoxy goes back at least to 1797, or if you prefer, to Thornton and Ricardo in 1802 and 1809 (Fetter, 1965; Morgan, 1943). But the inspiration of this paper comes secondly from Rostow's sharp reaction to a remark I made in his seminar at the University of Texas at Austin, shortly after having read A. W. Acworth's *Financial Reconstruction in England, 1815–1822* (1925), suggesting close parallelism between Britain, 1815 to 1822 and 1918 to 1925. Analogues run between the Bullion report (1810) and the Cunliffe report (1925); the postwar booms of 1814 and 1919, followed by collapse in 1816 and 1920, and then recovery for a couple of years in both cases; the Parliamentary committee report favouring Resumption in 1819 and the Chamberlain–Bradbury report of 1924; the Peterloo 'massacre' of 1819 and the coal strike of 1925 plus the General Strike of 1926; deflation following for four more years to 1823 after resumption in 1819, for six years until the 1931 depreciation in the case of 1925. Rostow denied that the troubles of 1815 to 1822 were anything like those of 1918 to 1925 or 1931. The latter were monetary, the former non-monetary. One could cite weightier authority than Acworth who says in his preface that he has 'refrained from pointing comparisons, contrasts with the last seven years' (1925, p.v.), for example T. E. Gregory in his introduction to Tooke's *History of Prices* (1928), who states:

> If the economic and, in particular the monetary problems we are facing today have a startling resemblance to those which were the subject-matter of contention for two generations a century ago, the experience of the Napoleonic and post-Napoleonic days has an interest for us in two respects. The two periods illumine one another, and we can pass from the depreciated exchanges of 1797–1819 to those of 1914–1925 . . . with the feeling that our comprehension of the past and present is increased by comparing one with the other.
>
> But these volumes have a renewed interest in another . . . respect. The interpretation of the events of the period . . . gave rise to an intellectual conflict in which now one side, now the other seemed for a time to have carried off the final victory.

It is true that the major participants in the decision to stabilise the pound seem not to have thought about the analogy – *pace* Acworth. I recall no reference to it in Keynes (1930, 1932, 1933), Leith Ross (1968), Grigg (1948), the Moggridge accounts (1969, 1972), the Norman Biographies – Clay (1957), Boyle (1967) – or Howson (1975). A peek is worth two finesses, however, so I wrote to Moggridge and asked. He kindly replied that only Hawtrey evoked the analogy between 1919 and 1925, and he did so several times. Nonetheless there seems to be enough evidence to reopen the question, to indict, if not at this stage to convict.

If I were more ambitious, I might try to extend the analogy to the British recoinage of silver in 1696 which involved appreciation and depression (Hawtrey, 1927, pp. 290 ff) or that of Demaretz in France in 1715 when the livre was raised from 20 to 14 to the louis d'or (Luethy, 1959, I, p. 281). I urge these extensions on the reader, not excluding Professor Rostow.

Apart from the closeness of the 1815/1918 analogy, it is hard to accept the suggestion that money and banking were passive and accommodating. Resumption was subject to 'extremely heated controversy', particularly as it was accompanied by sharp deflation, probably intensified by the decision in 1821 to return to a full gold-coin standard instead of Ricardo's bullion plan (O'Brien, I, p. 71).

The decision to resume gold payments was postponed at least six times. Nor did all but a few unorthodox minds agree on policy choices. There were clearly many who were unorthodox – William Cobbett who detested paper money, the national debt and banks; Sir John Sinclair, who 'went off in all directions at once, as he so often did', wanted a large note issue but was concerned about the 'coinage of paper money' (Fetter, 1965, pp. 22, 29); the eighth Earl of Lauderdale, an advocate of silver money, or at best bimetallism, a perpetual Cassandra of the economic situation in England (ibid., p. 15). In his review of a book by Lord King, Francis Horner, the chairman of the Committee that wrote the Bullion Report of 1810 stated: 'In great commercial cities, opinions have been avowed by persons who ought to be acquainted with the money trade that precious metals are unnecessary and that the provisions of the law of 1797 should be made permanent,' (ibid., p. 56). On the other side of the debate, Wheatley was, if penetrating and original, an extreme bullionist who held that monetary expansion had no effect on output, and foreign payments no impact on the exchange rate because of frictionless real transfer (ibid., p. 38). Most participants in the discussion, however, were prepared to concede some merit to the opposite case. Ricardo would have advocated devaluation if the pound had been depreciated in 1819 by 30 per cent, as it had been in 1813 (Viner, 1937, p. 205n.). 'Even so ardent a disciple of Ricardo as McCulloch thought the old par a mistake' (ibid., p. 175). Thomas Attwood of the Birmingham School, who resisted Resumption and wanted monetary expansion, would halt such expansion whenever it was sufficient to call every labourer into action; any further stimulus would be nugatory or injurious (ibid., p. 212 n.). Even Tooke, says Gregory, was *never* (his italics) an extreme bullionist (1982, p. 16). He was however a good hater (ibid., p. 120), a magnificent controversialist, with a thesis to uphold and an enemy to vanquish.

Rostow, of course, has been over this ground years ago. He wrote Part I of Volume I of the classic Gayer, Rostow and Schwartz, *Growth and Fluctuations of the British Economy, 1790–1850* (1953, I, p. vi). In this work he broke down Restriction from 1797 to 1819 into a series of short periods, largely, for our purposes, 1803 to 1806, 1807 to 1811, 1812 to 1816, and 1817 to 1821, and submitted each one to an identical period-by-period analysis of prices, foreign trade, investment, industry and agriculture, finance and labour. Finance was only one factor out of six, and that taken up penultimately.

Moreover, he follows Tooke closely. I counted 10 long quotations from that authority in the 110 pages, in addition to 60-plus citations. Tooke's time periods are somewhat different, 1799–1803, 1804–8, 1809–13, 1814–18, and 1819–22, and his schema is divided in three: the effect of the seasons, which discusses the harvest; the effect of war, dealing largely with the need to finance British and foreign troops fighting the French; and finally currency, which in his view essentially has nothing to do with prices or the exchange rate. Rostow follows him and Silberling in the analysis of the exchange rate. Extraordinary expenses abroad consists of bills and specie remitted for British armies, subsidies and loans for allies, and grain imports of more than £2 million in any year. The sum of these tracks very well with the price of silver and the exchange rate on Hamburg, as Viner shows (1937, p. 143), and the depreciation of the pound is not markedly different whether one takes the premium of the market above the mint gold price, the premium on silver, or the Hamburg exchange rate. Tooke and Rostow have a solid victory in this over many of the bullionists, including especially Ricardo and Wheatley, who dismissed extraordinary foreign expenditures as a source of depreciation because they assumed a frictionless transfer mechanism. The directors of the Bank of England on the other hand were also wrong in telling the Bullion Committee that foreign payments led to a 100 per cent loss of specie. But the division of the period into short subperiods leads to overemphasis of the short run and neglect of the truths of the long.

Tooke has little difficulty in indicating a whole series of years at the beginnings and ends of his mini-periods, when currency issues and prices were going in different directions. In some of his more ironic passages, he goes down into quarters and months, finding for example, that the gold premium and the exchange rate were improving in the spring of 1814 when the circulation was rising, and that prices collapsed in the spring of 1819 when the Bank of England circulation was still unchanged (1838, II, pp. 80–1, 96–7). I shall have something more to say about these speculative periods later. For the moment, however, one should observe that if 1797 to 1822 is divided into one expansionary and inflationary period from 1797, and particularly from 1808 to 1814, followed by deflation to 1822, as Viner does (1937, Chs iii, iv), it would have been evident that the sum of Bank of England commercial paper under discount and advances to the government rose from a low of £14.1 millions in 1798 to £41.4 millions in 1815 (ibid., p. 167); and that thereafter total advances (a somewhat different concept) declined from £42.9 millions in 1814 (£42.5 million in 1815) to £14.8 millions in 1824. To focus on the short run and leads and lags neglects long-run truth. Bank of England circulation is not a good measure of the money supply for a number of reasons – the debated question whether the note issues of the country banks are substitutes or complements for notes of the Bank; the even more hotly debated issue whether or not to count £1 and £2 notes, issued for the first time to conserve gold early in the war, and replaced by gold coin at an unknown rate beginning in 1816; and the gradually evolving role of deposits at the Bank.

It is none of our task to resolve these questions and decide by how much the money supply rose to 1814, and fell thereafter, or whether in fact the Bank responded passively, as Tooke and his Banking School believe it should and did, or whether the Bank behaved perversely in following the real-bills doctrine erroneously up to 1814, and then, beginning to get ready for resumption, withdrawing money and stockpiling gold. It is enough to point out the analogy between the two periods, 100-plus years apart, and to suggest that if anything, economic analysis of the resumption issue was more sophisticated after the peace of Vienna than after Versailles.

Modern monetary theory may have been said to have begun with Henry Thornton's *An Inquiry into the Nature and Effect of the Paper Credit of Great Britain* in 1802 rather than in 1936 with the *General Theory*. Thornton not only developed the doctrine of the lender of last resort, well before Bagehot, but he also had a nice sense of the long run and the short. Much of the work is devoted to the quantity theory which he later brought to his shared authorship of the Bullion Report (1810), but he also warned against too-precipitous contraction of the Bank of England circulation which may well produce convulsions leading to outflows of specie, rather than the inflow predicted by the monetary theory of the balance of payments (1802, pp. 116, 122, 226–7). Tooke admired *Paper Credit*, he asserted, and called Thornton profoundly acquainted with the principles and details of banking, adding, however, that he had not necessarily from his occupation as a banker, any knowledge of markets (1838, I, 313–14). The remark could be turned against Tooke, who was a merchant and business man, in insurance and docks, but whose understanding of banking came from the perspective of a customer, rather than the inside.

Unlike 1925, when there was little or no organised opposition to the return of sterling to par, and only the somewhat chaotic and unconvincing arguments of Keynes and McKenna (Moggridge, 1972, pp. 42 ff), two groups opposed Resumption in 1819 and earlier, and wanted it reversed in subsequent years. In numbers and position they were so prominent that it is hard to characterise them as 'a few unorthodox minds'. The Birmingham school was interested in employment, maintaining an embryonic Keynesian view (of the 1930s, not 1920s) that expansion of bank circulation was necessary to increase employment and that it was impossible to achieve such expansion with Resumption. The agriculturalists had what was close to a Populist position, with emphasis on higher prices to lighten the burden of debt, both mortgage and national debt, the service of which required high taxation. It even contained a bimetallist, who sometimes appears to be in favour of the silver standard, the Earl of Lauderdale (Smart, 1911, I, p. 478, 622) who was the sole member of the 1819 Lords Committee to vote against Resumption (Fetter, 1965, p. 93 note). In this he was a precursor of the Junkers who favoured bimetallism for Germany at the end of the century (Williamson, 1971, p. 21), and of course the American Populists of William Jennings Bryan's day.

It does not seem to me to be entirely correct to say that the Birmingham School had no interest in the inequity between creditor and debtor from inflation and deflation (Fetter, 1965, p. 75; Checkland, 1948, p. 3). Checkland himself notes that Thomas Attwood conceded the case for resumption, provided all debts and obligations would be adjusted (1948, p. 5; Viner, 1937, p. 186). He further talked in terms of stabilising money in terms of wheat, all prices, the rate of interest, or the wages of agricultural labour, all but the third of which comes close to the agricultural position. But the main interest of Birmingham was employment.

There was no doubt that Birmingham was hurt by real factors. War expenditure had been cut, particularly affecting the city that manufactured small arms, hardware, and the 'toy trade'. Machinery was displacing handwork. Exports had been reduced not only by the miscalculations of 1814, comparable to those of 1919, but by tariff increases in the United States and on the Continent. Britain had made rather feeble efforts to guarantee entry of her products in the territory of her wartime allies, seeking, like the United States in the Lend-Lease settlements nearly a century and a half later, to use its bargaining power for trade advantage. It did not succeed (Sherwig, 1969, p. 311). The failure was complained of contemporaneously by Brougham and in 1835 by Cogden (Acworth, 1925, pp. 121–2). A Birmingham petition of labourers, with 11 000 signatures collected in 48 hours, was presented by Brougham to Parliament in 1817, complaining that the city was unemployed or down to 2 to 3 days work a week. Another petition of Birmingham citizens in 1820, drafted by the banker Thomas Attwood, called for a reconsideration of Resumption. (These petitions have left a less lasting impression in history than the well-known petition of the Merchants of London for freer trade, presented in 1820 too, written by Thomas Tooke, and presented to Parliament by Alexander Baring (Smart, 1911, pp. 744–7)). A motion for repeal was introduced into the House of Commons by Baring, and was defeated twice, the second time on a roll-call vote of 141–27. In the course of the debate, Edward Ellice said he would have preferred resumption at £5 10s for gold, compared to the parity price of £3 17s 10 1/2d. This would have been a depreciation of more than 40 per cent (Fetter, 1965, pp. 100–1). Lord Folkestone for the agriculturalists would have settled for £4 0s 6d in 1819. Tooke states that undertaking Resumption at the market price of 1819 'however *palpably unjust*, would have least have been *intelligible*' (1838, II, p. 65, his italics). In 1828 Mr Denison said the proper course to be taken in 1819 was not widely agreed. He held to £4 10s or £4 15s while a colleague in the House of Commons, agreeing with a noble Lord in the other House (Lord Lauderdale?) thought that it ought to be £5 5s or £5 10s (ibid, II, pp. 67, 68). Thomas Attwood himself wanted abandonment of the gold standard altogether, but failing that he sought devaluation by raising the price of gold to £8, qualified to £6 in 1821 and to £5 in 1826 (Checkland, 1948, p. 15). The first number qualifies as unorthodox.

Here was a sharp contrast with 1925 when the issue was never posed in terms of alternative exchange rates but only resumption or no resumption at the price for gold set by Isaac Newton in 1717. It will also be remembered that when Britain finally went off the gold standard in September, 1931, Tom Johnson, an ex-Labour minister, is said to have remarked 'They never told us we could do that' (Moggridge, 1969, p. 9).

The problem of money as a standard of deferred payment for contracts came to national attention early when Lord King in 1811 for political reasons wrote a letter to his tenants giving them notice that he wanted his rents paid in gold equivalents because of the depreciation of paper currency. Paper currency had not been made legal tender officially because of the frightening example of the assignats in France, but the government responded to Lord King's initiative by legislation preventing Bank of England notes being received for a smaller sum than specified on the notes passed (Levi, 1880, pp. 123–33, Fetter, 1965, p.59). When inflation turned to deflation 'one William Cobbett' (*sic*, Smart, 1911, I, p. 739) petitioned Parliament for relief by reducing his debt to its 1813 value. He had bought and improved an estate to the extent of £30 000, of which £13 000 was borrowed. With prices less than half their 1813 level 'on account of the Resumption Act' he was about to be ruined. The petition was ignored, and he did lose his farm at Botley in Southampton (*Encyclopedia Britannica*, 1970, V, p. 989). But Cobbett was more interested as a Radical in the problems of farm labourers and factory workers. He did not 'hate Peel like Castlereagh and Pitt, but held him primarily responsible for severe distresses of common people. Returning to gold without any liquidation of debt charges or reduction of other burdens had been the main cause of semi-starvation. . .' (Cole, 1924, p. 396).

A short digression on Cobbett may be worthwhile, even though he is assuredly one of the few minds that Rostow characterises as unorthodox. In 1819 he had written from the United States where he had taken refuge from the 1817 act repealing Habeas Corpus, that 'resumption would result in a big fall in prices which would be universally ruinous...ruin to all who held stocks of goods or who owed large sums or who had heavy mortgages'. Later when the Resumption Act passed (and he had returned to Britain), he wrote saying that at least one million would die of hunger, that the act would never be completely carried out, and that if it were so, he 'would suffer Castlereagh to broil him alive while Sidmouth stirred the coals, and Canning stood by to make a jest of his groans' (Doubleday, 1847, pp. 248–9). A gridiron became his symbol and logograph for his newspaper, the *Political Register*. The key word in his promise is the word 'completely', meaning the need to eliminate the note issues of the country banks and the Bank of England (Fetter, 1965, p. 108) and do something about the burden of the national debt. A Feast of the Gridiron was promised to his Radical followers and held in April, 1826 (Cole, 1924, pp. 280–3). But by this time Cobbett had returned to his hatred of paper money, inspired by his reading of Thomas Paine's *Decline and Fall of the English System of Finance* (1803), and embodied in his *Paper Against Gold* (1815), written when he was in Newgate prison for sedition.

When prices were rising in 1824 and 1825 he tried to bring them down by urging trade unionists to convert paper money into gold at every opportunity, and trade unions to appoint a 'gold man'. In August 1832 he debated Thomas Attwood, the Birmingham expansionist, who wanted larger issues of paper money while Cobbett wanted to eliminate both paper money and debt. Attwood opened the debate before 1 400 people in a speech lasting four and a half hours, and Cobbett came back the next day with a moderate two hours of rebuttal (ibid., p. 223, 263, 396–7). E. P. Thompson notes that it is not difficult to show that Cobbett had some very stupid and contradictory ideas but he quotes with approval Raymond Williams' attribution to Cobbett of an 'extraordinary sureness of instinct' (1963, pp. 749, 758), and Cole calls him 'largely right' (Cole, 1924, p. 280). Both men write, to be sure, from a leftist perspective.

The classical writers were by no means unaware of the problem of equity between creditor and debtor. Thornton said that the question of whether resumption should be undertaken or not turned on whether depreciation had lasted a long time, such as 15 or 20 years, during which bargains had been made in depreciated currency, or merely two or three years (1802, p. 345). In 1802 when *Paper Credit* was written there had been but two years of 10 per cent or so depreciation (premium on the mint price of gold). This then subsided until 1809 when it rose to 40 or 50 per cent until 1814. What Thornton would have thought about the equity of resumption in 1819 in the light of this uneven record is an interesting puzzle but academic. He died in 1815. Ricardo and McCullogh were concerned less with mortgages and private bargains than with the national debt, as was a wide section of opinion in the 1810s. There was no such issue, so far as I am aware, in public opinion in the 1920s. Ricardo advocated a capital levy to restore equity. In 1817 the income tax had been abandoned, and in any case had not been progressive (Acworth, 1925, Ch. V, esp. p. 57). In his first tract in economics, J. R. McCulloch proposed reduction of interest on the national debt because much of it had been advanced in depreciated currency (Smart, 1911, p. 510). This would not have affected the capital value of repayment of short-dated issues. Tooke was scornful of all such talk, especially in agricultural land: 'What it has since been the fashion to call an equitable adjustment of contracts means in reality an indemnification of bad speculations' (1838, I, p. 326). Nor did his heart bleed for the industrialists who suffered losses from the fall in prices of industrial goods, some running as high as 50 per cent upon the return of Napoleon from Elba:

> That rise of prices of exportable produce and manufactures which proved so ephemeral as being founded upon the most unwarranted expectations of demand *in consequence of the peace* (his italics), and of the renewal of commercial intercourse with the Continent, has been the occasion of the most absurd conclusions conceivable. . . The disastrous effects of these ill-judged and extravagantly extensive speculations began to manifest themselves in numerous failures which took place toward the end of 1814. (ibid., II, 6–8)

The analogue, of course, is with the boomlet of 1920–1 when a great number of industries in Britain, notably cotton textiles, steel and shipping, went into debt at very high prices of output and capital assets that could not be sustained, and piled up interest charges that were a heavy burden for the rest of the decade (Pigou, 1948, pp. 12; Youngson, 1960, pp. 25–6).

Speculation ran the prices of agricultural produce and exports up and down. It did the same with gold, silver and foreign exchange. Once resumption was in the offing, the premiums on gold, silver and Hamburg exchange declined sharply, so that the depreciation of sterling from par was less than five per cent. In 1924 after the change of government from Labour to the Conservative party, the pound sterling rose against the dollar to a depreciation of the order of 10 per cent. In these circumstances, the temptation to go the rest of the way is strong indeed. Tooke calls the gap a 'trifling' distance or divergence (1838, II, pp. 65, 76). In commenting on Peel's view that failure to undertake resumption would have been a fraud on creditors Hawtrey uses the same word: 'It would have been a mean-spirited course to go back on the century-old standard on account of so trifling a premium on gold' (1927, p. 351).

'Fraud' and 'mean spirited' introduce into the question the moral issues which were present both in 1819 and in 1925, 'Defenders of the metallic standard contended themselves with an appeal to arbitrary dogmas and moral issues' (Viner, 1937, p. 216). Fetter quotes Brougham: 'To tamper with the public faith; to sully the honour of the country; to declare a national bankruptcy? Good God! Who in his senses would recommend it?' (1965, p. 105). Compare Sauvy on resumption in 1925: 'A question of prestige, a question of dogma, . . . almost a question of honor' (1965, p. 121). Another French view states that it came from the need to look the dollar in the eye . . . 'an affair of *amour propre* rather than monetary policy' (Perrot, 1955, p. 35).

Tooke initially held to the view that the elimination of the three or four per cent premium on gold or discount on sterling could not have reduced prices by more than that percentage (1838, I, p. 4). He later admitted that by drawing gold from the Continent, Britain could have raised the price of gold, or lowered commodity prices on a world-wide basis. Ricardo had tried to limit the British demand for gold by urging that Resumption take place on the bullion standard, so that convertibility would not be made into coin. This raises the issue of the £1 and £2 notes again, and how much gold was required to retire them from circulation. Tooke admits the possibility of deflation from this source but argues that the amounts of British gold and silver lost to or gained from the rest of the world never amounted to more than 12 to 15 million pounds as contrasted with a world money supply of gold and silver somewhere between £1200 and £2000 million, or close to one per cent and surely no more than two per cent (1838, I, 131–5). The counter to this contention is that the world was, for the most part, on the silver standard, and British gains and losses in gold were a much higher percentage of the world gold supply. Soetbeer's tables of the average ratio of gold to silver in Hamburg goes from 15.11 in 1817 to 15.95 in 1821 (US Senate, 1879, p. 709) which suggests an increasing scarcity of gold, above that of world money in general. From the modern theoretical views of Mundell and Laffer embodied in the expression 'World Monetarism', some pressure on the world money supply, more in gold currency than in silver, thus came from British gold acquisitions from 1819 on. Ricardo put this effect at five per cent, and agreed with Tooke that it was the result of Bank mismanagement, that is acceptance of the decision to redeem in coin as well as bullion (Viner, 1937, p. 175).

Insistence of the Banking School that it was real factors that produced these drastic up and down swings in prices, and especially series of crop failures or gluts in a row encounters another serious objection, that all prices rise and fall more or less together. This is true in Britain, as between agricultural and industrial prices, and between Britain and the Continent, where general price levels rise and fall in wider swings than can be accounted for by exchange-rate differences, which in their turn, on the Banking School showing, were generated by extraordinary foreign payments – another real factor. On the other hand, the classical explanation is probably not much help here either. It was not that prices rose and fell with Bank of England policies of monetary expansion and contraction, although there was some of that as far as the government was concerned. There was some expansion up to 1814 to finance government, and some contraction when the government in connection with Resumption, acceded to the Bank's request to pay down its advance by ten million pounds. For the most part, however, and particularly for private discounts, the Bank was passive, as indeed the Banking School and the real-bill doctrine believed it should be. Speculation drove prices and prices drove money. As Temin explains in his discussion of the depression in the United States in 1929–33, it was not the LM curve which moved independently and reduced nominal income; it was the shift in spending, the IS curve, which reduced income and led to a decrease in the money supply (1976). A Currency School approach under which the attempt would have been made to limit fluctuations in money to those dictated by the state of the specie reserve would have moderated the swing of prices responding to speculation, but not eliminated them. Speculation in agricultural produce, agricultural land and export commodities responding to variations in harvest and to changes in the fortunes of war could be financed for some considerable distance on the up-side and without limit on the down by the possibility of monetising personal credit. The country-bank note issues responded in this way. Bills of exchange could equally do so. The fact that agricultural and industrial prices rose and fell together suggests that it was not variations in crops alone that affected prices, but that there were important forces working on the side of money as well, despite the passiveness of monetary policy.

The same issue arises with Europe. European prices rose and fell with British ones. Tooke attempts to rebut the argument that this bespeaks the primacy of monetary over real factors, advanced by Matthias Attwood, a London banker and brother of the Birmingham banker, Thomas Attwood, in debate on 10 July 1822 on Mr. Western's motion to reconsider Resumption, by stating that the same real factors were operative on the Continent as in Britain, and that in fact the decline of prices in 1819 originated on the Continent not England (1838, II, 87, 89, 95). The charge has a familiar ring to those who recall the debate as to whether the financial crisis of 1836 originated in the United States or Britain, and the similar issue over 1929. It is evident that variations in weather can leap the Channel with little difficulty and that one can have long and short crops simultaneously in England and the Continent. The coincidence that the same real factors in industrial products would move non-agricultural prices in similar directions is hard to credit, unless speculation financed by monetised personal credit be regarded as a real instead of a monetary factor.

On these scores I find it hard to accept the view that

(a) monetary policies were more conscious after 1918 than before;
(b) that non-monetary factors are paramount in economic history (I propose to say more on this question at another time and place);
(c) that modern concepts of monetary policy did not exist down to 1914;
(d) that the monetary system was substantially passive and responsive; and
(e) that economic reconstruction after 1815 was altogether different from that after 1918.

I should perhaps go further, and suggest here, as I have in the case of eighteenth- and nineteenth-century France (1980), that the clash between monetarism and Keynesianism is an ancient one, going back at least to John Law a century before Henry Thornton. I expect it will still be around a century hence.

Perhaps I should give the last word to the Rostow of about 1941 who wrote:

> During these years (1819–21) and in the following three decades there was much controversy on the allegedly deflationary consequences of the Act of 1819. These speculations (along with those of 1810) evoked perhaps the most fruitful monetary discussion of the nineteenth century. (Gayer *et al*, 1953, p. 165)

This would seem to dispose of the 'few unorthodox minds'.

REFERENCES

Acworth, A. W., *Financial Reconstruction in England, 1815–1822* (London: P. S. King, 1925).

Boyle, Andrew, *Montagu Norman* (London: Cassell, 1967).

Checkland, S. G., 'The Birmingham Economists, 1815–1850', *Economic History Review*, second series, I, 1 (1948) pp. 1–19.
Cole, G. D. H., *The Life of William Cobbett* (New York: Harcourt, Brace, no date, preface dated 1924).
(Cunliffe Report), British Parliamentary Reports on International Finance, *The Cunliffe Committee and the Macmillan Committee (1931) Reports* (New York: Arno Press, 1978).
Doubleday, Thomas, *A Financial, Monetary and Statistical History of England from the Revolution of 1688 to the Present Time* (London: Effingham, Wilson, 1847).
Fetter, Frank Whitson, *Development of British Monetary Orthodoxy, 1797–1815*, (Cambridge, Mass.: Harvard University Press, 1965).
Gayer, Arthur D., W. W. Rostow, and Anna Jacobson Schwartz, *The Growth and Fluctuation of the British Economy, 1790–1850, An Historical, Statistical and Theoretical Study of Britain's Economic Development* (Oxford: Clarendon, 1953) (largely unchanged from the manuscript of 1941).
Great Britain, Parliamentary Debates, *Report from the Select Committee on the High Price of Gold Bullion*, Ordered by the House of Commons to be Printed, 8 June 1810 (reprinted New York: Arno Press, 1978).
Gregory, T. E., 'Introduction' to Tooke and Newmarch, op. cit.
Grigg, P. J., *Prejudice and Judgement* (London: Jonathan Cape, 1948).
Hawtrey, R. G., *Currency and Credit* (1919), third ed. (London: Longmans, Green, 1927).
Howson, Susan K., *Domestic Monetary Management in Britain, 1919–38* (Cambridge University Press, 1975).
Keynes, John Maynard, *Essays in Persuasion* (New York: Harcourt Brace, 1932).
Keynes, John Maynard, *Essays in Biography* (1933) new edition with three additional essays (London: Hart-Davis, 1951).
Keynes, John Maynard, *A Treatise on Money*, 2 volumes (New York: Harcourt Brace, 1930).
Keynes, John Maynard, *The General Theory of Employment, Interest and Money* (New York: Harcourt Brace, 1936).
Kindleberger, Charles P., 'Keynesianism vs Monetarism in 18th and 19th Century France', *History of Political Economy*, Vol. 12, No. 4 (Winter 1980), pp 499–523
Leith-Ross, Sir Frederick, *Money Talks, Fifty Years of International Finance* (London: Hutchinson, 1968).
Levi, Leone, *The History of British Commerce*, 2nd edn, (London: Murray, 1880).
Li, Ming-Hsun, *The Great Recoinage of 1686 to 1699* (London: Weidenfeld and Nicolson, 1963).
Luethy, Herbert, *La Banque protestante en France dès la revocation de l'édit de Nantes à la révolution*, Tôme I, *Dispersion et régroupement (1685–1730)*, (Paris, S.E.V.P.E.N., 1959).
Moggridge, D. E., *British Monetary Policy, 1924–1931, The Norman Conquest of* $4.86 (Cambridge University Press, 1972).
Moggridge, D. E., *The Return to Gold, 1925, The Formulation of Policy and Its Critics* (Cambridge University Press, 1969).
Morgan, E. Victor, *The Theory and Practice of Central Banking, 1797–1913* (Cambridge University Press, 1943).
O'Brien, D. P. (ed.), *The Correspondence of Lord Overstone*, vols I, II, III (Cambridge University Press, 1971).

Perrot, Marguerite, *La monnaie et l'opinion publique en France et en Angleterre, 1924–36* (Paris: Colin, 1955).
Pigou, A. C., *Aspects of British Economic History, 1918–25* (London: Macmillan, 1948).
Rostow, W. W., *The World Economy* (Austin: University of Texas Press, 1978).
Rostow, W. W., 'Money and Prices: An old Debate Revisited,' in *Why the Poor get Richer and the Rich Slow Down: Essays in the Marshallian Long Period* (Austin: University of Texas Press, 1980).
Sauvy, Alfred, *Histoire économique de la France entre les deux guerres*, Tôme I, *1918–31* (Paris: Fayard, 1965).
Sherwig, John M., *Guineas and Gunpowder, British Foreign Aid in the Wars with France 1793–1815* (Cambridge, Mass.: Harvard University Press, 1969).
Silberling, N. J., 'Financial and Monetary Policy in Great Britain during the Napoleonic Wars', *Quarterly Journal of Economics*, XXXVIII (I, II, 1924) pp. 214–23, 397–439.
Smart, William, *Economic Annals of the Nineteenth Century* (1911) Volume I, 1801–1820, Volume II, 1821–1830 (reprinted, New York: Kelly, 1964).
Temin, Peter, *Did Monetary Forces Cause the Great Depression?* (New York: W. W. Norton, 1976).
Thompson, E. P., *The Making of the English Working Class* (New York: Knopf, 1963).
Thornton, Henry, *An Enquiry into the Nature and Effect of the Paper Credit of Great Britain* (1802) together with the Evidence, edited with an introduction by F. A. Hayek (London: Frank Cass, 1962), (reprint of London: George Allen & Unwin, 1939).
Tooke, Thomas, and William Newmarch, *A History of Prices and of the State Circulation from 1792 to 1896*, reproduced from the original with an introduction by T. E. Gregory (New York: Adelphi, no date, introduction date 1928, six volumes, first two volumes originally 1838).
United States Senate, *International Monetary Conference of 1878, Proceedings and Exhibits*, Washington, G.O.P., 1879 (reprinted New York: Arno Press, 1978).
Vilar, Pierre, *A History of Gold and Money, 1450–1920*, translated from the French edition of 1969 by Judith White (London: NLB, 1976).
Viner, Jacob, *Studies in the Theory of International Trade*(New York: Harpers, 1937).
Williamson, John, *Karl Helfferich, 1872–1920, Economist, Financier, Politician* (Princeton University Press, 1971).
Youngson, A. J., *The British Economy, 1920–1957* (London: George Allen & Unwin, 1960).

6 Caliban: The Devaluation of Sterling in 1949

A. CAIRNCROSS

I

To those who took part in it, the devaluation of sterling in September 1949 was one of the most dramatic episodes in the post-war history of the United Kingdom. It seemed likely at the time that it would also prove one of the most important in terms of its effects. There might be room for disagreement as to the need or the purpose or the wisdom or even the significance of the devaluation. But it was unmistakably a turning-point. So rare and startling an event as a fall of 30 per cent in the parity of sterling, the currency in which one-third of the world's commerce was conducted, could not fail to exercise a powerful influence on international transactions of all kinds. Yet many of those who have looked back on the devaluation have doubted whether it accomplished any lasting changes and have concluded that it was of quite minor importance in post-war economic development. How does it look now in retrospect after thirty years that have seen one more major devaluation of sterling as well as day-to-day fluctuations that rob devaluation of its drama?

I shall begin with a narrative of events that describes how the decision was actually taken. It is important, in assessing decisions of this kind, to recognise that they are not the automatic outcome of a careful analysis of the facts (including facts that cannot possibly be known until after the event) and that those who take them are not necessarily moved wholly or largely by economic considerations. Devaluation is a peculiarly interesting case-study in governmental decision-making precisely because it reveals so clearly the nakedness in the face of uncertainty of Ministers who of necessity have only an imperfect understanding of the economics of trace and payments.

Next I shall turn to the economic background to devaluation and the trends underlying it. The main question for consideration here is how far the pressures that led to devaluation were ephemeral, reversible and resistible and how far they were enduring and likely to be cumulative.

This discussion leads naturally into a consideration of the effects of devaluation. These effects are not easily assessed because of their submergence from the middle of 1950 onwards once the outbreak of war in Korea sent the world economy out of balance. But so far as they can be assessed after the event they have to be looked at in the framework of expectations when the decision to devalue was taken. The wisdom of the decision has to be measured not just in terms of the effectiveness of the instrument – devaluation – but also in terms of its appropriateness to the circumstances and how correctly the circumstances were appreciated.

The first discussion of devaluation in Whitehall goes back to June 1945 when R. W. B. ('Otto') Clarke, who had recently moved full-time to the Treasury, circulated a memorandum entitled 'Towards a Balance of Payments'. In this memorandum he looked forward to a recovery of international trade to pre-war volumes by 1949–50 and argued that the United Kingdom should be able to get back into balance within five years if there were an early and modest devaluation of sterling. Keynes, who did not see 'any serious risk of an overall shortage of gold and dollars in the first three (post-war) years', took issue with Clarke over the need for a devaluation. In his view a comparison of inflation rates in Britain and America indicated some overvaluation of the dollar and he concluded that British exporters would retain a residual cost advantage at the end of the war.

Even if Keynes was right both about the short-term dollar shortage and about the competitive position of British exporters, that should not have disposed of the issue if the scale of the necessary adjustment in Britain's trade made it necessary to reinforce her competitive position. On the other hand, it could have been argued that, however great the trade imbalance at the end of the war and however necessary an eventual devaluation of sterling to its removal, it was preferable to defer an adjustment for some years. To have devalued immediately would have done little or nothing to accelerate the process of reconversion from war to peace. Price was not the significant limiting factor in the recovery of exports from the low level to which they had sunk. At the same time, imports were largely under the direct control of the government. The balance of trade would have responded very slowly and probably very little to a devaluation while the terms of trade might have changed sharply for the worse. Higher import prices would also have given an additional fillip to inflation unless the government had intervened with higher subsidies; and this would have been particularly awkward at a time when there was already an enormous budget deficit.

In the successive exchange crises over the next two years, not much was heard of the possibility of devaluation. But at the beginning of 1948 the Treasury began to prepare a contingency plan and opened a 'Sterling War Book'. In June 1948 Otto Clarke gave it as his view that:

> We shall ourselves decide that we should devalue. I am myself very largely convinced of the desirability of this, as the only means of mobilising ordinary commercial incentives for the task of righting our dollar balance of payments.[1]

But Otto, who was at that time an Assistant Secretary, did not speak for the Overseas Finance Division of the Treasury under Henry Wilson Smith. Later in the month the Treasury abandoned all work on the contingency plan.

There were of course many people outside Whitehall who felt that sterling ought to be devalued. There were doubts about the continued use of exchange control in support of the parity. Some critics of government policy argued against a fixed rate on principle or took it for granted that a change in the rate would dispose of any balance of payments problem and remove the need for a whole catalogue of government controls.[2] There was also a widely held expectation of devaluation in financial circles, especially in North America, and the gap between the official and the black market rates for sterling was regarded as evidence of the strength of this expectation. 'Cheap' sterling had by 1949 become an important preoccupation of the government, especially because of the commodity shunting operations that flourished because of its availability. But in fact 'cheap' sterling reflected the blocking of capital transfers through exchange control rather than the maintenance of an unrealistic rate of exchange; and the idea that a floating rate would automatically put an end to an external deficit, like the later idea that it would automatically allow convertibility to be restored, was never argued out.

It was a commonly held view, none the less, that the case for devaluation was to be measured in terms of its power to remove a deficit in the balance of payments. At the time I took exactly the opposite point of view, that it should be considered precisely because the deficit had almost disappeared. I was then Economic Adviser to the Board of Trade and closely involved in discussions on commodity and trade problems. When it became apparent at the end of 1948 that the current account had already reached rough balance and was likely to be in surplus in 1949 I suggested that the time was approaching when sterling should be devalued so as to redirect sterling area exports towards dollar markets and that it would be wise to act before the issue came to be publicly debated. In my judgment we had perhaps six months in which to make up our minds.

The minute of 24 December 1948 in which I set out my reasons for coming to this conclusion had no effect. Three months later I revived the suggestion, making sure that the minute was seen by the President, Harold Wilson. Again, nothing happened. The senior officials in the Board of Trade were dead against the idea. The President showed no enthusiasm and made no move to discuss it with me. About the same time, however, Robert Hall, then Director of the Economic Section of the Cabinet Office, began to campaign for devaluation and converted some of his colleagues, including Edwin Plowden (then Chief Planning Officer) and Roger Makins (Head of the Economic Division in the Foreign Office). In the months that followed I kept in close touch with him but was of little practical help since the Board of Trade, both at ministerial and official level, stuck to the other side. The Bank of England was strongly against devaluation and the Treasury was doubtful and divided.

At the beginning of May 1949, the Chancellor of the Exchequer, Sir Stafford Cripps, reacting to growing speculation and rumours of a forthcoming devaluation, had felt it necessary to scotch the rumours in a speech in Rome which seemed to leave no scope for any subsequent change of front. Nevertheless, a few days after Sir Stafford's speech, George Bolton, an executive director of the Bank of England, was cabling the Treasury from Washington on 12 May to warn them of 'the spate of rumour regarding exchange readjustment, sterling depreciation, etc.'. Public debate had been joined when the reserves, at their lowest level since the war, were hopelessly inadequate to withstand sustained pressure. In spite of exchange control a speculative run on the pound was just as real a danger as it had been two years previously in the brief spell of convertibility in mid-1947.

Later in May the British Ambassador in Washington, Sir Oliver Franks, reported to Cripps and Bevin (the Foreign Secretary) that a number of influential American economists favoured a devaluation of sterling and that it would be desirable to engage in consultations with the US government before things got out of hand.[3] Official consultations started with the visit to Washington at the beginning of June of Robert Hall and Henry Wilson Smith.[4] This was followed by ministerial consultations in London early in July attended by John Snyder, Secretary of the US Treasury, Averill Harriman and Ambassador Lewis Douglas.

By this time, there were indications of a recession in trade that might have a serious effect on sterling. Hugh Dalton (then Chancellor of the Duchy of Lancaster) noted in his diary in mid-June, after a meeting of the Economic Policy Committee of the Cabinet,

> a lot of items in (the) dollar balance sheet all going wrong at once: our exports to the U.S. very low in April and recession will keep them low; colonial dollar surplus has vanished, U.S. no longer buying Malayan rubber and tin: Commonwealth countries spending too much, especially Australia and South Africa; forestalling, postponement of orders, etc. on devaluation talk.

By mid-June the drain on the reserves was gathering speed. At the meeting of the Economic Policy Committee on 17 June to which Hall and Wilson Smith reported, Cripps is quoted by Hugh Dalton as saying that 'within twelve months all our reserves will be gone. This time there is nothing behind them and there might well be "a complete collapse of sterling" '. Attlee, not easily perturbed, turned to Dalton as they left the meeting with the words '1931 over again'. To which Dalton replied: 'It reminds me awfully of 1947', (i.e. of the convertibility crisis in the summer of that year, when Dalton was Chancellor of the Exchequer).[5]

But there was no sign at that stage that any member of the Cabinet was taking immediate devaluation seriously. As late as

7 July Cripps was reiterating in the House of Commons that 'the Government has not the slightest intention of devaluing the pound'. Even in mid-June John Strachey, the Minister of Food, was still demanding additional dollar expenditure on foodstuffs. Harold Wilson had gone out of his way, in a long report on his visit to Canada, to dismiss the idea of devaluing the pound.[6] Some Ministers, including Harold Wilson, were giving more thought to the possibility of an autumn election than to the merits of devaluation. For them the question was: Could an election be held before devaluation or would devaluation delay an election until the spring?[7]

Cripps was anxious to be seen to be taking action to stop the dollar drain before the periodical statement of the reserve position due on 5 July was published. On 20 June he put round a paper to the Economic Policy Committee, which met every Friday morning, indicating that the dollar reserves would run out by January 1950 or at latest by March if current trends continued. His proposals for dealing with the situation included the summoning of a Commonwealth Conference in July, a cut of 25 per cent in dollar expenditure, to be announced on 5 July when the next quarterly statement on the dollar drain was due, and the suspension of fresh dollar payments, apart from exceptional cases, until 30 September. This was not a strategy likely to appeal to all his colleagues and was difficult to justify in preference to devaluation especially as it meant reviving and tightening controls that could be dispensed with after devaluation. While no one came forward to argue for devaluation, Nye Bevan, the Minister of Health, was no doubt speaking for others on 23 June when he expressed himself in favour of 'something different from everlasting cuts'. Nevertheless the proposals were accepted. The Commonwealth Conference was held in July and agreed to make the cuts proposed.

Officials remained divided. The head of the Treasury, Sir Edward Bridges, summing up official opinion on 18 June, told Ministers that 'most of us, with differing degrees of emphasis are opposed to devaluation *now*' but he did not exclude the possibility of a forced devaluation in the autumn or of devaluing some time later in more propitious circumstances. He was anxious that devaluation should be regarded not as a panacea but in the context of other measures designed to reduce the overload on the economy. It would be fatal if one devaluation was followed by a second and it should therefore not be attempted when conditions were too inflationary as those opposed to devaluation maintained they were. Under such conditions prices and wages would rise and the initial competitive gains would speedily disappear. The disadvantages were certain, the advantages uncertain. Devaluation would contribute little to the development of export earnings in the United States, especially when the outlook in the American market remained obscure. This uncertainty posed a further difficulty in deciding how far the rate should go in the event of devaluation and the Bank of England insisted that there should be no question of a floating rate, even for a limited period.

Those who opposed devaluation were chiefly concerned to see immediate cuts in public expenditure. Without such cuts, devaluation would not work; with them, it would prove unnecessary. Bridges pointed specifically to the food subsidies, suggesting that they should be cut by £100 million. Supporting measures in the credit field would also be necessary and should include a rise in Bank Rate, higher interest rates generally and restriction of bank credit. Those who favoured devaluation (named by Bridges as Edwin Plowden, Leslie Rowan and Robert Hall) recognised the need for some accompanying measures but thought in terms of milder cuts in government expenditure and efforts to contain the rise in costs by a form of incomes policy.

Robert Hall himself put the case rather differently. He pointed out that although the process of reconversion after the war was largely complete and was likely to be followed by the recovery of some of our most important competitors, there was no end to the dollar deficit in sight, not even in the so-called 'Four Year Plan' for the years 1948–52 recently submitted to the OEEC. The country had run through borrowings and gifts from abroad at a rapid rate all through the post-war years and was still living on ERP aid without fully appreciating the precariousness of the situation. Moreover there was plenty of evidence that exporters were handicapped by high costs. The Canadians were constantly complaining that American goods were cheaper and in the markets outside North America there were similar complaints. How if not by devaluation was it proposed to close the gap, both in export prices and in the dollar balance of payments?

The Governor of the Bank of England, C. F. Cobbold, was strongly against devaluation. In his view the fundamental issue was whether after devaluation we could be 'reasonably certain of seeing equilibrium in our balance of payments and avoiding pressure against sterling at the new rate over, say, the next two years'. He wanted a new agreement with the United States and Canada to 'take some of the rest of the world's demand for dollars off our back' by assuming some of the burden of sterling liabilities. On the one hand, our cost structure was too high and inflexible and on the other, overseas holdings of sterling were excessive: too much sterling was 'chasing too few dollars'. He accepted the need for complementary action in the monetary field if the pound was devalued but expressed doubts about direct action to restrict credit. By the end of July, when a decision had been all but taken, he was reported by Sir Wilfred Eady to be very much alarmed by the absence of any proposals for a cut in government expenditure and determined to resist a tightening of monetary policy without complementary budgetary action. If there were no reduction in government expenditure he would refuse outright to restrict credit or raise interest rates.

A few days later, on 3 August, he wrote to the Prime Minister to express his fears of a second devaluation if no action were taken to reduce inflationary pressure and deal with overseas sterling balances. These fears would lead him to recommend a larger devaluation than would be appropriate if it were undertaken as 'part of a general plan' (that is with the necessary accompanying measures).[8] American pressure for devaluation was founded on the hope that it would be a step to convertibility and the relaxation of controls generally. But this was an illusion since convertibility called for a strong pound whereas the pound would be 'convalescent' after devaluation and this would make it necessary to tighten restrictions on the use of sterling by third countries. Devaluation so soon after the Commonwealth Conference, which had just been held, was 'a hasty retreat to an unprepared line of defence'. It would cause other countries to move in line with sterling so that there would be no improvement in the balance of payments with third countries. In dollar markets there was 'no reason to foresee any immediate increase in the dollar income of the Sterling Area'. Imports were already controlled and unlikely to contract. The immediate effect of devaluation on net dollar earnings, in his view, seemed likely to be unfavourable.

This view of the effect on net dollar earnings was shared by others, including Douglas Jay, Economic Secretary of the Treasury. In a brief to the Chancellor before the meeting of the Economic Policy Committee on 8 July he argued that 'the issue [of devaluation] turns entirely on whether or not we should earn more dollars as a result and I do not feel that this has yet been established'. In June he had dismissed the 'thoroughly hypothetical economic gains' of devaluation and criticised the case submitted against it as 'altogether understated'. But by mid-July he had swung round. After a meeting on 21 July at the Treasury on the possible use of income tax rebates on dollar exports, he said to me: 'I wish to God we had done it a year ago'.

The chances of an early expansion in dollar earnings as a result of devaluation were much debated, particularly by those who were opposed to devaluation. Even after a decision in principle had been taken on 21 July to devalue, Treasury officials reported that it was unlikely that devaluation would affect the loss of reserves for six months.[9] Yet when a letter was sent to Stafford Cripps at the end of July by the Prime Minister it opened with a reference to 'the ever-accumulating evidence that the universal expectation of devaluation is holding back purchases of British exports day by day and discouraging the holding of sterling all over the world'. Thus while some were concentrating on time-lags, low price elasticities and non-price elements in marketing, others focussed on expectations, capital movements and short-run effects.

Opinion changed quickly in the last week of June and the early days of July. On 22 June when I had lunch with Robert Hall he was in despair. The main opposition at official level came from Cobbold and Wilson Smith (who regarded devaluation as 'a desperate gamble') but it was not clear to him what alternative policy other than 'old-fashioned deflation' they had in mind. There was a danger that the sharp division of opinion might continue long enough to allow the reserves to run down to a negligible level at which there would be no escape from devaluation in the worst possible circumstances. Ministers were unconvinced; and the Prime Minister, whom he briefed, would be more likely to echo his briefs if he left them unread. The one ray of hope was that Roger Makins (now Lord Sherfield) in the Foreign Office thought that he might carry Bevin. Max Nicholson, the Lord President's Permanent Secretary, said to me that same evening: 'We'll *have* to devalue'. Since he had Herbert Morrison's ear, he, too, might be persuaded. James Helmore, Second Secretary in the Board of Trade, was wavering and I had managed to get it across to the President that I was by no means the only protagonist of devaluation.

Treasury Ministers in the meantime were adamant. The Chancellor thought devaluation wrong in principle and the expression of a policy of laissez-faire. He associated it in his mind with Wall Street and believed that by planning and control it was possible to achieve all that could be got by devaluation.

Yet the position was beginning to look more hopeful. Robert Hall claimed at the end of June to have converted Douglas Jay on condition that there would be no cut in the food subsidies. He thought that opinion among officials was now fairly solidly in favour, with one or two conspicuous exceptions, while of the Ministers, Morrison and probably also Bevin could be counted as supporters. Harold Wilson, reacting against overstatements of the case for cuts and deflation by his officials, was coming round and his Parliamentary Secretary, John Edwards, was strongly in favour of devaluation, regarding it as the traditional alternative to wage-cuts. Evidence of a movement in outside opinion reached me in the form of unsolicited declarations by Paul Bareau of *The Economist*, and by Richard Kahn and other economists at a Nuffield Conference, that devaluation was obviously coming.

Nothing of this was apparent from the meeting of the Economic Policy Committee on 1 July, which pursued the will o' the wisp of 'a comprehensive agreement' with the United States and Canada, nor from Stafford Cripps' public rejection of devaluation five days later in the House of Commons. When the Secretary of the US Treasury, John Snyder, arrived on 7 July the Chancellor's line was that devaluation would only be feasible within the limits of a 'general settlement', the nature of which was left extremely vague. Although Cripps conducted the talks over the next two days with his usual skill he had not slept for some days and had already made arrangements to go off to a Swiss sanatorium in less than a fortnight's time.

The talks were remarkable chiefly for the calculated absence of any reference to devaluation which the public took to be the main subject of discussion. This gave rise to a long and heated debate when the communiqué came to be prepared on the afternoon of the second day (9 July). Officials wrestled for an hour and a half and Ministers for an equal period over what mention should be made of devaluation. Snyder wanted no reference to the subject because there had been no discussion of it. Cripps rejoined that that was all he wanted to say. Snyder, petulant and angry, felt caught in a logical trap. If they broke up without any reference to devaluation in the communiqué, the press would stick to its view that the purpose of Snyder's visit was to urge devaluation on the government; while to say that the subject had not been discussed might be taken to imply either endorsement of British views or feebleness on Snyder's part. After a 30-minute adjournment Snyder had in the end to agree, Cripps pointing out that nothing could be of more assistance in stopping the drain on the reserves.[10]

In the course of July Hugh Gaitskell (Minister of Fuel and Power), now in a key position in Cripps' absence, joined the ranks of those favouring devaluation and he and Douglas Jay set about proselytising their colleagues. Gaitskell's conversion was largely the work of Paul Rosenstein-Rodan in the course of a long walk on Hampstead Heath but others (including Lord Kaldor who put the case to him on 18 July) have claimed the credit. At the time I was told that what convinced Gaitskell was the argument that the demand for British exports in dollar markets had an elasticity in excess of unity, an argument which he had previously doubted. His diary, however, implies a rather more sophisticated analysis.[11]

Two days after Cripps' departure, on 21 July, Gaitskell, Jay and Wilson, the economic ministers in charge, decided in principle to devalue. Of the three, Gaitskell's was the decisive voice. At the beginning of 1949 Harold Wilson seemed the likely successor to Cripps as Chancellor but as Douglas Jay subsequently wrote of the events of July 1949 'it was this chapter which left no doubt in the minds of those few who knew the facts that, if Cripps' health failed, Hugh Gaitskell was the only possible Chancellor'.[12]

At that point the line to be taken in Washington was that the decision reflected the Cabinet's judgment that this was the right thing to do and that the US Government was of the same opinion. This meant rejecting the position suggested at the end of June by the Chancellor and taken up enthusiastically by the President of the Board of Trade in July that a bargain might be struck with the Americans under which they would be required to offer further help as the price of devaluation. There was something typically English about this proposal to do the one thing that would get you out of a mess as a *quid pro quo* for a major concession by somebody else.

The 'further help' sought from the Americans might have been supposed to have included a substantial loan. But this does not seem to have been suggested at any time, no doubt because of disenchantment with previous experience of loan negotiations. The draft communiqué on 9 July said flatly that the British did not want a loan from the United States and this was only cut out at the suggestion of Bill Martin (at that time Assistant Secretary of the US Treasury) who was in the US delegation.

At first devaluation was thought of for some undefined date in September. Gaitskell in July was so perturbed by the loss of reserves that he wanted immediate action; but once it had become clear that the earliest date was 24 August he agreed that it would make little difference if action were deferred until 7 September, that is until the conclusions of talks in Washington with the Americans and Canadians. Others were less confident that the reserves would be adequate by that date to permit a controlled movement to a new exchange rate, especially in view of the exposed position of the sterling area at the junction of the dollar and non-dollar world.

The timing of devaluation was ultimately settled by Cripps himself. Once the Prime Minister had given his agreement to devaluation he wrote to the Chancellor in Switzerland telling him that

> all of us are now agreed, including the responsible officials, that [devaluation] is a necessary step (though not of course the only step) if we are to stop the present dollar drain before our reserves fall to a [dangerous] level.

The letter was delivered by Harold Wilson in the course of a motor tour on the Continent, his private secretary Max Brown flying out during the first week-end in August to communicate to him the latest available information. I had suggested to Max (and others took the same view) that it would be best to devalue before the talks that were due to take place in September with the US and Canada, both in order to get useful results from the talks and to avoid any accusation of acting under pressure from the US Government. But Stafford Cripps plumped instead for a date (18 September) when he would be back in the United Kingdom from the IMF annual meeting in Washington and could make the announcement to the British public in person. The delay extended the rundown in the reserves which was unusually heavy in the first half of September. It was also by no means obvious that the Chancellor was the right man to explain the inevitability of devaluation or to underline its advantages when he had come out so strongly and repeatedly against it.

A meeting of Ministers was held at Chequers immediately Cripps returned to England on 19 August. Cripps was still reluctant to agree to devaluation but ultimately agreed, subject to three conditions, all of them involving the attitude likely to be taken by the United States. He insisted that it was necessary to secure the backing of the United States in approaching the IMF since it would not be possible to give due notice to the IMF of the government's intentions. The United States would also require reassurance that the new rate would be held. Finally, the rate selected should not be so low as to invite retaliation by the United States. At that stage Cripps was against any rate lower than $3 to the £1 and Bevin favoured a rate of $3.20. Cripps went on to explain his choice of 18 September as the date for devaluation. How, he asked, could he defend such a step on the eve of his talks in Washington when nothing had changed? By waiting until after the talks he could at least link the decision with the views expressed there. This was only one of many discussions in the summer of 1949 in which the role of the United States (and to a slightly smaller extent, Canada) absorbed the attention of Ministers to the almost complete exclusion of the rest of the world.

The decisions reached at Chequers were confirmed by the Cabinet ten days later, on 29 August before Cripps and Bevin left by sea for Washington. The secret was well kept: there has never been any suggestion of a leak during the critical two months from the time when the case was put to the Prime Minister on 21 July.

Meanwhile important issues remained to be decided: the scale and make-up of accompanying measures; what changes in government expenditure were involved or necessary; the size of the depreciation; whether the sterling area should move together; whether and how the new rate should be controlled. Some of these matters were settled very late. A few days before devaluation, on 14 September, the President of the Board of Trade did not know the rate, which had only been decided by Bevin and Cripps on 12 September at the British Embassy in Washington. Little consideration was given to floating the pound.[13] No soundings were taken of other countries' intentions.

The researches of the Treasury had, however, revealed some curious situations. Ceylon, for example, was in the unfortunate position that parity had to be maintained with the rupee as well as with sterling so that her reserves were liable to disappear in a day as the money went round and round if Britain devalued and India did not. In Honduras the currency was convertible into dollars at a guaranteed rate while the reserves were held in sterling. Argentina was speculating in sterling because it had been given a dollar guarantee at the end of June. European central banks had absorbed large additional holdings of sterling in consequence of the precautionary movement of private funds in the expectation of devaluation.

As might be expected, the main struggle was over accompanying measures. The Prime Minister clung to the view that the external difficulties of the United Kingdom were quite unrelated to domestic policies: to suppose otherwise was 'nineteenth century economics'. Other Ministers regarded devaluation as an alternative to deflationary measures which were consequently redundant. Dalton, in particular, to judge from his diary, saw absolutely no need for any accompanying changes in the budget. No country in the world, he maintained, had carried financial austerity and rectitude so far as the United Kingdom and to suggest cuts in public expenditure was to demonstrate how politically unreliable the government's advisers really were.[14]

This reluctance to accept the need for accompanying fiscal measures strengthened the suspicion of officials hostile to devaluation that it was being advocated as 'an easy way out' when the real need was to trim back government expenditure and release resources. Repeatedly officials drew the attention of Ministers to the need for accompanying measures. Bridges told the Chancellor on 6 July:

> We are all concerned that the proposals now before the Economic Policy Committee will not get us out of our difficulties. These proposals are in effect a continuation of the policy of exhortation to the people of this country to increase their productivity and to exercise restraint in their demands for increased wages and profits, coupled with a proposal to devalue the pound while maintaining full employment.

The minimum needed was 'a definite instruction to the Bank of England to bring about some restriction of credit and a limit of government expenditure to the estimates put forward at the time of the Budget'. Current forecasts suggested that without any change in policy the estimates would creep up by £140 million over the original total for 1949–50. As for credit restriction, 'the present policy of very cheap money has meant that the monetary system has put no obstacle whatever in the way of inflationary forces generally'.

The Chancellor politely took note of this point of view in red ink, without further comment. After his departure to Switzerland Bridges tried again in a private minute to the Prime Minister, insisting on the importance of a cut in public expenditure. This was spelt out three days later in a paper submitted on 26 July along with the Treasury Second Secretaries, as well as Edwin Plowden and Robert Hall, arguing that public expenditure should at least be kept within the estimates and preferably cut by five per cent as proposed by the Lord President, Herbert Morrison. There should also be 'a moderate rise in money rates of interest to make the present Bank Rate [then two per cent] effective'.

Later still, when the ministerial brief for the Washington discussions was being prepared, Treasury officials insisted on including a paragraph on the need for stronger measures if only to carry conviction with the Americans. The paragraph got as far as the Economic Policy Committee but no further. In the end, no commitment to cut public expenditure was made in advance of devaluation and nothing was done to tighten monetary policy until 24 October when the expenditure cuts were at last announced. Even then it was limited to a letter from the Chancellor to the Governor calling on the banks and accepting houses to 'use every endeavour to ensure that inflationary policies were held in check'.

On the other hand, it was recognised that some form of incomes policy was highly desirable and Bevin and Cripps eventually persuaded the TUC to accept a standstill in wages so long as prices did not rise by more than five per cent. This made it necessary to work out measures conforming to this acceptance and refrain from action that would have more than a limited impact on the cost of living.

The only deflationary measure on which Cripps and Bevin agreed before devaluation was an increase in the price of bread coupled with a reduction in the extraction ratio. Although Stafford Cripps favoured wholemeal bread and a high extraction ratio, Bevin who was inclined to belch, thought that the working man would accept a higher price of bread more readily if offered a whiter loaf and the trade unions were thought also to regard the colour of bread as a first class political issue. After some argument between the two, Cripps conceded the point with the unrealistic proviso that no increase in dollar expenditure should be involved.[15] Their proposal that the price of the loaf should be raised by 1½ p. and the extraction ratio reduced to 82½ per cent was, however, rejected. The loaf went up by 1 p. No other measures were agreed upon until after devaluation.

Other measures were, however, discussed. These included the imposition of a tax on capital gains (since devaluation would bring stock profits); an increase in profits tax to balance the wage freeze; the possibility of a rebate of tax on profits derived from exports (dismissed as contrary to GATT); a price stop over the first month following devaluation (this was an earlier proposal of the Chancellor). When the Chancellor at last put round a paper in mid-October he proposed a cut of £280 million, half falling on government expenditure, half on capital investment.[16] The cut in expenditure, however, took credit for an increase in profits tax and a small prescription charge under the National Health Service. It left the social services and food subsidies virtually intact, except for animal feeding stuffs and fish, and made only a very modest reduction in defence. The cut in investment was largely on paper except for housing where it was bound to be somewhat problematic and was in fact restored subsequently. The cuts were announced on 24 October and to the casual reader seemed to be made up largely of miscellaneous trimmings such as the Treasury might normally make in examining departmental estimates.

The expenditure cuts could be the subject of an instructive case-study in their own right and have been dealt with above in very summary fashion. At the meeting of the Cabinet on 28 July at which the Lord President's memorandum calling for a five per cent cut was discussed, the Economic Policy Committee was asked to 'scrutinise government expenditure with a view to securing such economies as were consistent with the continued application of major government policies'. Some ministers, however, insisted that the main cause of the dollar drain was not the government's internal financial policy but the fall in sales of sterling area commodities for dollars. On 4 August the Prime Minister put round a paper (CP(49)170) asking for proposals to meet the aim of a five per cent all-round cut in expenditure by the civil departments. The government was satisfied that measures of retrenchment must be introduced 'if only to offset the increases which must automatically follow from the expansion of policies already approved'.

Little more was heard of the five per cent cuts until after devaluation. Then at the request of the Chancellor, Robert Hall prepared a paper on the internal financial situation (EPC(49)102) which was circulated to the Economic Policy Committee on 5 October. This attempted to work out the size of the cut in government expenditure and investment that should accompany devaluation. He started from the fact that the government had spent £221 million more in the first six months of the fiscal year than in the corresponding period in 1948 and that the Budget surplus, to judge from supplementary estimates was likely to be about £160 million less than had been hoped. There were also indications of a fall in personal savings: the small savers were drawing down their deposits at a rate of about £40 million per annum. All this pointed to the need for cuts of the order of £200 million merely in order to limit the pressure of demand to what had been judged appropriate in the 1949 Budget. The changes in the foreign balance over the past six months pointed to a similar figure. As a supplementary memorandum pointed out (EPC(49)110), the visible balance had worsened since the six winter months of 1948–9, when the current account was roughly in balance, by over £20 million per month or £240 million per annum. Although exports were lower, unemployment was falling quite sharply: in the first eight months of 1949 it had come down by 115 000 compared with 30 000 in the same eight months in 1948. The home market was booming, with industrial production up by six or seven per cent in spite of the fall in exports, and more imports were being absorbed. Investment, which had been consistently under-estimated, was at least up to expectations. Quite apart from devaluation, a stiff dose of disinflation was called for.

But devaluation made still larger cuts necessary. To the estimate of £200 million for disinflation, Robert Hall suggested adding a further £100 million to free resources for improving the balance of payments and changing the pattern of production. It was important to act quickly or the chance of profiting from the new exchange rate would slip away. Failure to remove the inflationary tendencies at once would be irremediable whereas if the cuts made proved to be excessive there would be no difficulty in relaxing them later, for example, in or before the next Budget.

Robert Hall was obviously a little doubtful whether he had pitched his total high enough. On 10 October he warned the Chancellor that if he did not start with the idea that he would have to go for the whole of the £300 million he would never get anywhere with his colleagues. Politically difficult items might, however, be knocked off the list at a later stage in the bargaining process. Three days later, in a minute to Plowden, he was querying his own total. Government expenditure was running at a level that made him suspicious that some supplementary estimates were being delayed; investment might again have been under-estimated; the additional expenditure in which departments might be involved by devaluation was not fully known and departments also had a way of circumventing restrictive policies and failing to keep within agreed limits; in addition, there could be no guarantee that wages and salaries would hold steady.

Robert Hall's assessment was attacked on a number of grounds: there were those who disliked quantification in principle although the need to quantify the cuts in expenditure was inescapable. There were others who looked to higher import prices to do the job of disinflation without assistance from cuts in government expenditure: they found it hard to accept that there would be no net disinflation once the higher cost of imports had to be met from a larger volume of exports. The economies forced on consumers would be offset by a fresh demand on resources. There was also some disposition to argue that exports might be re-directed to dollar markets at the expense of sterling markets without any increase in volume and hence without any need to cut other claims on resources. This would have been a valid argument had it been possible to disregard the low level of reserves, the commitments to sterling area countries already entered into, and the relatively modest allowance made by Robert Hall for the diversion of resources from domestic to external use. But £100 million hardly seemed excessive as an initial bid. Others argued that increased production – possibly via longer working hours – would do the trick. Finally, Ministers fell back on the proposition that devaluation brought higher profits to trading departments such as the Ministry of Food and urged that these profits should be brought into the budgetary reckoning. It was accepted in the end that the starting-figure of £300 million might be abated by £15 million on this account.

It was assumed throughout that the budgetary change could be equated with the change in the level of final demand. The Chancellor, in asking for economies of £280 million, referred to a reduction in consumption but was clearly thinking of the claims on resources since half of his total was to take the form of a cut in investment.

When details of the cuts were given by Cripps to the House of Commons on 26 October, Anthony Eden maintained that the proposals had been' . . . . just scratched together in the last fortnight and they represent the maximum that can be agreed without Cabinet resignation'.[17] This was an exaggeration: but it had an element of truth. The cuts in expenditure, as distinct from investment, were fought over until the very last minute. Nye Bevan, for example, accepted a prescription charge but successfully resisted (till another day) a charge to hospital patients and a charge for dentures and spectacles, all three of these being designed to raise £10 million. Many of the cuts were not to come into effect at once and there were some that might never take effect. For example, the withdrawal of the feeding stuffs subsidy (put first at £30 million and later at £36 million) was to take effect only after the next Annual Review in February 1950 but how much of the cost would then fall on the farmers would depend on the outcome of the Review. The subsidy on fish was to be discontinued after decontrol at 'a convenient date' in the spring of 1950. Defence was credited with a cut of £30 million per annum but this meant only that an intended supplementary, estimated by the Treasury at £30 million (a 'conjectural figure' accepted by the Ministry of Defence 'because they cannot think of a better') would now be limited to £17.5 million.

At the end of the day, the score-board for expenditure cuts read £122.5 million instead of the target of £140 million and £79 million of the total represented feeding stuffs, defence and additional profits tax. 'Administrative economies' were put at £28 million and the £10 million for prescription charges was the main other item.

II

Before I turn to examine how the devaluation worked, there are some points in this narrative worth emphasising:

(i) Those who favoured devaluation did so for quite different reasons, and often for bad reasons. Some wanted devaluation to improve the competitive position of British industry although exports were already paying for imports. Some hoped that devaluation would improve the competitive position of British exports in dollar markets, or simply in the United States. Some saw no other way of resisting the speculative pressure against the pound. At the meeting of the Cabinet on 29 August at which the crucial decision to devalue was confirmed, Cripps himself accepted that:

> An atmosphere had . . . been created . . . in which the pound could not reach stability without devaluation.

(ii) These arguments were usually advanced as if devaluation were a sufficient device for the purpose favoured, without regard to other necessary accompanying measures, or to less drastic and more effective ways of achieving the same purpose. In the end the compelling factor in the situation was lack of adequate reserves; but the corollary was not drawn that ways must be found of reinforcing reserves either at once or at least in time to withstand future pressure of the same kind. The rundown in reserves was attributed rather too readily to a falling-off in sterling area sales in the North American market while the speculative movement of funds in anticipation of a devaluation of sterling was never analysed and the causes of it little discussed.

(iii) The debate in Whitehall was dominated by short run considerations when it was arguable that the decisive factors were long-term. It should have been obvious that at some point in the post-war years it would be necessary to reconsider the sterling-dollar rate of exchange as a contribution to the solution of the so-called 'dollar problem'. That point was most likely to be reached when the first surge in British (and non-dollar) exports was beginning to lose momentum or when exports had reached a level at which the prime requirement was not to expand the total but to effect a redistribution between dollar and non-dollar markets. In 1949 for the first time there was a margin in hand for this purpose, represented by the prospective surplus on trade with non-dollar markets which accrued in the form of a balance of 'soft', inconvertible currencies side by side with a deficit in trade with dollar countries that had to be discharged in dollars. The United Kingdom was thus in danger of running out of dollars as a result of settling its deficit in 'hard' currencies and at the same time running up useless balances in 'soft' currencies through the sale of 'unrequited' exports. It was necessary to make the soft currencies harder and the hard currencies softer; and there could be no more effective way of doing this than by making hard currencies dearer in terms of soft currencies. This in turn could best be brought about by devaluing sterling against the dollar and inducing other countries to devalue their currency simultaneously.

(iv) From this point of view, the British balance of payments was largely irrelevant to the case for devaluation since what was in question was the value of the dollar rather than the value of the pound. The issue was not how to restore British trade to balance, since it was already in balance, but how to respond to the so-called dollar shortage. At some stage this response would have to include currency re-alignments but it would have been premature to embark on these when exports were rising strongly and there was nothing in hand to permit of a *redirection* of exports to dollar markets.
(v) Except in the papers prepared for the meeting of the Economic Policy Committee on 1 July, there does not seem to have been a careful weighing of the pros and cons by officials, much less by Ministers.

In the last resort, it was the loss of reserves that settled the matter, given the government's priorities. Although the Economic Section had given thought to the choice of rate it was in the end largely a matter of accident that \$2.80 rather than \$3 to the £1 was the rate selected. The significance of getting other countries to move simultaneously was rarely stressed. The measures to accompany devaluation were considered separately and almost as an afterthought (although two months later the Chancellor had so far forgotten the sequence of events that he insisted that the economy cuts were decided upon 'side by side' with devaluation).
(vi) As in 1967 devaluation took place in spite of repeated declarations by the Chancellor that he would not countenance it. This in itself hardly contributed to careful pre-planning. In contrast to 1967, the Chancellor did not resign, although Cripps might have been thought more ready to do so than Callaghan.
(vii) Both in 1949 and 1967 devaluation was delayed well beyond the point of maximum advantage: in 1949 until after a strong expectation of devaluation had developed and in 1967 until after heavy forward sales of sterling had been made. On both occasions Ministers were unwilling to contemplate action that would have had the advantage of surprise. As Cripps pointed out in his Mansion House speech on 4 October:

> Our action had been discussed, debated, and indeed almost expected, throughout the world . . . Though the actual date and the degree of change in the sterling exchange rate may have taken people by surprise – no one can suggest that it was a matter suddenly sprung upon an unsuspecting world.

While this is substantially correct, it hardly lay with Cripps to say so, since those who *were* taken by surprise were those who took him at his word. The uncertainty that seemed to him to justify devaluation need never have been created had he taken action earlier.
(viii) Devaluation was seen by Cripps as an act of foreign policy quite as much as of economic policy. He was constantly insisting that 'the relationship between the dollar and the sterling worlds is not one to which the United Kingdom alone can find a remedy. It is a problem', he told the House of Commons in July, 'in which our friends and partners in the U.S.A. and the Commonwealth are especially involved'. In this he was undoubtedly right: the problem was part of the post-war dollar problem and intimately concerned the United States, and her trading partners in the Commonwealth and elsewhere. But to say this was not, as Cripps at times implied, to voice an objection to devaluation. For if that were so, it was necessary to come forward with some other equally powerful instrument for re-structuring the world economy. And the most that was ever suggested by those who preferred a 'general settlement' to outright devaluation was trivial and peripheral in comparison.
(ix) Finally, it is instructive to see who finally decided. Not Cripps, though he acquiesced. Not Bevin, though he had shown in 1931 that he had no inhibitions about devaluation. Not Morrison, whose part is still obscure. Not the Prime Minister, who had perhaps the oddest view of them all as to what was involved. Three young and relatively junior Ministers, all of them economists, accidentally in a position to decide and accidentally led by a Minister of principle and determination who was not even a member of the Cabinet: none of them, except possibly Jay, much influenced by official advice.

III

Let us now turn to look at the economic background to devaluation. We can begin by examining the UK's trade accounts and balance of payments (see Table 6.1). The annual figures are in no way suggestive of a crisis in 1949. Exports continued to rise, the deficit on visible trade continued to fall and there was a small surplus on current account:

Even if we concentrate exclusively on trade with the dollar area (Table 6.2) there is little that makes 1949 look unusual. Undoubtedly there was a setback in exports and the trend in the visible

TABLE 6.1 *British trade and payments, 1947–51. (£m)*

	1947	1948	1949	1950	1951
UK exports and re-exports	1145	1602	1841	2250	2748
UK imports	1560	1794	1978	2383	3491
Surplus or deficit on visible trade	−415	−192	−137	−133	−743
Surplus or deficit on invisibles	− 28	193	168	433	340
Balance on current account	−443	1	31	300	−403

SOURCE Annual Abstract of Statistics for 1958.

TABLE 6.2 *British trade with the dollar area, 1947–51 (£ m)*

	1947	1948	1949	1950	1951
UK exports and re-exports	130	196	195	324	393
UK imports	567	406	442	439	742
Surplus or deficit on visible trade	−437	−210	−247	−115	−349
Surplus or deficit on invisibles	− 73	− 42	− 49	27	− 87
Total surplus or deficit	−510	−252	−296	− 88	−436

SOURCE Annual Abstract of Statistics for 1958.

deficit was reversed. But the size of the changes was hardly enough of itself to smack of crisis. Finally if we analyse the gold and dollar deficit we obtain the picture shown in Table 6.3.

The most these figures suggest is a slight wobble in 1949 in the favourable trend between 1947 and 1950. The dollar deficit of the outer sterling area, of which so much was made at the time, was, if anything, less in 1949 than in 1948. There was a check to the gradual replacement of a deficit by a surplus, but it was in no way catastrophic. The biggest single change between 1948 and 1949 was in gold sales to the UK and this reflected a gold loan of £80 million by South Africa in 1948. If this is left out, the gold and dollar deficit was much the same in 1949 as in 1948. Moreover, what stands out in both years as the biggest single factor in the deficit is the United Kingdom's own deficit on current account. And if one looks ahead to 1954 to see what pattern would emerge in the 1950's as a

TABLE 6.3 *UK gold and dollar deficit, 1947–54 (£m)*

	1947	*1948*	*1949*	*1950*	*1951*	*1954*
UK deficit on current account with dollar area	−510	−252	−296	− 88	−436	−72
Deficit of rest of sterling area with dollar area	−306	− 65	− 54	+170	+102	+27
Payments of dollars to OECD and other countries	−260	− 95	− 89	− 12	− 67	−23
Gold sales and loans to UK: receipt of IMF dollars	+144	+150	+ 68	+100	+ 78	+98
Total	−932	−262	−371	+170	−323	+30

SOURCE Annual Abstract of Statistics for 1958.

sustainable one it was in this item that the biggest change fell to be made.

But the annual figures do not tell the whole story: there were large fluctuations within the year. The gold and dollar reserves, for example, fell from £471 million at the end of March to £406 million at the end of June, £372 million on 20 August and £330 million by 18 September – a fall of 30 per cent within six months. The movement in the dollar deficit from quarter to quarter tells a similar story as in Table 6.4.

How are these figures to be reconciled with the comparative stability of the annual totals? Most of the discussion at the time laid emphasis on the depressed state of the US market from the spring of 1949 until the autumn; so we may begin by looking at the

TABLE 6.4 *Dollar deficit excluding ERP aid, etc. (£m. at $4.03 to £1)*

	1947	*1948*	*1949*
Quarter to March 31	227	147	82
Quarter to June 30	242	107	157
Quarter to Sept 30	381	76	133
Quarter to Dec 31	174	93	

SOURCE Document EPC (49) 61 of 11 June 1949.

fluctuations in trade between the sterling area and the United States from quarter to quarter. Estimates are given in the ECA study of the sterling area published in 1951 and although they are only approximations they indicate the magnitude of the swings during the year.[18] (See Table 6.5).

TABLE 6.5 *Trade of sterling area with United States 1948–50 ($m. per quarter)*

	Sterling area exports to US	*Sterling area imports from US*	*Balance of trade*	*UK imports from US*	*Rest of sterling area exports to US*	*Excess of R.S.A. exports over UK imports*
1948 average	346	501	−155	161	274	113
1949 Q1	345	504	−159	170	297	127
Q2	281	561	−280	222	217	− 5
Q3	231	413	−182	155	162	52
Q4	297	385	− 88		252	
1950 Q1	326	348	− 22	122	280	158
Q2	361	318	43			
Q3–Q4	457	321	136	140	352	212

SOURCE Based on Table 35 and p. 77 of *The Sterling Area: an American Analysis* (London: ECA, 1951).

It will be seen that the trade deficit nearly doubled in the second quarter and improved thereafter quarter by quarter until by the second quarter of 1950 the net improvement was over $320 million per quarter. However, the average quarterly deficit in 1949 was only $22 million worse than in 1948, the second half of the year showing a deficit rather below the 1948 average.

It is not possible to assign the deterioration in the second quarter with any precision to its various sources, but it is clear that it cannot all be attributed to the trade deficit with the United States. The figures in Table 6.4 show a rise in the dollar deficit in the second quarter by £75 million compared with the first quarter and £52 million compared with the average for 1948. Even if we take the second basis of comparison the rise in the trade deficit with the United States by $125 million (or just over £30 million per quarter) does not account for more than about half the change in the total dollar deficit.

To some extent the higher deficit in the second quarter was foreseen. In a brief for the Chancellor before the meeting of the Economic Policy Committee on 17 June, Sam Goldman pointed out that the Treasury had been expecting the deficit to increase since early April because of heavier expenditure on food and materials (for stockpiling), the usual seasonal reduction in the dollar surplus of the Colonies, bigger losses to Belgium and Switzerland and an unfavourable turn in the working of the South African Loan Agreement. April had been in line with the target but in May there was an overshoot of $80 million divided in roughly equal terms between the United Kingdom, the colonial territories and the rest of the sterling area. It is rather remarkable that so small an addition to the drain on the reserves should so quickly have produced an exchange crisis and is one more illustration of the inadequacy of the reserves in the post-war years.

In addition to the special factors mentioned in the brief, we can distinguish four different elements in the deterioration during the second quarter:

(i) A large part of the increase in the dollar deficit in the second quarter – about $60 million was due to a 38 per cent increase above the 1948 level in British import expenditures in the United States. Some of this corresponded to the stockpiling of food and raw materials already referred to. Since there was never any intention of maintaining this level of expenditure over the year some falling back was to be expected and did occur. In addition, the alarm generated by the growing deficit led the British Government to cut their import programme and this reinforced the fall.

(ii) The check to activity in the United States reacted on imports, particularly of raw materials, and on commodity prices, so that sales of materials such as rubber, tin, and wool to the United States were depressed on both scores. Imports into the United States from the outer sterling area fell by $80 million in the second quarter and by a further $55 million in the third. When business conditions improved later in the year, inventories of materials were built up again and the movement was strengthened by the expectation that prices would recover. Imports into the United States from the outer sterling area countries rose between the third and fourth quarters from $162 million to $252 million although devaluation had lowered the dollar price of most of the commodities supplied. Full recovery to the 1948 level did not, however, take place until the first half of 1950.

(iii) The expectation of devaluation made for a deferment of purchases payable in sterling and of actual disbursements in sterling. It also encouraged a corresponding acceleration of imports from the dollar area and the immediate discharge of dollar obligations. This speculative element must have influenced the purchases of materials referred to under (ii), delaying them before devaluation and accelerating them thereafter. British exports to the United States may also have suffered prior to devaluation, if only through delays in payment. American companies in London were known to be taking no chances in transferring their profits to dollar accounts as fast as possible. The fall in gold sales to the United Kingdom in the middle quarters of 1949 by 27 per cent and 20 per cent below the 1948 level reflects the same influences. Since gold sales were much the same in 1948 as in 1949 it is natural to suspect that the distortion in the pattern of sales over the year was associated with the expectation of devaluation that developed from the spring onwards.

(iv) Finally, one has to take account of all the governmental measures designed to reduce the drain on the reserves and of devaluation itself. The American and Canadian Governments, for example, had undertaken in September to review their stockpiling programmes for tin and rubber so as to enlarge the field for imports. The Commonwealth governments had agreed to cut their dollar outgoings by 25 per cent from the 1948 levels. The British Government had also made various cuts in order to improve its dollar deficit. On top of this, devaluation was likely to exercise a progressively larger influence on the deficit although not much might have been expected to happen in the first quarter, abstracting from the speculative factors referred to under (iii).

It is not easy to demonstrate the relative importance of these four factors. But the evidence suggests that the speculative element was probably at least as important as the check to domestic activity in the United States; and to that extent devaluation was a capitulation to market opinion and the first of many demonstrations of the weakness of government in face of an exchange crisis.

As the ECA study of *The Sterling Area* explained later,

> underlying the whole situation was the fact that at the existing exchange rate (£1 = $4.03) the free market demand for goods and services from the Dollar Area was greatly in excess of what could be paid for. Only by the use of controls was it possible to

> limit the actual size of the current deficits – there was no natural tendency to equilibrium. Progress in the rearrangement of trade patterns and the narrowing of the dollar gap had been substantial, but the difficulties in making the necessary controls work effectively when market forces were pulling so strongly against them were great. Objections against the use of controls, too, were beginning to be strongly heard in some non-sterling countries.[19]

In this passage, the controls referred to relate to import and exchange controls operated within the sterling area but the thesis holds true also of domestic controls designed to limit expenditure on dollar imports, and used by a much wider group of countries. It was the perception, not always very clearly, that devaluation was a necessary ingredient in the restoration of international equilibrium that fuelled speculative pressure; and it was the speculative pressure that in the end compelled devaluation. But if it had not been for the additional uncertainty generated by the mild depression of 1949 it is doubtful whether the pressure would have been sufficient to force devaluation in 1949 and it might have been possible to refrain from action before the outbreak of the Korean war in June 1950. Thereafter, to judge from the frequency with which *re*valuation was urged, the issue might not have arisen for some considerable time.

IV

The war in Korea began nine months after devaluation and swept through the world economy like a tornado. World prices, international trade and payments, national budgets – all were pulled into new orbits; and by the time the storm died down the devaluation of sterling was a distant, almost forgotten event and its effects hard to trace with certainty in the new pattern of trade flows.

These effects must be judged against the expectations entertained in advance. To those who looked to devaluation primarily as a means of stopping the dollar drain it justified itself in the increase in the gold and dollar reserves by 70 per cent in the first nine months and the still larger increase in the nine months that followed. Those who stressed the need to improve Britain's competitive position could claim that most of the advantage conferred by a 30 per cent devaluation outlasted the Korean war. Between 1949 and, say, 1954 the American GDP price deflator rose by 13.3 per cent while in

Britain it rose by 16.4 per cent, so that nearly the whole of the cost advantage remained. Even those who looked to devaluation to pave the way for a current account surplus in the balance of payments could take satisfaction from the outcome: a surplus in all but one of the five years 1950–4 and a cumulative surplus of well over £500 million.

But what of those who hoped that devaluation would lay the basis for a new relationship between the sterling and the dollar worlds? Some evidence of the change after 1949 appears in Table 6.3 which shows a fall in the UK deficit on current account with the dollar area in 1950 by nearly $300 million. The fall was reversed in the Korean war but re-appeared when that was over. Similarly the rest of the sterling area also showed a marked improvement in its balance of payments with the dollar area although again there was a setback in the Korean war.

Another way of bringing out the change that took place is to compare trade with the dollar area and trade with the sterling area as in Table 6.6. The most notable feature of this comparison is the sharp change in 1950: the proportion of British exports sold in dollar markets rose abruptly and the proportion of imports from dollar markets fell equally abruptly.

TABLE 6.6 *British trade with the dollar and sterling areas, 1948–57 (per cent)*

	Ratio of UK exports to the dollar area to exports to the sterling area	*Ratio of UK imports from the dollar area to imports from the sterling area*
1948	21.2	61.3
1949	17.9	58.6
1950	27.2	48.4
1951	24.8	55.3
1954	27.1	41.4
1957	36.9	62.2

SOURCE Based on Table 35 and p. 77 of *The Sterling Area: an American Analysis* (London: ECA, 1951).

The reaction in 1951 presumably reflects the disturbance to trade and prices brought about by the Korean War. But if one takes an average of the three following years (1952–4) and compares it with the average for 1948–9 there is a striking shift in both ratios in exactly the way one would expect: up from 19.5 per cent in 1948–9 to 28.2 per cent in 1952–4 for exports and down from 60.0 per cent to 44.6 per cent for imports.

It is true that there were other factors in the shift quite unconnected with devaluation. Sterling area sources of supply were recovering from war-time dislocation and post-war difficulties so that there was an upward trend in the area's trade, not only outwards but inwards. On the other hand, one might have expected the British authorities to take a more relaxed attitude to imports costing dollars as their reserves improved and this may help to explain the sharp rise in the proportion of dollar imports in 1951 and the later recovery in 1954–7. Discrimination did not extend to dollar exports, however, and the continuing climb in the proportion of British exports reaching dollar markets is evidence of the durability of the competitive advantage brought by devaluation.[20]

British trade, however, is only half the story: the change in parities went far beyond sterling, and the sterling area. In Western Europe, for example, only Sweden and Switzerland abstained from devaluing in September, Sweden having already devalued by 30 per cent the previous year. Denmark, France, Ireland, the Netherlands and Norway all devalued by 30 per cent and Germany by 20 per cent. Belgium, Italy and Portugal made more modest devaluations while Austria, Greece, and Iceland made larger ones. The rest of the world also took the opportunity to make devaluations against the dollar: even the Canadian dollar was devalued by 9 per cent. The trade-weighted devaluation of sterling may be estimated at approximately 9 per cent too – rather larger on the import side and smaller on the export side.

The net result might have been expected to be a marked check to the growth of US exports and a spurt in US imports. The record bears out that this was happening in 1950 as shown in Table 6.7.

Even if we allow for a downward trend in US exports as Europe recovered and an upward trend in US imports with the renewed growth in GNP, the size of the adjustments on both sides of the account in 1950 is striking. But the very speed with which they followed devaluation makes it doubtful how far they were caused by it. In the first half of 1949 exports were running (on a seasonally adjusted basis) at $17.9 billion per annum and had already fallen to $15.5 billion in the third quarter (that is before devaluation). In each of the next three quarters they remained below $13.5 billion and only rose above $14.0 billion in the final quarter of 1950. Imports of goods and services fluctuated between $9 billion and $10 billion per

TABLE 6.7 *US trade and national income, 1948–54*

	Exports from US (including services) ($ billion)	*Imports into US (including services) ($ billion)*	*Current balance of US ($ billion)*	*US/GNP at constant prices (1948 = 100)*
1948	16.88	10.37	6.51	100.0
1949	15.86	9.64	6.22	98.9
1950	13.91	12.01	1.90	105.7
1951	18.93	15.09	3.84	112.4
1954	18.00	16.01	1.99	113.6

SOURCE National Income and Product Accounts of the United States, 1929–74
NOTE Billion is used in the American sense.

annum in the five quarters between the beginning of 1949 and April 1950 but had risen from $9.5 billion in the last quarter of 1949 to $10.6 billion in the second quarter of 1950 and $13.4 billion in the third. It would seem from these quarterly movements that most of the turn-round in 1950 that can be disentangled from the effects of the Korean war came on the import side. Some of the rise in imports can be attributed to the recovery in economic activity in the United States in the winter of 1949–50. But it is not unreasonable to treat devaluation as contributing to the rise, particularly when one finds it continuing after hostilities had ceased. Making all allowances, the reduction in the current surplus of the United States after 1949 was materially assisted by the series of devaluations in 1949.

Thus whether we start from the composition of British trade or from the American current account there is evidence of a change in the balance between the dollar and the non-dollar world that persisted into the 1950s and was an indispensable element in post-war reconstruction.

From the British point of view the adjustment was by no means painless. Although in trade-weighted terms the devaluation was under 10 per cent, import prices rose between June 1949 and June 1950 by 17 per cent while export prices rose by only 5 per cent. The shift in the terms of trade represented a real cost even if it was small by comparison with the much larger shift that followed the outbreak of the Korean war.

Finally, what of the danger that costs and prices would rise so as to extinguish the competitive gains of devaluation and raise the spectre of a *dégringolade* of the exchange? In spite of the rise in import prices and the relaxed stance of monetary policy the cost of living was remarkably steady. In the year to September 1949 retail prices had risen by 3.2 per cent; in the year that followed the rise was only 2.0 per cent. Food prices which had risen by 8.8 per cent in the year before devaluation rose only by a further 4.5 per cent in the following year. The government kept well within its bargain with the trade unions who had agreed to hold wages steady if the cost of living rose by under 5 per cent. The trade unions for their part were almost equally successful during the first post-devaluation year. Basic hourly rates for men rose by one per cent and although hourly earnings, measured in the biennial October survey, increased rather faster, there was no acceleration compared with the previous year, the rise being limited to $3\frac{1}{2}$ per cent.

Thus the advocates of devaluation could claim that things had worked out more or less as they had predicted; and the politicians who were so hard to persuade could take comfort that they had largely avoided the accompanying measures which their advisers kept insisting were indispensable.

NOTES

1. P. Hennessy and M. Brown, '19-month progress to devaluation', *The Times*, 8 January 1980.
2. See, for example, J. Jewkes, *Ordeal by Planning* (London: Macmillan, 1948) p. 233.
3. P. Hennessy and M. Brown, 'Deciphering the "Rose" Code', *The Times*, 3 January 1980.
4. In the Annex to their Report, Robert Hall quotes William McChesney Martin as confirming 'that practically all officials of the U.S. Government were firmly convinced that devaluation of sterling was inevitable'. (Annex to Report on a Visit to the United States in June 1949 by H. Wilson Smith and R. L. Hall, (EPC(49)63.)
5. Hugh Dalton's diary (MSS, at LSE).
6. His report claimed that 'the [Canadian] government advisers . . . accept the view that devaluation would merely add to the difficulties in which the already adverse terms of trade have involved us'; and that 'practically all the leading Canadian financial advisers (unlike some of their opposite numbers in the United States) reject devaluation as a means of overcoming Anglo-Canadian economic difficulties'. Nevertheless he referred later in his report to 'the unfortunate and fairly general – though erroneous – expectation of devaluation'. While emphasising that 'our prices of consumer goods are far too high' to compete with American goods in the Canadian market, he refrained from any suggestion that only devaluation could close the gap and while in

Canada had 'repeated the Chancellor's recent clear statement on devaluation' (paras. 20 and 40 of EPC(49)65, dated 23 June 1949).

7. Nye Bevan was arguing in favour of an early election in May and in recording this in his diary, Dalton added (24 May): 'Douglas Jay argued this way with me last week. If we have to devalue sterling the cost of living will jump up and that will lose us the election'.
8. On 26 August he indicated that he wanted a rate midway between $2.50 and $3 to the £1.
9. They added: 'unless the devaluation was so savage, e.g. down to $2.50, as to affect the internal standard of living in the country.'
10. The Communiqué issued on 10 July said that:

> It was agreed that (a number of supplementary suggestions) should be the subject of further consideration. In this connection no suggestion was made that sterling should be devalued.

11. P. Williams, *Hugh Gaitskell* (London: Jonathan Cape, 1979), p. 199. On 20 July Gaitskell set out five reasons for devaluing the pound:

    (a) Exchange control had not prevented a substantial dollar drain and would not by itself bring the money back;
    (b) It was clear that the U.S. Government would offer no help in the short term and would offer long-term aid only on stiff conditions;
    (c) The controls over dollar expenditure by Commonwealth countries were looser than had been supposed and were weakened when sterling prices were relatively high;
    (d) Since devaluation would make exports to dollar markets much more profitable, the prospects of an expansion in dollar earnings were favourable;
    (e) There was a danger of a currency collapse if the reserves continued to fall.

12. W. T. Rodgers (ed.), *Hugh Gaitskell 1906–1963* (London: Thames and Hudson, 1964), p. 95.
13. The possibility was raised in an appendix to the memorandum circulated by the Chancellor to the meeting of the Economic Policy Committee on 1 July. In a memorandum by the Economic Section of the Cabinet Office on 2 August ('The Choice of a New Exchange Rate') it was suggested that the I.M.F. might be willing to accept a regime of variable exchange rates for an experimental period before a fixed rate was settled. The Bank of England, however, opposed this idea on the grounds that the reserves were too low.
14. Dalton noted in his diary that, after the Economic Policy Committee meeting on 19 July the officials were asked to leave the room. Stafford Cripps then told the Committee that he did not trust his own officials and advisers in the Treasury (and presumably also in the Bank). 'They were all really, by reason of their training and their belief in a "free economy", much more in agreement with the Americans than with British Ministers'. Dalton advised him to make use of Douglas Jay and Stafford agreed. Other entries in Dalton's diary make it clear that Ministers were deeply suspicious of their advisers and that the grounds for this usually lay in an almost paranoiac reaction to any hint that

public expenditure should be cut. At the end of July the Prime Minister complained to Dalton that he was 'being served up from the Treasury and the Bank arguments which he thinks are fallacious on evil effects of our public expenditure'. Dalton assured him that the arguments *were* fallacious.

15. The dispute is described in the article by Hennessy and Brown, 'Cripps and the search for a whiter loaf', *The Times*, 4 January 1980. But it took place at least a week before the meeting at the British Embassy at which the new rate for the dollar was settled.
16. The Chancellor based his total of £280 million on a calculation by Robert Hall that final demand was running at least £200 million above what had been assumed in the 1949 Budget and that a further cut of £100 million was required to free resources for the improvements in the visible balance that devaluation would permit. The £300 million was whittled down to £280 million and the final cuts by another £20 million. It would be broadly true to say that the cuts did little more than aim at restoring the pressure of demand to what had been contemplated in the Spring before any question of devaluation arose.
17. Hansard, 26 October 1949, Col. 1360.
18. *The Sterling Area: an American Analysis* (London: ECA, 1951) p. 76.
19. ibid., p. 75.
20. Allowance should, however, be made for the increase in American GNP by 13 per cent between 1949 and 1951 after a growth of only 1 per cent in the previous two years.

7 The End of Full Employment*

R. HALL

I

'The Government accept as one of their primary aims and responsibilities the maintenance of a high and stable level of employment after the war'. This is the opening of the White Paper on Employment Policy (Cmd. 6527) issued in May 1944 by the British Coalition Government, in which the three main parties were represented. This marked a revolutionary change in economic policy and undertook a commitment which no previous British Government would have contemplated. For the next three years the problems were those of transition, but as excess demand slackened the new policy had to be implemented. In November 1947 Sir Stafford Cripps succeeded Mr Dalton as Chancellor of the Exchequer and retained the portfolio he already held as Minister of Economic Affairs. As Director of the Economic Section of the Cabinet Office (later transferred to the Treasury and called Economic Adviser to H.M.G.), I became in effect his economic adviser, remaining in this capacity under successive Chancellors until my retirement in 1961. This paper is a short account of how the policy worked in practice and some reflections on later events.

* Much has already been written about the period covered by this paper but I cannot pretend to have read more than a small part of it. For the years 1947–61 the account given is from direct personal experience. In the years following I give my own views, those I think of someone well placed as an observer. For much of this time I was closely connected with the National Institute of Economic and Social Research and I have consulted its quarterly Reviews for the narrative.

When I wrote the first draft I did not know that Sir Alec Cairncross was preparing a lecture (since published as the Ellis Hunter Memorial lecture) called 'Farewell Full Employment'. Sir Alec himself persuaded me to go on with my own version, and I am indebted to him for many comments and suggestions.

The economic thinking of the White Paper was a combination of traditional theory and of the cyclical theory associated with the name of Maynard Keynes. In a market economy, employment is the result of bargains between employers and workers, and the traditional view was that the labour market, like all others, would tend to be cleared by price – here wage – movements. In equilibrium there would be no unemployment in a country with adequate resources. But as the parameters of the system – the pattern of demand for output, the supply of resources, and the methods of production technically available – are constantly changing, unemployment would be expected because of the time needed to adjust to these changes. Its amount would be a function of the speed and severity of the changes and of the adaptability of the system. This is usually called transitional or structural unemployment.

This general equilibrium analysis, first clearly expressed in the Walras–Pareto equations, gives the student a much clearer picture of the interdependence of the forces at work in a market economy than Marshall's simile of balls in a bowl, each affected by all the others. The difficulty of applying them to actual affairs is to know to what extent real individuals and their behaviour conform to the definitions in the equations. The disparities can be lumped together as 'market imperfections'. In the present context an obvious illustration is the definition of unemployment itself, raised by phrases like 'involuntary unemployment' which implies an objective test of a state of mind. Fortunately for its official economists, in Britain the official figures of unemployment had a clear meaning and for most of the period under review were consistent enough for their trend to be a good indicator.

This traditional view of unemployment as a necessary, and for the individual a transitory concomitant of change, was gradually found to be unsatisfactory because of the tendency in developed economies to swing between booms and slumps. The combination of human misery and unused resources in the slumps made it increasingly difficult to defend the market system. Wicksell and his followers began to argue that a system which depended on money for the whole functioning of the market was inherently unstable, but their ideas were little known in England and the rapid change there was due to the publication in 1930 of Keynes's *Treatise on Money*. The *Treatise* was full of stimulating ideas and, like all great path-breaking works, allowed those who followed to find their own applications – much more so, in my own view, than the *General*

Theory. The methods of economic management which were generally followed in market economies for thirty years after the end of the Second World War were all based on what came to be called Keynesian principles, those of demand management. This is essentially a counter-cyclical policy and had a tremendous appeal to politicians and economists who had lived through the Great Depression of the 1930s.

The White Paper accepted the division between transitional and cyclical unemployment, and proposed to deal with these by separate policies. The transitional or structural was to be tackled partly by what came to be called regional policy, giving special inducements to industry to establish new works in the areas which had been most affected by the decline of British heavy industry: and partly by measures to increase the adaptability of labour through assistance with training for new skills and with moving to new places. These policies were vigorously prosecuted by the Board of Trade for regional policy and by the Ministry of Labour and National Service for training. They are not further considered here until the last part of the paper. There was also a brief reference to seasonal unemployment.

The anti-cyclical policy was explained at some length and various suggestions were made about how the balance between government revenue and expenditure could be altered to act as a counter-weight to any swings in demand from expenditure in the private sector. As might be expected in a document much influenced by Keynes, both through his writings and because at that time he was a leading figure in the Treasury, the main variations were expected to come from capital expenditure and from variations in the foreign balance.

The foreign balance itself is discussed in a separate section. Britain, then as now, was dependent on imports for much of its food and raw materials: and it was also committed to the general reduction of barriers to international trade envisaged in the plans for post-war reconstruction sponsored by the US and the UK.

Changes in the terms of trade and the strength of competition both in home and export markets are disturbing influences, but not directly susceptible to internal action as are changes arising at home. It was hoped that a concerted plan for stabilising the prices of primary products would do much to reduce the extreme swings in the terms of trade experienced in the 1930s. The disturbing effects of changes in the relative competitive positions will usually be felt when some countries run balance of payments surpluses, which must be matched by deficits elsewhere. This puts pressure on deficit countries to deflate, reducing employment. The White Paper pointed to the undertakings which it was hoped would be given by the main trading countries during the negotiations envisaged after the war, to the effect that they would all seek to maintain high and stable levels of employment and collaborate in the solution of any difficulties which might arise.

Finally, the White Paper called on the community as a whole to cooperate in making the new policy effective, and warned that without this it would not succeed. Paragraphs 53 and 54 called on trade unions not to exploit the new security to be given to their jobs, by high wage demands or restrictive labour practices: and on employers not to seek high prices by restrictions on output. Paragraph 56 called on all citizens not to neglect the duty of fending for themselves, nor to allow any weakening of personal enterprise. These warnings were fully justified by events.

II

THE POLICY IN PRACTICE

Mr Dalton's second Budget of 1947 was designed to check the state of excess demand which had dominated the early post-war scene. All Budgets after this until recently were formulated on the basis of a judgement about what was needed to bring or keep the economy to a desired state of activity. This continued until about 1974, when the present phase was entered, quite different from anything previously experienced in the post-war period. The Budget, as the occasion for a general review of public expenditure and revenue, was naturally the main vehicle for implementing the cyclical part of the new policy. But almost all Budget speeches emphasised that events might easily turn out to be other than forecast, and that if this happened changes would be made accordingly. From time to time such changes were needed, often in what was popularly called a mini-Budget.

The White Paper did not suggest any figure to correspond to the words 'full' or 'high' for the amount of employment which was to be taken as the target figure. This is a crucial question, and in the early operation of the policy its importance was not fully understood. It has remained controversial ever since. Sir William Beveridge, in his book, *Full Employment in a Free Society* had put forward a figure of three per cent as a maximum level for unemployment. The figure, which had to be a guess as there was no experience to go on, was made up of one per cent for unavoidable seasonal fluctuations, one per cent for frictional or transitional reasons, and one per cent which might occur because of disturbances from outside the economy.

This three per cent maximum was given a sort of official status by Hugh Gaitskell who succeeded Cripps as Chancellor, in a written reply to a Parliamentary question on 22 March 1951. This was the result of pressure from the UN Economic and Social Council, and caused him much anxiety. There was still a good deal of doubt about whether the new policy would succeed, and any figure given by the Government would be a hostage to fortune. At the end of 1951 the Labour Government was replaced by the Conservatives. In oppostion they had made play with the forecasting errors in the annual Economic Surveys, and were anxious to reduce their own exposure. Since then there have been no official targets, though attitudes can be deduced from what happened.

The policy, widely accepted, was quite simple, to decrease taxes or increase government expenditure if unemployment rose to an unacceptable level, and to reverse direction if the economy became over-loaded. But 'acceptable' and 'over-loaded' mean the same things as 'full' and 'overfull'. Those responsible for advising Ministers had to learn as they went along. At that time it was thought by all parties that it would be difficult to maintain high employment levels, and all thought that unemployment was likely to be the most sensitive politically of all subjects in the economic field. For this reason, and also because all governments find it easier to reduce than to increase taxes, the pressure to keep to a low unemployment figure was stronger than that for caution.

In practice it turned out to be much easier to keep below three per cent than most people had expected. But during the first decade it was gradually observed that instead of the old business cycle, a new cycle had been introduced because of the way in which intervention was operated. The best indicators of this were given by the unemployment figures themselves, and by the index of industrial production, which is more sensitive to changes in aggregate demand than the GDP. The balance of visible trade was also relevant, though it behaved rather more erratically.

The production peak of this cycle, following a stimulation of demand, occurs while unemployment is falling. But owing to bad timing of intervention, demand is still increasing while output is flattening out. The demand constraint (lack of orders) has been replaced by a supply constraint (shortage of resources). This shows itself in various bottlenecks in the system, since the output of all the materials, components, etc. needed for the complex of final output does not keep in step. There are complaints of lack of skilled labour, of components and of capacity. The economy has reached the limits set by its adaptability, and any further stimulus, while it may reduce unemployment at the extensive and intensive margins, has offsetting disadvantages. The remaining unemployment is structural rather than cyclical, and should be attacked, if it is thought worth doing, in ways which do not add to aggregate demand, that is by shifting expenditure rather than increasing it.

One of the disadvantages is an alteration in the trade balance because of increased imports of manufactures and semi-manufactures, and perhaps also because of a diversion of output from export to home markets. In the period under discussion, this was often accompanied by pressure on sterling, a more effective danger signal than the other symptoms. Policy is now changed from stimulus to restraint. As this gradually takes effect, the imbalances in the system are reduced and the secular increase in productivity, which went on until quite recently, leads to the release of labour so that unemployment begins to rise. The balance of payments and confidence in sterling improve and concern about unemployment causes policy to be reversed and a new cycle begins.

In the typical post-war cycle, the stimulation always turned out to have been overdone, so that industrial production catches up the arrears of checked growth in a short time. The braking process, a more difficult operation for political reasons, was much more gradual, so that industrial production stagnated rather than fell. In a contraction the Chancellor of the Exchequer tended to be a lonely figure, while in an expansion all his colleagues are only too anxious to help.

It follows from the above analysis that the unemployment target for 'a high and stable level of employment' cannot be sustainable (and therefore stable) beyond the limits set by the adaptability of the structure and these limits have to be determined empirically. Further, it can only be stable if the interventions are differently timed. In practice they were usually 'too much, too late'. This was partly due to the time taken to get a clear picture of what was happening, no doubt because in the early years not enough attention was given to the crucial importance of the target figure. But in any case, the politicians who have to take the responsibility for the way the economy is managed have to think about a lot of other things besides the smooth running of the systems. They also tend to have rather a short time horizon. Thus when restrictive measures are needed, a collection of expenditure cuts are chosen where they will cause least outcry: additions to taxes are made on the same criteria: and there were often attempts to modify access to credit in a selective way. All these take time to bite, and some bite less than planned. But when the time comes for a reversal of policy, the atmosphere becomes one in which it is difficult to retain control so that in the event, more turns out to have been done than was planned. This explains the speed with which expenditure and output rose once the signs were changed to 'Go'.

Several attempts were made to improve the methods of control. In 1959 a Committee was appointed, chaired by Lord Plowden, 'to review the principles which govern the control by the executive of public expenditure'. The main part of its conclusions were published in a White Paper (Cmd. 1432) in July 1961. These were that the system of decision-making encouraged departmental Ministers to think only of spending, leaving the Chancellor to struggle with the aggregates and their implication for the whole economy. 'Chopping and changing in Government policy is frustrating to efficiency and economy . . . and impairs cost-consciousness and financial discipline in the public service'. There was also a considerable delay in implementing measures to change spending, so that they tended to bite out of phase.

We recommended that there should be regular Ministerial appraisals of public expenditure as a whole, over a period of years ahead, and in relation to prospective resources. These should be submitted to senior Ministers for approval (or pruning), and it was thus hoped that the limits within which spending Ministers could act would be laid down well in advance. Finally, the greatest practicable stability of decisions on public expenditure once taken should be observed. It followed from this that, as far as possible, short term changes in public expenditure should not be an instrument of stabilisation policy. In effect, the instruments should be confined to taxation and monetary policy.

As would be expected after more than ten years' experience, these proposals showed a considerable advance on the original White

Paper as a practical analysis of the problems. An official Committee was established to make the regular forecasts and surveys recommended. Another change was the regulator, a tax introduced by Mr Selwyn Lloyd in 1961. None of the existing taxes were ideal from the point of view of smooth changes in final expenditure. The regulator was operated by empowering the Government to raise or lower almost all indirect taxes by up to ten per cent by administrative action. These powers have been used from time to time.

Nevertheless, the policy of alternating stimulus and restraint in a way which led to the Stop–Go cycle was pursued by all Governments (with one exception) until about 1974. Over this period the unemployment rate only reached three per cent for very short spells of unusual weather. The policy can therefore be regarded as a success from the point of view of the objective, full employment. It was also acceptable politically, in the sense that no Government lost an election on this issue.

The possible exception was during the Chancellorship of Mr Roy Jenkins, who replaced Mr Callaghan after the 1967 devaluation. This came after a long period of balance of payments difficulties, the result of an exchange rate which had become too high and an over-stimulated economy. Mr Jenkins, determined to allow room for the expected increase in exports, introduced a severe Budget in 1968. After the usual time-lag the balance of payments responded and was clearly improving by mid-1969. The cycle, which behaved somewhat erratically, began to show a new pattern. From 1968 to 1971 industrial production remained almost static and unemployment began to rise to figures high by the standard of previous administrations. This combination would have been regarded as an indication of a demand constraint, needing a stimulus. Mr Jenkins, however, kept the economy on a tight rein until the Government was defeated in the 1970 election.

It would have been instructive, from the point of view of demand management, if the new Government had continued what looks like an attempt to get away from Stop–Go and run the economy with more margin at the peaks. It is very unlikely that the rising unemployment had anything to do with the defeat of Labour, certainly not expected by Mr Wilson or the professional forecasters. Mr Heath would not in any case have been expected at that time to change the policy – he came to office when his party was opposed to an incomes policy (discussed below) and were more or less monetarists. At first no stimulus was given. Industrial production remained flat and unemployment at the end of 1970 began a rapid rise, reaching a peak of just over 900 000 or about four per cent, figures not approached since the beginning of the war.

This was too much for the Government and was followed by a reversal of policy, a very rapid increase in industrial production and a fall in unemployment. This was, in the event, the last of full employment as an objective of policy, discussed later in this paper. Apart from the Jenkins period, little notice had been taken from a practical point of view of the Plowden Committee. The review of public expenditure had been developed, but the pressures to expand it and lay up future trouble, remained. The economy was over-expanded in the run-up to the 1964 election. The incoming Government nevertheless embarked on a rapid increase in public spending, to be financed from a four per cent annual increase in the GDP which was called for in a national plan. It was widely rumoured at the time that this very improbable growth rate was agreed by Ministers to reconcile the conflicting claims of spending Ministers. In fact, output rose very little and expenditure had to be cut from 1967 on. Mr Heath's administration of 1970 started with a deflationary stance but quickly turned to the fastest and shortest expansion of the whole period. The strong tendency of democratic governments to take short views meant that nothing was learnt from the uneven progress of the whole period.

Nevertheless the performance in maintaining a high, if not very stable, level of employment can be considered as satisfactory, and certainly better than had been expected at the outset. This had been helped a good deal by the success of the policies for international economic collaboration which had been called for in the White Paper, where it was said that the maintenance of full employment depended on these. As far as full employment was concerned, the substance of the obligations accepted under the aegis of the UN was that trading countries would all try to maintain high and stable levels of employment, not resorting either to competitive devaluations or to increasing barriers to trade, through which the 'export of unemployment' was attempted during the Great Depression.

The Keynesian approach was generally accepted among developed countries, though there was controversy about how 'full' was full employment, and about the extent to which duties or obligations should be symmetrical. Although every balance of payments surplus must have a corresponding deficit, most developed countries would prefer a surplus, at least on current account. Deficit countries had an obligation to correct their positions by deflating or, if their costs were out of line, by devaluation. But it was inherent in the system that surplus countries had equal obligations to be more expansionist or to revalue.

The various organisations under the UN umbrella were too large, cumbrous and diverse in their outlook to be effective, with the exceptions perhaps of the GATT and later the IMF. The practice developed of discussing macroeconomic problems among the more important of the developed countries, especially through the OEEC (later the OECD). There were also even more informal contacts such as those of central bankers through the Bank for International Settlements and the annual meetings of Commonwealth Finance Ministers before the IMF/IBRD annual meetings. I was for some years chairman of the 'group of economic experts' established by OECD, where people who thoroughly understood their own countries' outlook could discuss without actually committing their Ministers and it was evident that we all shared the same framework of ideas and objectives, though with differences of emphasis, especially about the relative importance of stable employment and stable prices.

Broadly speaking, then, the international economic climate was a benign one. Such recessions as there were did not spread and this in itself made them milder. Primary product prices did not show such great swings as were feared, and the terms of trade of developed countries, especially the UK, improved a little. Exchange rates were generally stable and international trade expanded almost steadily. The general prosperity was no doubt facilitated by the attitude of the US after Marshall Aid in easing the dollar shortage which had been such a problem in the early post-war years. Unfortunately, towards the end of the period, there were signs that these generally easy circumstances were under strain. The different rates of inflation in the main trading countries finally caused the break-down of fixed exchange rates in 1971, and some part of the inflation was caused by the easy supply of dollars itself.

If the external conditions postulated by the 1941 White Paper had been so happily met, the same cannot be said of the internal ones, quoted above. The most obvious failing, and probably that which sowed the seed for the collapse of full employment, was the cost inflation which accompanied it. By 1948 the Attlee Government was worried enough to publish another White Paper calling for restraint in wages and prices, the fore-runner of a long series of documents and exhortations, especially in Budget Speeches, on the general theme that if incomes went up faster than productivity, prices would inevitably rise.

Sir Stafford Cripps managed to persuade the trade unions to severe restraint after the 1949 devaluation, but this was followed by high settlements in 1951, stimulated by the rise in import prices after the outbreak of the war in Korea. The basic difficulty, now much more generally recognised than at the time, is that full employment strengthens the power of unions to secure wage increases, while weakening the incentive of employers to resist. If the Government is committed to maintaining employment, this involves keeping marginal employers in business: and employers generally will not be affected by a wage increase as long as competitors have to pay it too. The cost of a stoppage is much greater than the hypothetical gain from resistance. The traditional method of controlling the general level of prices through the money supply can only be effective through the circuitous route of higher interest rates and direct measures of a fiscal kind to reduce aggregate demand, putting pressure on employers to reduce output and employment. In a perfect labour market the resulting unemployment would lead to wage cuts or at least to lower increases, but the labour market in Britain has never been perfect and has steadily become less so. Thus full employment and price stability are inconsistent unless the Government can persuade or compel the trade unions not to exploit the situation. Such persuasion or compulsion goes under the broad title of incomes policy.

After 1951 the terms of trade reversed again and in the next decade wage settlements were quite moderate by later standards. I myself became increasingly worried about the threat to price stability, partly for the traditional reasons about the social objections to inflation – the most respectable members of society were urging everyone to put their savings into government securities which were certain to lose their value – but even more because I thought that if full employment were continued, with the money base accommodating itself to the price level, wages were indeterminate and settlements would escalate, with the eventual result of a flight from money. I thought also that an incomes policy would be much less destructive of political stability and much more precise in controlling cost inflation than monetary policy and unemployment. But I had no success in persuading any of the Chancellors under whom I served to take this up. A third White

Paper, stressing the relationship between wage and price increases, was published in 1956 (Cmd. 9725). This fell flat as Ministers did little to support it. In 1957 Mr Thorneycroft set up a Council on Productivity, Prices and Incomes to report on developments and make recommendations, in the hope of influencing public opinion. This was also ineffective, mainly because the early reports put the blame on the Government for running the economy too full. Mr Thorneycroft himself agreed with this view, but he resigned (in effect on this issue) before he had time to make any experiments. The Prime Minister, Mr Macmillan, would never have countenanced using unemployment as an instrument of policy, which monetarism entails. No doubt on his prompting, Mr Selwyn Lloyd was the first Chancellor to attempt an incomes policy.

Why was so little concern shown by Ministers and the public? It was because wage increases and the resulting price rises had been what now seems so moderate. As Table 7.1 shows, the retail price index went up by 70 per cent in the 14 years from 1948, and had only doubled by 1967. During a time of general prosperity and a steady rise in the standard of living, few felt themselves incommoded by the behaviour of prices or even the steady erosion of the value of government securities. There was much discussion among senior officials, certainly from 1956 onwards, but opinions about how serious it was or what could be done were divided. Some thought along Phillip's curves lines, that is that a little more unemployment would do the job, and many that any sort of incomes policy would be very difficult to carry out successfully unless public opinion was much more strongly aroused than it was. Mr Selwyn Lloyd, less opposed to planning than his Tory predecessors, inaugurated the long series of experiments when in 1961 he called for a temporary pause to pay increases while a more durable policy was prepared, and imposed this on the public sector.

From then until the most recent change of government, in 1979, when Mrs Thatcher embraced full-blown monetarism, some form of incomes policy was in operation except for short periods, of which the most notable was at the beginning of the Heath administration in 1970. The variations are far too numerous and complex to be detailed, but the broad pattern was:

1. A short period of standstill or freeze, more or less observed, on wages, prices and other incomes.
2. This was followed by a more detailed policy, laying down a

TABLE 7.1 *The British economy 1948–79. Selected indicators*

	Industrial production	*Unemployment*	*Balance of visible trade*	*Retail price index*	*Chancellor*
1948	50.3	1.33	−151	23.1	S. Cripps
1949	53.6	1.35	−137	23.8	S. Cripps
1950	56.8	1.59	−51	24.5	Cripps/Gaitskell
1951	58.1	1.09	−689	26.7	Gaitskell/Butler
1952	56.4	1.57	−279	29.2	R. A. Butler
1953	60.0	1.46	−244	30.1	R. A. Butler
1954	63.0	1.45	−204	30.6	R. A. Butler
1955	66.1	0.97	−313	32.0	Butler/Macmillan
1956	66.6	1.03	53	33.6	H. Macmillan
1957	67.8	1.30	−29	34.8	Macmillan/Thorneycroft
1958	67.3	1.79	29	35.9	P. Thorneycroft
1959	70.6	1.9	−115	36.1	Thorneycroft/H-Amory
1960	75.5	1.6	−401	36.5	H-Amory/S-Lloyd
1961	76.4	1.4	−140	37.7	Selwyn-Lloyd
1962	77.2	1.9	−100	39.3	S-Lloyd/Maudling
1963	79.4	2.4	−89	40.1	R. Maudling
1964	86.1	1.7	−510	41.4	Maudling/Callaghan
1965	88.7	1.3	−233	43.4	J. Callaghan
1966	90.2	1.4	−77	45.1	J. Callaghan
1967	91.2	2.2	−567	46.2	Callaghan/Jenkins
1968	97.0	2.3	−682	48.4	R. Jenkins
1969	99.6	2.3	−172	51.0	R. Jenkins
1970	99.7	2.5	−42	54.2	Jenkins/Macleod/Barber
1971	99.8	3.3	261	59.3	A. Barber
1972	102.0	3.6	−722	63.6	A. Barber
1973	109.5	2.6	−2383	69.4	A. Barber
1974	108.5	2.6	−5235	80.5	Barber/Healey
1975	*100.0*	3.9	−3236	100.0	D. W. Healey
1976	101.4	5.2	−3601	116.5	D. W. Healey
1977	102.8	5.6	−1744	135.0	D. W. Healey
1978	103.6	5.5	−1175	146.2	D. W. Healey
1979	104.2	5.5	−3312	166.0	Healey/G. Howe

NOTES *Industrial Production*: Index 1975 = 100. After 1975, the index is of manufacturing, to eliminate N. Sea oil production
Unemployment: Percentage of working population, UK
Balance of Visible Trade: £ Millions (Actual prices)
Retail Prices: Index 1975 = 100

SOURCE Central Statistical Office, 1980 Supplement

'norm' for increases in all of these, and some machinery for policing these and empowered to give dispensations in certain types of situations.
3. The difficulty of imposing the policy on the trade unions and pressure from these to return to what they called 'free collective bargaining' led to its collapse.
4. A change of government, soon followed by a new set of experiments.

It will be seen that after the 20 years from 1947 to 1967, retail prices had doubled. They doubled again in about 7 years to 1974–75, and with the exception perhaps of 1978, they have been rising faster than this since 1975. Thus the course of incomes policy has been attended by aggravation of the malady. British economists are deeply divided between those who think this shows that incomes policy makes inflation worse, and those who think it would have been even higher without the policy. The latter group are divided again, some (like myself) thinking that if the policies had been better conducted they would have been more successful. As all the arguments are hypothetical they cannot be resolved, though Mrs Thatcher will provide more evidence about whether monetarism is a practicable solution. The position of the trade unions is discussed below.

The second stipulation of the White Paper was in effect that trade unions (and employers) should examine and reform their restrictive practices. As far as employers are concerned, the proscription of retail price maintenance has clearly led to much greater efficiency in the distributive trades and the Monopolies Commission had done a good deal to reduce collusive practices among employers. Restrictive practices by trade unions have continued to flourish, facilitated partly by the attempts to enlist their cooperation in incomes policy and partly by Labour Governments strengthening the legal privileges enjoyed by the unions in return for so-called concordats between the unions and the government. This is again discussed below.

The third condition in the White Paper was that full employment should not weaken individual initiative and responsibility. If this has happened, it must be attributed to the welfare state as a whole, rather than to full employment itself. The community is certainly much better off, better educated and more mobile than it was 30 years ago. On the other hand, the grip now held by the trade unions has considerably reduced the scope for individual initiative. In attempting to compare the adaptability of the economic structure in 1973 with that in 1947, I came to the conclusion that the experience under Mr Jenkins, already referred to, suggested that when the economy levelled out it was at an unemployment figure not much different from that which ought to have been aimed at in earlier cycles. This suggests that adaptability remained much the same, the factors for improvement offsetting those against. It was a feature of the whole period that when a plant closed or made a big staff reduction, there was an outcry against the unemployment, but that in a short time those displaced had found other work.

Since about the end of 1973, developments in the world and the UK have been very different. The outside world has become less benign and the ability of the British economy to adapt has diminished. The course of events is so recent that they can be treated quite briefly.

Unemployment, which reached a low of 2.3 per cent at the end of 1973 with an overheated economy, rose steadily to over five per cent by 1976 and has remained since in the 5–6 per cent region. Industrial production has limped along, and if the effect of North Sea oil is eliminated it has been well below the 1973 level. Public opinion has been rather apathetic, as neither party when in office has been able to do anything about it.

These radical changes were forced on the Government in the first instance by the sudden increase in oil prices, the first of a series of shocks still going on. An orderly adjustment to the balance of payments deficits thus imposed has been too much for the western world and its former international co-operation. All major developed countries have felt themselves constrained to try to keep down their own deficits, so that international trade is now aggressively competitive. This state of affairs seems likely to continue at least until the price of oil has made other energy sources fully competitive.

Meanwhile, the problem of inflation, given successive upward twists by the oil prices, has got worse for everyone. Though the rates between countries are as uneven as they were when they forced the abandonment of fixed parities in 1971, almost all currencies are under pressure. For once, governments themselves agree with their central bankers that this problem must take precedence over that of employment. Monetary methods against inflation use unemployment as an instrument of policy.

Faced with this external climate, British power to control its own economy is considerably limited. This could be overcome if it became more adaptable. The world of the planner is a vasty deep of spirits for all occasions. But – 'will they come when you do call for them?'. The calls for more restraint in wage demands and more output in the works still go out, now even from Mrs Thatcher. But the spirits of these are deafer than ever.

The steady acceleration of prices has already been mentioned. After an agreement with the trade unions, there was some improvement in 1977–8, but in 1979 the TUC voted for a return to 'free collective bargaining', and since then price increases have been around 20 per cent annually. Mr Healey, and his successor, Sir Geoffrey Howe, have repeatedly said that there can be no hope of full employment until we have the reality of much lower inflation. Although the present administration has pinned its faith to monetarism, Mr Healey was a strong advocate of incomes policy. What must have restrained him from giving any stimulus was the extent of import penetration. As real incomes rise, they bring with them a more than proportionate increase in manufactured imports. The British people do not want to buy what they are willing to produce.

Undoubtedly, the troubles have been mainly caused by the combination of external events and the failure of incomes policy. These have been exacerbated by the high exchange rate, a temporary effect required by monetary policy. But there would be fairly general agreement that the frictions in the market are much worse than they used to be. This is obviously believed by all those who now call for protection and leaving the Common Market. For my own part, I find it impossible to believe that the changes outlined in the previous paragraph could themselves account for the responses to unemployment being so different from those of the previous 30 years, unless the forces making for response were much weaker.

III

In seeking an explanation, my own view is that the period during which the international position became more difficult, the rate of inflation accelerated, and (as I think) the British ability to cope with change decreased – coincides with the growth in the power of the trade unions and with their ability and willingness to use it. This is a power which is employed only in a negative way, except for the short periods when there have been attempts to support an incomes policy. But the effective use of the power is to stop, or threaten to stop, some part of the economic system, in order to secure inflationary wage demands or to resist the introduction of improved methods of production: a threat similar to that made by blackmailers or some kinds of terrorists, to bring themselves and their victims to a common disaster. But because the trade union movement was founded and nourished in an atmosphere of struggle against employers, and its cohering force is 'solidarity', which means that union members should always support one another in any conflict with employers, the movement is much less successful, when it makes a bargain, in getting its members to stick to their promises or undertakings. It enjoys legal immunity against actions which employers might bring in the courts, if the behaviour concerned was in the opinion of the union in furtherance of a trade dispute: an agreement cannot be enforced.

When Sir Stafford Cripps became Minister of Economic Affairs in 1947, he set up the Economic Planning Board, with equal representation of the TUC, the CBI as the employer's organisation, and senior civil servants (including myself). Sir Stafford felt strongly that the planning needed for full employment, and for solving the problems and exploiting the opportunities which would attend it, would require the understanding and cooperation of both sides of industry. Unfortunately, the Board turned out to be little more than a talking shop. Nearly all the papers which it discussed gave the Government's views on the economic outlook or aspects of it. Ministers never attended and the civil servants were not authorised to commit them or say much about their intentions. All the right things were said about stable prices, productivity and the balance of payments, but there were no specific commitments, nor anything resembling joint planning. As already explained, the early years of the full employment policy were reasonably satisfactory, so that these deficiencies were not remarked, and after the advent of the Conservatives the Board was even more neglected and was finally abolished.

When Mr Selwyn Lloyd became Chancellor in 1960 and concern about inflation was getting stronger, these ideas were revived. By that time it was becoming evident that British productivity was lagging behind that of our competitors and needed stimulation. A new body, the National Economic Development Council (NEDC) was set up with similar membership to that of the Planning Board, but with Ministers representing Government, and with its own staff. (The Planning Board was serviced by Treasury officials, nearly all of whom had other duties as well.) This body has remained in existence, and through a number of subsidiaries dealing with individual industries, has done a great deal of work on productivity problems. This work must have helped towards more adaptability and done something to counteract the forces working the other way. But the basic weakness of the Planning Board, that it did not commit itself to planning decisions requiring implementation, remained.

The main change in the power of the unions came not from their position on the NEDC, but from the attempts to control inflation through some form of incomes policy. The end sought was desirable but the means chosen turned out to have the opposite effect from that intended. As it was generally accepted that it would be difficult to operate sanctions against a powerful trade union, all the experiments sought to enlist the cooperation of the unions, and have been accompanied by controls of some kind on prices, salaries and dividends so as to make the restraints hoped for from the unions seem to be fair. It was much easier administratively to control prices and dividends than wages. Here the guide-lines or norms were usually effective at the outset of each experiment, but they were soon weakened indirectly by subterfuges such as allowances for 'productivity' deals, the unions agreeing to be less obstructive about new methods: and as time passed, by direct breaches of the understandings, for which there were no effective sanctions. The burdens of management were increased by investigations to enforce price controls, and these controls and for a long time the taxation of the stock appreciation which arises automatically from inflation, brought the real profits of industry almost steadily downwards.

This process fixed firmly in the minds of trade union negotiators and their constituents the belief that they were making sacrifices by agreeing to wage restraint. Although few would deny that the control of inflation is beneficial to the whole community, the distribution of the wage increases in any wage round gives a temporary advantage to the first comers at the expense mainly of those who come later. The gradual realisation of this has driven the workers in many occupations, who at one time would hardly have thought of holding the community to ransom, to show that they too can cause the sort of damage once thought of as mainly in the power of key industries such as coal mining, electricity generation, and transport. As the principle of solidarity forces the first comers to support the threats or action of everyone else, the benefits are soon eroded and the stage set for new claims to meet the rising cost of living.

Added to the sense of making sacrifices by collaborating in incomes policy, and the realisation that industrial power to damage the community was not a prerogative of a few powerful unions, was the steady increase under the two Labour administrations (1964–70 and 1974–9) of direct negotiations between the Government and the Council of the TUC. The main object of these was to make concessions to the unions which would strengthen their bargaining position in a variety of ways, in return for agreement to collaborate in incomes policies. This process, termed a Social Contract by the Prime Minister, Mr Wilson, was similar to the bargaining on price and dividend control in return for wage restraint. The concessions made by the Government were enshrined in legislation while the agreements made by the TUC lasted at most for a few years. If it had been made clear at the beginning that the legislation would be repealed as soon as wage increases exceeded a stipulated rate, the unions would have had a strong incentive to introduce some order and discipline into their archaic and often anarchic structure. To do this after 1974 would have been impossible given the dependence of Labour on trade union support. But if the long series of experiments in incomes policy had been directed to something of the kind, I believe that labour relations and inflation in Britain would not be in such a disastrous state.

Meanwhile, the rate of inflation continues to rise, in the sense that the pressure on union negotiators to start at a higher figure than last year's, and the probability that this will apply to settlements also, is very strong. The most recent example of the inability of the TUC to keep to its side of a negotiated agreement is also the most dramatic. This agreement, directly reached as if it were a treaty between two independent powers, is in the form of a joint statement called 'The Economy, the Government and Trade Union Responsibilities' published (not as a White Paper) by the (official) Stationery Office in February 1979. This came at the end of three years in which an agreed incomes policy had had some success – the rate of inflation had fallen from about 24 per cent in 1975 to about eight per cent in 1977. The statement pointed to this success and discussed the next stage, in terms which would have been broadly acceptable to any government during the period covered by this paper (except that eight per cent would not have been thought anything to boast about in the earlier years). It spoke, in terms by this time all too familiar, of the need to increase productivity and adaptability: the need to avoid strikes except as a last resort: and to bring the rate of inflation to an annual rate of five per cent and hold it there. Perhaps the gem is the following sentence: 'The TUC, which is as committed to reducing inflation as to any other of the policies adopted by Congress, recognise with the Government the danger that could be caused by the escalation of pay settlements'.

The ink was hardly dry on this unexceptionable document when the Trade Union Congress passed a resolution against incomes policy and in favour of a return to 'free collective bargaining'. Meanwhile a series of strikes, really against the Government's pay policy, were going on. The Government was defeated in the general election in May, partly because of the irritation with the unions because of the disruption caused by strikes. The new Government, which inherited a round of wage increases of the order of 20 per cent, is committed to monetary policy and as this begins to bite, the forecasts are for unemployment to rise to figures comparable to all but the worst years of the Great Depression. So much for full employment.

8 A Comparative Analysis of Stagflation in France and Germany, 1971–9

J. MARCZEWSKI

The purpose of this chapter is to show, by using data on France and Germany in the 1970s, how to apply a quantitative method for examining the causes of stagflation.

THE INFLATIONARY GAP OF TOTAL RESOURCES

A modern economy can be defined as a set of agents who trade goods and services among themselves for money. When considered over a period of time, for example a year, these exchanges form flows: 'real' flows composed of goods and services, and 'monetary' flows composed of money in the broadest sense of the word. These flows follow the circuit in opposite directions. The rates of the two types of flows are not constant, and they vary differently over time. There is inflation when the rate of increase of monetary flows is greater than that of real flows. A converse situation is known as deflation (Marczewski, 1978a, p. 1).

This can be expressed by the formula:

$$\Delta M - \Delta R > 0 \quad \text{for inflation and}$$
$$\Delta M - \Delta R < 0 \quad \text{for deflation,}$$

where ΔM and ΔR represent respectively the increase in monetary and real flows.

Recent economic events demonstrate that the increase in monetary flows can be accompanied by a slowdown or even a decrease in real flows. Thus we have to consider a third variable: the rate of growth of real flows, *r*. Accordingly there are four possible types of economic development:

	$\Delta M - \Delta R > 0$ *Inflation*	$\Delta M - \Delta R < 0$ *Deflation*
$\Delta r > 0$	Inflationary growth (IG)	Deflationary Growth (DG)
$\Delta r < 0$	Stagflation (S)	Recession (R)

The difference $\Delta M - \Delta R$, that is the difference between the 'nominal' growth of the aggregate considered and its 'real' growth calculated on the basis of data at prices of the preceding year, constitutes what is generally known as the inflationary (or deflationary) gap. This gap can be calculated for any aggregate or item in the national accounts. For studying inflation on the national level the most appropriate concept available is the Inflationary Gap of Total Resources. The latter represent the sum of GDP and Imports and therefore include all transactions carried out within the national economy (Marczewski, 1978b, p. 285). The inflationary gap can then be expressed either in absolute terms at current prices or as a percentage of total resources. Table 8.1 (lines 1.1 and 1.2) shows the results of such a calculation for the years 1971 to 1979 in France and Germany.

The information which can be derived from a statistical series of total inflationary gaps (TIG), expressed as a percentage of total resources, basically does not differ from that given by a general price index (Table 8.1, lines 2.1 and 2.2). In addition, there is – as one should expect – a close correlation between these two indicators (0.97 for France and 0.87 for Germany). As Table 8.1 shows, inflation fluctuated in both countries in the same direction for all the years considered without any exception. But, since 1972, the French inflation has been increasingly stronger than the German one (Table 8.1, line 1.3). This explains why the coefficient of correlation between the inflationary gaps in France and Germany is rather weak (0.37).

A comparison of the inflationary gap with the real growth rate also shows a remarkable similarity of economic evolution in both

TABLE 8.1 *Total inflationary gap and GDP growth rates in France and Germany 1971–9*

	1971	1972	1973	1974	1975	1976	1977	1978	1979	Average 1971–9
(1) Total inflationary gap as a percentage of total resources										
1.1 France	5.3	4.9	7.1	14.0	10.0	9.2	8.6	7.8	9.4	8.5
1.2 Germany	6.2	4.6	6.2	8.4	5.3	3.4	3.2	2.6	4.3	4.9
1.3 Ratio $\frac{1.1}{1.2}$	0.9	1.1	1.1	1.7	1.9	2.7	2.7	3.0	2.2	1.7
(2) Growth rates of GDP in prices of the preceding year (%)										
2.1 France	5.3	5.8	5.4	2.8	0.3	4.9	2.9	3.3	3.2	3.7
2.2 Germany	3.3	3.6	4.9	0.4	−1.8	5.3	2.6	3.5	4.4	2.9
(3) Consumer price index (%)										
3.1 France	5.5	5.9	7.3	13.7	11.7	9.6	9.4	9.1	10.8	9.2
3.2 Germany	5.4	5.6	7.1	7.0	6.2	4.5	3.8	2.6	4.1	5.1
(4) Types of economic development										
4.1 France	S	DG	S	S	R	DG	R	DG	S	
4.2 Germany	S	DG	IG	S	R	DG	R	DG	IG	

DG = Deflationary growth; IG = Inflationary growth; S = Stagflation; R = Recession.
SOURCES Computed from INSEE, 1977 and 1979, vol. 3. p. 6 and SB, 1978 vol. 1, pp. 124, 134, 143, 166, 1979, vol. 1., pp. 9, 17, 10.

countries (Table 8.1, lines 4.1 and 4.2). There are however two exceptions: in 1973 and 1979 stagflation in France coincides with inflationary growth in Germany. On the other hand, till 1976, the rate of real growth was notably higher in France than in Germany (3.9 per cent and 2.3 per cent). But this latter advantage for France has disappeared during the years 1976–9 (France 3.6; Germany 4.).

However, the specific utility of TIG as an instrument for studying inflation appears really when an economic historian or an economic politician endeavours to find out the causes of a given inflationary process. Indeed, TIG is not a pure number. It is a cardinal magnitude which can be broken down in several ways in order to show the contribution of specific economic agents and transactions to a divergent evolution of real and monetary flows.

THE BREAKDOWN OF TIG

The aggregate Total Resources may be considered alternatively as the sum of production costs (gross factor incomes, indirect taxes less subsidies, imports) or as the total value of goods and services sold for a final use (private and public consumption, capital formation and exports). Each of these subaggregates can in turn be divided according to the nature, origin or destination of the flows it is composed of. A partial inflationary gap can then be calculated for each of these subdivisions in order to determine the operations which have contributed significantly to the creation of the gap and the agents who may be considered as directly responsible for them. It would of course be desirable to pursue further the analysis by examining the causal relationship and actual motivations of the agents concerned. But this goes beyond the scope of the present paper.

THE INFLATIONARY GAP OF COSTS

Table 8.2 shows the structure and the evolution of the inflationary gap of costs in France and Germany, 1971–9. The structure of the gap is in both countries almost identical.

TABLE 8.2 *Structure and evolution of the inflationary gap of costs in France and Germany, 1971–9 (as a percentage of total inflationary gap)*

	1971	1972	1973	1974	1975	1976	1977	1978	1979	1971–9 Average
(1) Wages and social insurance costs										
1.1 France	56.4	47.2	52.9	42.2	67.0	46.8	49.5	49.4	42.0	50.4
1.2 Germany	61.9	56.6	56.9	47.6	48.7	24.5	57.1	51.9	23.3	48.1
(2) Households net income from property and entrepreneurship										
2.1 France	18.8	23.1	10.3	8.0	18.0	10.2	15.2	19.0	16.1	15.4
2.2 Germany	14.8	0.7	3.7	6.2	26.3	19.6	28.4	12.0	n.a	14.0
(3) Net undistributed income of enterprise										
3.1 France	−3.0	6.4	4.6	−5.0	−7.9	−2.7	8.3	3.7	6.7	1.2
3.2 Germany	−4.7	19.1	3.2	−4.9	0.6	20.8	−12.1	23.3	n.a	5.7
(4) Government net income from property and entrepreneurship										
4.1 France	1.9	1.1	1.2	0.3	−3.0	−0.1	−1.3	−1.5	−2.3	−0.4
4.2 Germany	−0.7	−3.7	0.5	−2.0	−4.6	−5.1	−5.6	2.0	−0.7	−2.2

TABLE 8.2 *Continued*

	1971	*1972*	*1973*	*1974*	*1975*	*1976*	*1977*	*1978*	*1979*	*Average 1971–9*
(5) Taxes on production less subsidies										
5.1 France	13.4	15.0	9.0	4.6	7.9	12.7	3.1	14.9	13.2	10.4
5.2 Germany	16.0	18.2	6.8	7.6	17.6	5.1	14.0	15.0	11.4	12.4
(6) Capital consumption										
6.1 France	8.9	9.5	8.8	10.4	14.5	17.4	4.7	10.2	8.0	10.3
6.2 Germany	9.1	5.6	5.8	6.4	8.5	8.6	8.7	12.7	9.8	8.4
(7) Imports										
7.1 France	8.9	−4.2	13.5	39.0	1.7	17.3	20.7	3.8	17.5	13.1
7.2 Germany	3.6	3.5	23.1	39.2	2.9	26.5	9.5	−16.9	35.3	14.1
(8) Net factor income and taxes payed to the rest of the world										
(France)	−5.3	1.9	−0.3	0.5	1.8	−1.6	−0.2	0.5	−1.2	−0.4
Total resources	100%	100%	100%	100%	100%	100%	100%	100%	100%	

SOURCES Computed from INSEE, 1977 and 1979, vol. 3, pp. 6,8,10,12 and SB, 1978, vol. 1, pp. 122, 143, 145 and 1979 vol. 1, pp. 17 and 64.

1. Labour costs

The increase on labour costs per unit produced represents in both countries about a half of TIG. It is however slightly higher in France (50.4 per cent) than in Germany (48.1 per cent). The contribution of labour costs to TIG varies in both countries in the same direction for all the years considered without any exception. However the coefficient of correlation between these two series (0.41) is weak as in the case of the correlation between the total TIGs of France and Germany. Increases in the labour costs contribution coincide generally with higher TIGs. This means that labour costs per unit produced rise faster than prices. Conversely, decreases in the contribution of labour costs lead to a slowdown of inflation. The exceptional years when this relationship does not work (1974 and 1979) are marked by a particularly strong intervention of another factor of inflation: the cost of imports caused by the massive raise in oil prices. It has reduced the relative contribution of labour costs to TIG despite the continued and rapid raise in wages.

It must not be forgotten however, that the German TIG, expressed as a percentage of total resources, is much smaller than the French one (Table 8.1, line 1.3). Consequently, in order to compare in absolute terms the inflationary impact of a given cost raise in both countries it is necessary to divide the German figures by the ratio of the two TIGs (Table 8.1, line 1.3) for the respective year (Table 8.3). It appears then that the inflationary impact of labour costs is, on the average, weaker in Germany than in France by 37 per cent. The difference was particularly important during the last four years when the German inflationary gap of labour costs fell below 32 per cent of the French one. It is probably worth stressing that for the same period the German economic growth overtook the economic growth of France (Table 8.1, lines 2.1 and 2.2).

Table 8.4 confirms that the rate of growth of nominal labour costs per unit produced is on the average 2.5 times higher in France than in Germany. For the last four years this ratio reached 3.7. We must admit therefore that, in both countries, there is a close relationship between the rate of increase in nominal wages per unit produced and the rate of inflation. In fact, the coefficient of correlation between TIG, expressed as a percentage of total resources (Table 8.1, lines 1.1 and 1.2) and the rate of growth in

TABLE 8.3 *Inflationary gaps of German labour and import costs as a percentage of the corresponding French data*

	1971	*1972*	*1973*	*1974*	*1975*	*1976*	*1977*	*1978*	*1979*	*Average 1971–9*
(1) Wages and social insurance costs										
1.1 as a percentage of French TIG	72.8	53.4	49.5	28.5	25.8	9.0	21.2	17.3	12.5	32.2
1.2 as a percentage of French labour costs inflationary gap	129.1	113.1	93.5	67.5	38.5	19.3	42.9	33.3	29.8	63.0
(2) Imports										
2.1 as a percentage of French TIG	4.2	3.3	20.1	23.5	1.5	9.8	3.5	−5.6	16.2	8.5
2.2 as a percentage of French import costs inflationary gap	47.6	−79.0	148.8	60.2	90.3	56.5	17.1	−148.2	92.5	31.8

SOURCES Table 8.1 and 8.2.

TABLE 8.4 *Increase in nominal labour costs per unit produced in France and Germany, 1971–9 (annual growth rates, per cent)*

	1971	*1972*	*1973*	*1974*	*1975*	*1976*	*1977*	*1978*	*1979*	*Average 1971–9*
(1) Wages and social security costs total										
1.1 France	13.1	11.9	15.5	19.2	17.6	16.0	13.5	12.8	13.1	14.7
1.2 Germany	13.0	9.9	13.5	10.0	4.0	7.3	6.9	6.7	7.2	8.7
(2) Wages and social security costs per unit of GDP										
2.1 France	7.4	5.8	9.5	15.9	17.2	10.5	10.3	9.1	9.5	10.6
2.2 Germany	9.3	6.1	8.1	9.5	5.9	1.8	4.1	3.0	2.6	5.6
(3) Ratio $\frac{2.1}{2.2}$	0.8	1.0	1.2	1.7	2.9	5.8	2.5	3.0	3.7	2.5

SOURCES Computed from INSEE, 1977 and 1979, vol. 3, pp. 6 and 11 and SB, 1978, vol. 1, pp. 139, 141 and 1979, vol. 1, p. 58.

TABLE 8.5 *Real wage growth in France and Germany, 1971–9 (annual rate, per cent)*

	1971	1972	1973	1974	1975	1976	1977	1978	1979	Average 1971–9
(1) Nominal income of wages earners										
1.1 France	13.1	11.9	15.5	19.2	17.6	16.0	13.5	12.8	13.1	14.7
1.2 Germany	13.0	9.9	13.5	10.0	4.0	7.3	6.9	6.7	7.2	8.7
(2) Employment										
2.1 France	1.4	1.6	2.2	1.5	−0.8	1.2	1.2	0.6	0.6	1.1
2.2 Germany	0.4	0.5	0.6	−0.2	−3.5	0.0	0.3	1.2	1.8	0.1
(3) Nominal income of wage earners per capita										
3.1 France	11.5	10.1	13.0	17.7	18.5	14.6	12.2	12.1	13.0	13.6
3.2 Germany	12.6	9.4	12.8	12.0	10.8	7.8	6.7	5.4	5.5	9.2

(4) Real income of wage earners										
4.1 France	5.7	4.0	5.3	3.5	6.1	4.6	2.5	2.8	2.0	4.1
4.2 Germany	6.8	3.6	5.3	4.7	4.3	3.2	2.7	2.8	1.1	3.8
4.3 Ratio 4.1/4.2	0.8	1.1	1.0	0.7	1.4	1.4	0.9	1.0	1.8	1.1
(5) Growth of real GDP per capita										
5.1 France	4.4	4.9	4.6	2.2	0.2	4.5	2.5	2.9	2.8	3.2
5.2 Germany	3.1	3.6	4.8	0.4	−1.5	5.7	3.0	3.2	4.4	3.0
5.3 Difference 4–5										
France	1.3	−0.9	0.7	1.3	5.9	0.1	0.0	−0.1	−0.8	0.9
Germany	3.7	0.0	0.5	4.3	5.8	−2.5	−0.3	−0.4	−3.3	−0.8

SOURCES Computed from INSEE, 1977 and 1979, vol. 3, pp. 6, 11, 62, 63, 201 and 202 and SB 1978, vol. 1, pp. 201, 252 and 284, and 1979, vol. 1, pp. 94, 65, 12, 87 and 284.

nominal wages per unit produced (Table 8.4, lines 2.1 and 2.2) is significant as well for France (0.84) as for Germany (0.88).

It might be objected however that the relative moderation of nominal wage growth in Germany is not a cause but rather a consequence of the slower price rise in this country. It is quite true that wages at time interval t_1 result from collective bargaining performed at t_0 where trade unions and employers have been considering expected prices and wages for future time intervals $t_2, t_3, \ldots t_n$, derived from the past evolution of prices and wages at $t_{-1}, t_{-2}, \ldots t_{-n}$.

But, once the wage rate is fixed by a common agreement, it remains unchanged for some time and, in conjunction with other independent variables, determines the conditions of demand and supply and therefore prices, at least to the extent to which the latter are not fixed exogenously. A less or more moderate attitude of trade unions in wage bargaining is therefore a decisive factor in the determination of the total inflationary gap.

Moreover, the relative moderation of the German trade unions in nominal wage bargaining did not deprive their members of a substantial improvement in their standard of living (Table 8.5). Even if the real wage rate growth appears to be slightly slower than in France (line 4.3), it has been achieved, contrary to the French case, without any deterioration in other fundamental aspects of the country's economic growth, such as the balance of trade, the financial capacity of enterprises to invest, and consequently, the employment rate and future well-being of workers.

The French balance of trade (Trade 8.6) represents on the average 0.1 per cent of GDP. It was negative in 1974, 1976 and 1979. The German balance equals 2.6 per cent of GDP and remains positive during the whole period. Given that, in both countries, the structure of exports and imports is broadly similar, and that they have been submitted to the same external shocks (massive oil price raises in 1974 and 1979) and constraints (slowing down of world trade after 1973), the explanation of such a considerable difference must be looked for in their internal evolution. The steady increase in the labour-cost ratio between France and Germany (Table 8.4, line 3), which was not always compensated immediately by a corresponding change in the ratio of exchange rates (Table 8.7 lines 2 and 3) – as a consequence of conventional monetary links between the franc and the mark (the European 'snake' and the EMS) – explains the relative weakness of the French performance in

TABLE 8.6 *Balance of trade, France and Germany, 1971–9 (as a percentage of GDP at current prices)*

	1971	*1972*	*1973*	*1974*	*1975*	*1976*	*1977*	*1978*	*1979*	*Average 1971–9*
France	0.9	0.8	0.6	−1.5	0.7	−1.1	−0.3	0.7	−0.1	0.1
Germany	2.1	2.2	3.2	4.4	2.8	2.5	2.5	2.9	0.9	2.6

SOURCES Computed from INSEE, 1977 and 1979, vol. 3, pp. 164–7 and SB 1978, vol. 1, pp. 10, 13, 124, 143, and 1979, pp. 12, 17.

TABLE 8.7 *Exchange rates and labour costs indices in France and Germany, 1973–9*

	1973	*1974*	*1975*	*1976*	*1977*	*1978*	*1979*
(1) Total inflationary-gap index $\frac{\text{France}}{\text{Germany}}$ (1970 = 1)	1.00	1.05	1.10	1.16	1.22	1.28	1.34
(2) Labour costs per unit produced index $\frac{\text{France}}{\text{Germany}}$ (1970 = 1)	1.05	1.11	1.23	1.34	1.42	1.50	1.60
(3) Exchange-rate index $\frac{\text{DM}}{\text{FF}}$ (31.12.69 = 1)	1.16	1.21	1.12	1.38	1.47	1.51	1.54
(4) Exchange-rate index $\frac{\text{DM}}{\text{SI}}$ (31.12.69 = 1)	1.16	1.23	1.19	1.34	1.40	1.46	1.54
(5) Exchange-rate index $\frac{\text{FF}}{\text{SI}}$ (31.12.69 = 1)	1.00	1.01	1.07	0.97	0.95	0.97	1.00
(6) Exchange-rate index $\frac{\$}{\text{SI}}$ (31.12.69 = 1)	0.85	0.81	0.86	0.87	0.81	0.73	0.73
(7) Balance of trade France–Germany (annual change in billion of Francs)	−0.30	−4.30	−4.30	4.50	−6.60	2.40	0.50

SI = synthetic index of 11 most important currencies weighted by the contribution of respective countries in world trade in manufactured goods.
SOURCES Line 1: Table 8.1; Line 2: Table 8.4; Lines 3 to 6: computed from INSEE, 1976 and 1979, vol. 2, p. 23; Line 7: INSEE, 1979, vol. 3, p. 172.

balancing foreign trade. On the other hand, the moderate progression of its labour costs enabled Germany to raise progressively the exchange rate of the mark against all currencies with the single exception of the Swiss franc (Table 8.7, line 4). In this way, Germany managed to reduce considerably the pressure of world inflation on its domestic market (Table 8.3, line 2.2) and in particular to lighten the impact of massive increases in prices of oil and other raw materials in 1974 and 1979.

2. Income from property and entrepreneurship

In both countries, the growth of real wages during the first years of the period was noticeably higher than the growth of real GDP per capita (Table 8.5, line 5.3). However, this situation was reversed in Germany after 1975, whereas in France this change occurred only after 1978. In both countries the improvement of the relative position of wage earners was made up by a deterioration in the share of income from property and entrepreneurship, and especially of undistributed profits of enterprise. This evolution was particularly marked in France where a tremendous rise in labour and imports costs coincided with the impossibility of a proportional rise in prices constrained as they were by foreign competition or government regulation. The inflationary gap of net undistributed income became negative in 1971, 1974, 1975 and 1976 (Table 8.2, line 3.1). In other words, undistributed profits grew more slowly than prices, that is declined in real value. The decline was particularly deep and durable in the French non-financial corporations, while in Germany such enterprises were affected only for one year, that is 1975 (Table 8.8). This evolution had an important bearing on the propensity to invest in both countries.

3. Taxes on production less subsidies

The inflationary impact of this cost is on the average relatively higher in Germany than in France (Table 8.2, lines 5.1 and 5.2) but as the French TIG is larger, its absolute burden on production is lower in Germany than in France. In both countries, the changes in the inflationary gap of net taxes are, to some extent, inversely correlated to TIG, the relative burden of net taxes showing a tendency to be reduced during the years of strongest inflation.

TABLE 8.8 *Change in the real value of non-financial corporations' undistributed income at prices of the preceding year, France and Germany, 1973–9 (in millions of FF or DM)*

	1973	*1974*	*1975*	*1976*	*1977*	*1978*	*1979*
Net undistributed income of non-financial corporations							
1. France	1030	−18266	−14	−587	−757	−569	253
2. Germany	607	246	−69	217	518	407	n.a.

SOURCES Computed from INSEE, 1977, 1979, vol. 3. pp. 6, 10, 62–3 and 86–7 and SB, 1979, vol. 1, pp. 63–4.

4. Imports

In both countries, imports become an important factor of inflation only in the years of a massive rise in prices of imported oil and other raw materials (1973, 1974 and 1979). While the growth rate of imports in real terms is on the average faster in France (8 per cent) than in Germany (6.5 per cent), their apparent inflationary impact on production costs is relatively stronger in Germany (Table 8.2, lines 7.1 and 7.2). This is simply due to the fact that domestic costs rise faster in France. In absolute terms, the inflationary pressure of imports is less than half as strong in Germany (Table 8.3, line 2.2). The continuous appreciation of the mark (Table 8.7, lines 3 and 4) which reduces imports costs for German enterprises, plays a major part in this evolution. On the other hand, the moderate rise in living costs enables German workers to accept moderate nominal wage increases which explain the continuous appreciation of the mark. It is what is commonly called the 'virtuous circle' of the German economy.

THE INFLATIONARY GAP OF EXPENDITURES

Considered as the total value of final goods, Total Resources can be defined as the sum of expenditures accomplished by the final users of these goods (households, enterprises, government and the rest of the world). TIG can then be decomposed into partial inflationary gaps of households' consumption and capital formation, enterprise fixed capital formation and the change in inventories, government consumption and capital formation, and exports.

Table 8.9 shows the structure and the evolution of the inflationary gap of expenditures in France and Germany, 1971–9. The general structure of the gap in both countries is similar, but in Germany the contributions of government spending and exports are relatively larger, while in the case of France, the shares of households' consumption and enterprises' capital formation are predominant.

1. Households' Consumption and Capital Formation

Except for two years (1976 and 1978) the household consumption inflationary gap varies in both countries in the same direction. The

TABLE 8.9 *Structure and evolution of the inflationary gap in expenditures, France and Germany, 1970–9 (as a percentage of the total inflationary gap)*

	1971	*1972*	*1973*	*1974*	*1975*	*1976*	*1977*	*1978*	*1979*	*Average 1971–9*
(1) *Households*										
1. Consumption										
1.1 France	53.1	60.5	46.4	42.5	54.0	50.3	50.2	53.9	52.4	51.5
1.2 Germany	37.5	52.3	48.0	32.9	51.0	47.6	51.3	44.0	38.1	44.7
2. Fixed capital formation										
2.2 France	4.1	6.0	7.0	5.6	5.1	6.3	4.9	5.3	5.5	5.5
2.3 Germany	11.8	20.7	8.1	1.4	−3.5	3.3	2.9	7.9	6.8	6.6
(2) *Enterprises*										
3. Fixed capital formation										
3.1 France	10.9	11.5	10.6	11.4	9.5	12.4	10.9	9.4	9.1	10.6
3.2 Germany	9.6	−5.5	5.4	8.7	13.2	8.0	10.9	15.8	13.3	8.8

4. Change in Inventories										
4.1 France	−0.2	1.7	2.4	2.5	3.9	0.9	0.5	0.6	1.4	1.5
4.2 Germany	−0.1	0.7	−0.9	0.3	−0.1	6.8	−2.2	0.6	1.4	0.7
(3) *Government*										
5. Consumption										
5.1 France	16.2	16.0	14.7	11.9	15.7	13.1	15.0	15.7	12.6	14.5
5.2 Germany	25.4	19.6	21.6	19.4	19.1	13.6	23.1	19.4	16.0	19.7
6. Capital formation										
6.1 France	3.8	2.9	4.0	2.9	3.1	3.2	2.3	2.5	2.5	3.0
6.2 Germany	4.7	2.4	2.2	2.6	1.3	1.7	2.7	4.6	3.9	2.9
(4) *Rest of the world*										
7. Exports										
7.1 France	12.1	1.4	14.9	23.2	8.7	13.8	16.2	12.6	16.5	13.3
7.2 Germany	11.1	9.8	15.6	34.7	19.0	19.0	11.3	7.7	20.5	16.5
Total inflationary gap	100.0	100.0	100.0	100.0	100.0	100.0	100.0	100.0	100.0	

SOURCES Computed from INSEE, 1977 and 1979, vol. 3, p. 6 and SB, 1978, vol. 1, pp. 201, 252 and 284, and 1979, pp. 65, 94 and 120.

coefficient of correlation between the two series is positive and significant (0.50) as it is for wages (Table 8.2, lines 1.1 and 1.2) although consumer prices movements (Table 8.4, lines 3.1 and 3.2) are not correlated at all ($r = 0.08$). In both countries, the inflationary gap of consumption is on the average approximately equal to the inflationary gap of wages. But in France the gap of consumption is slightly larger than the gap of wages, while in Germany this relationship is exactly the inverse. This is probably due to the fact that the proportion of wage earners in the total population is in France slightly lower (34 per cent) than in Germany (36 per cent) and perhaps also because German workers have a higher propensity to save.

There is no significant correlation between the inflationary gaps of consumption and wages either in France (0.25), or in Germany (0.14). As the most dynamic factor of inflation, the inflationary gap of wages varies generally in the same direction as TIG. On the other hand, consumption is the most stable item of expenditures and therefore its share in TIG varies mostly in the opposite direction.

The inflationary gaps of household capital formation which represents the construction of dwellings, vary also in both countries in the same direction. The only exception is the year 1973 when a slight increase in France coincides with a deep decrease in Germany. There is however no correlation between the two series (0.10).

2. Enterprises' Capital Formation

The real growth rates of fixed capital formation by enterprises are on the average almost identical in both countries: France, 2.4 per cent, Germany 2.5 per cent. But in France, a very rapid growth in the years 1971–3 (6.2 per cent) was followed by a marked slowdown in the years 1974–9 (0.5 per cent on the average) due to the negative development of non-financial-enterprise profits (Table 8.8). On the contrary, in Germany, the deep slowdown in the years 1974 and 1975 was succeeded immediately by an extremely rapid growth (6.8 per cent on the average) which corresponds to the rapid restoration of profits (Table 8.8). As to the inflationary gap, it is larger in France than in Germany. This is due to the combination of slower real growth of investment with faster rise in prices. Nevertheless, the two series are correlated (0.61). On the other hand, there is no correlation whatsoever between the inflationary gaps of inventories change. Their relative value corresponds roughly, on the average, to the ratio between price rises in both countries.

3. Public Expenditures

Surprisingly enough there is a correlation (0.59) between the inflationary gaps of public consumption in France and Germany. This correlation is higher than that between the two TIGs or labour-cost inflationary gaps. The German share of public consumption is however much larger than the French one. Public consumption contributes relatively more to inflation in Germany than in France, but in absolute terms its inflationary impact represents on the average only 80 per cent of the French one, although the real growth of this item is faster in Germany (3.8 per cent) than in France (3.3 per cent).

Conversely, while the relative shares of public capital formation in TIG are almost identical in both countries there is no significant correlation between them. This is quite understandable given the exogenous character of this variable in relation to most other economic magnitudes considered here. The real growth of the public capital formation in Germany is more than twice as fast as in France (0.89 vs. 0.38).

4. Exports

The inflationary gaps of exports in both countries are correlated ($r = 0.66$). Similarly to imports, the French exports rise faster in real terms (8.7 per cent on the average) than German exports (6.1), but their contribution to TIG is lower than in Germany. It means that contrary to other factors, foreign trade exerts relatively less inflationary pressure on France. This is understandable since domestic factors of inflation, and first of all labour costs, are much stronger in France. In absolute terms however, given the relationship between the respective TIGs (Table 8.1, line 1.3), the inflationary impact of exports on domestic economy is weaker in Germany than in France.

THE CAUSES OF STAGFLATION

As we have shown previously (Marczewski, 1978b, p. 291 and 1978c, p. 18), the transmission of inflationary pressures is accomplished through a variety of circuits. An inflationary circuit is created whenever a gap generated by the rise in a cost or an expenditure is passed on to other costs or expenditures, forming an inflationary flow. After having contributed to a certain number of transactions, the gap returns to the starting point and the process begins all over. The four most important circuits are: 'wages – households' consumption', 'incomes from property and entrepreneurship – private capital formation', 'taxes on production (less subsidies) – public expenditure', 'import costs – exports'.

It happens however that an inflationary flow created by a rise in a cost or in an expenditure does not come back to its starting point. For instance, an increase in wages instead of being spent on consumption of goods produced by the firm which bears the burden of rising labour costs is hoarded or diverted towards other home-produced or imported goods. Or an increase in import costs is not followed by an equal rise in exports. Or an expenditure on investment does not bring to the investors concerned any rise in profits. In all these cases, the inflationary circuit is interrupted. The firm or the nation which has financed the initial inflationary gap is compelled, after some time, either to reduce its activity or to replace the factors which have become too expensive by other means of production. This is the most common source of what is called now 'stagflation', that is inflation combined with a slow down of production and unemployment.

It may also happen that an inflationary circuit originated by an autonomous increase in demand (for instance a rise in propensity to consume or in government spending financed by Central Bank credit) is not followed by an equal increase in costs (wages, interests, rents or profits). Two extreme cases are then possible. Either the production system is perfectly elastic and then demand inflation is converted in what is known in Germany as a *Mengenkonjunktur* (Marczewski, 1941, p. 76) that is, a non-inflationary rise in supply. Or production is not elastic and the inflationary gap of demand takes the form of idle balances which cannot be spent on desired goods. This last case is very common in Eastern Europe and the USSR. All kinds of intermediate situations are also possible. The most usual is that in which there is at the same time a rise in production and in costs which may or may not be accompanied by an increase in liquidity. This is what we have called 'inflationary growth'. Conversely, there is 'deflationary growth' when a decrease in TIG is realised with a simultaneous increase in production. It implies a decreasing rate of cost inflation with an increasing demand and elastic production. Finally, there is a recession when a decreasing inflationary gap of costs coincides with a decreasing gap of demand and consequently with a slowdown of production.

In order to apply the preceding theory to the example of France and Germany in the period 1971–9, it is necessary to determine exactly the statistical content of the magnitudes to be compared. If we consider, as a first approximation, the productive system of a nation as a single unit comprising enterprises and government, then its relations with the outside world are reduced to buying labour services from, and selling consumption goods to households on one hand, and to buying imports from, and selling exports to the rest of the world on the other. All other transactions such as domestic investment, taxes, government spending, etc, are internal to the production system and do not have to be taken into account either as costs or as demands. The magnitudes to be compared are then: on the costs side, the inflationary gaps of wages and social security payments and imports; on the demand side, household consumption and exports. In a more refined calculation it would perhaps be correct to add to the costs the inflationary gap of businesses' interest and rent payments to households, but the amount concerned is small and does not vary very much from year to year.

As Table 8.10 shows, the comparison of costs and demands facing the French and the German productive systems seems to confirm, in 12 cases out of a total of 18 observations, our main hypothesis on the causes of stagflation. Stagflation appears whenever there is a simultaneous increase in costs ($\Delta C > 0$) and a decrease in the value of the difference between demands and costs ($D - C < 0$). The other combinations observed are:

$\Delta C > 0$	with	$D - C > 0$	: inflationary growth
$\Delta C < 0$	with	$D - C > 0$	: deflationary growth
$\Delta C < 0$	with	$D - C < 0$	: recession.

Of course the validity of this hypothesis implies a high demand elasticity of production. If this condition is not fulfilled, the excess of

Table 8.10 *Tentative explanation of the successive types of development in France and Germany, 1971–9 (as a percentage of corresponding TIGs)*

	1971	*1972*	*1973*	*1974*	*1975*	*1976*	*1977*	*1978*	*1979*
I FRANCE									
Demand									
Households' consumption	53.1	60.5	46.4	42.5	54.0	50.3	50.2	53.9	52.4
Exports	12.	1.4	14.9	23.2	8.7	13.8	16.2	12.6	16.5
Total D	65.2	61.9	61.3	65.7	62.7	64.1	66.4	65.5	68.9
Costs									
Wages and social security costs	56.4	47.2	52.9	42.2	67.0	46.8	49.5	49.4	42.0
Imports	8.9	−4.2	13.0	39.0	1.7	17.3	20.7	3.8	17.5
Total C	65.3	43.0	65.9	81.2	68.7	64.1	70.2	53.2	59.5
D−C	−0.1	18.9	−4.6	−15.5	−6.0	0.0	−3.8	12.3	8.4
Expected type of development	S	DG	S	S	R	DG	S	DG	IG
Effective type of development	S	DG	S	S	R	DG	R	DG	S

Table 8.10 *Continued*

	1971	*1972*	*1973*	*1974*	*1975*	*1976*	*1977*	*1978*	*1979*
II GERMANY									
Demand									
Households' consumption	37.5	52.3	48.0	32.9	51.0	47.6	51.3	44.0	38.1
Exports	11.1	9.8	15.6	34.7	19.0	19.0	11.3	7.7	20.5
Total D	48.6	62.1	63.6	67.6	70.0	66.6	62.6	51.7	58.6
Costs									
Wages and social security costs	61.9	56.6	56.9	47.6	48.7	24.5	57.1	51.9	27.3
Imports	3.6	3.5	23.1	39.2	2.9	26.5	9.5	−16.9	35.3
Total C	65.5	60.1	80.0	86.8	51.6	51.0	66.6	35.0	62.6
D − C	−16.9	2.0	−16.4	−19.2	18.4	15.6	−4.0	14.7	−4.0
Expected type of development	S	DG	S	S	DG	DG	S	DG	S
Effective type of development	S	DG	IG	S	R	DG	R	DG	IG

Sources Tables 8.2 and 8.9.

demand over costs ($D-C>0$) may not be able to trigger off an acceleration of GDP growth. The combination $\Delta C>0$ with $D-C>0$ will then result in stagflation instead of the inflationary growth. This is probably what has happened in France in 1979 as a consequence of a long period of declining profits (Table 8.8), lagging investments, and a particularly restrictive monetary policy (Table 8.11, line 1.3). It is also possible that the rate of real growth of GDP has been underestimated in the provisional national accounts for 1979.

The case of Germany in 1973 and 1979 is exactly opposite to that of France in 1979. With $C>0$ and $D-C<0$ there should have been stagflation. In fact there was inflationary growth based essentially on a strong rise in enterprises fixed capital formation and inventories accumulation, which were facilitated by a relatively liberal monetary policy (Table 8.11, line 2.3).

The exceptional cases of France and Germany in 1977 are very similar. The indicator $D-C$ is negative as it should be when the rate of growth is declining. But ΔC is positive, indicating a stagflation instead of a recession. Why did the accelerated increase in costs not bring an acceleration of inflation? Probably because the rise in demand was not strong enough in order to cover a sharp increase in costs. Prices lagged behind production costs which is particularly visible on Table 8.8 for France and Table 8.2, line 3.2 for Germany. Instead of inflating prices, the inflationary pressure compressed the quantities produced.

The same may have happened in Germany, in 1975. A particularly strong increase in the inflationary gap of demand was much more due to the decline in quantities sold than to the increase in prices, and the fall in sales was caused by the tremendous rise in costs in 1974. In any case further study is necessary in order to improve the indicators expressing the relationship between costs and demands.

We are trying now to extend the methodology described above to the analysis of world stagflation. It is obvious that massive oil price increases contribute to a rise of costs in all oil importing countries. To the extent that many of the latter (first of all the LDCs, and more generally the countries which do not master their domestic inflation) are unable to increase in the same proportion their exports, this increase in costs produces a stagflationary effect on their economy. Moreover some oil-exporting countries (Saudi Arabia, United Arab Emirates) are not able to increase their

TABLE 8.11 *Money supply (M_2) and total resources at current prices in France and Germany, 1971–9 (annual rates of growth, per cent)*

	1971	*1972*	*1973*	*1974*	*1975*	*1976*	*1977*	*1978*	*1979*
1. France									
1.1 Money supply (M_2)	17.9	18.5	14.5	16.0	16.5	17.3	12.3	13.2	13.4
1.2 Total resources	11.5	12.7	14.9	20.0	9.8	17.9	12.3	12.4	15.4
1.3 Ratio $\frac{1.1}{1.2}$	5.7	5.1	−0.3	−3.3	6.1	−0.5	0.0	0.7	−1.7
2. Germany									
2.1 Money supply (M_2)	11.5	12.5	13.6	14.7	13.6	15.5	12.1	13.5	13.9
2.2 Total resources	11.0	9.2	11.5	10.2	4.8	10.2	6.4	6.7	10.3
2.3 Ratio $\frac{2.1}{2.2}$	0.3	3.0	1.9	4.1	8.4	4.8	5.4	6.4	3.3

SOURCES France: Conseil National du Crédit, p. 138 and INSEE, 1977 and 1979, p. 6; Germany: OECD, p. 41 and SB, 1978, pp. 134 and 143, 1979, pp. 9 and 17.

imports proportionally to their exports. The world demand of imports is consequently reduced in absolute terms while production costs continue to rise. Only the oil-exporting countries and the countries which master their domestic costs will be able to expand their relative shares in the stagnant or decreasing world trade. The method above, when applied to an international matrix of trade and capital movements, should give us the possibility to find out at least a theoretical solution to this crucial issue.

REFERENCES

Conseil National du Crédit, *Trente-quatrième Rapport Annuel* (Paris, 1979).

Institut National de la Statistique et des Etudes Economiques (INSEE), *Les Collections de l'Inséé*, Série C, 'Rapports sur les Comptes de la Nation', vol. 1, 2 and 3, (Paris, 1971–9).

Marczewski J., *Inflation and Unemployment in France, A Quantitative Analysis* (New York: Praeger, 1978) (1978a).

Marczewski J., 'Inflation, Redistribution of Factors and Unemployment: Illustrated by the Case of France', *The Review of Income and Wealth*, series 24, number 3, 1978, pp. 283–312 (1978b).

Marczewski J., *Vaincre l'inflation et le chômage*, (Paris: Economica, 1978) (1978c).

Marczewski J., *Politique monétaire et financière du IIIème Reich* (Paris: Sirey, 1941).

Organisation for Economic Cooperation and Development, *Allemagne* (Paris: OECD, 1980).

Statistisches Bundesamt (SB), *Volkswirtschaftliche Gesamtrechnungen*, Fachserie 18, Reihe 1, Wiesbaden (1978 and 1979).

9 W. W. Rostow: A Selective Chronological Bibliography

BOOKS

1948 *Essays on the British Economy of the Nineteenth Century* (Oxford: Clarendon Press) reprinted (Westport, Conn.: Greenwood Press, 1981).

1952 *The Process of Economic Growth* (New York: W. W. Norton; Oxford: Clarendon Press, 1953) second editions, 1960.

The Dynamics of Soviet Society, with Alfred Levin and others (New York: W. W. Norton; London: Secker & Warburg, 1953) second edition, 1967.

1953 *The Growth and Fluctuation of the British Economy, 1790–1850*, with Arthur D. Gayer, Anna Jacobson Schwartz, with the assistance of Isaiah Frank, 2 vols (Oxford: Clarendon Press). Second edition (Hassocks, England: Harvester Press, 1975).

1954 *The Prospects for Communist China*, with Richard W. Hatch, Frank A. Kierman, and Alexander Eckstein (New York: Technology Press, MIT, John Wiley).

1955 *An American Policy in Asia*, with Richard W. Hatch (New York: Technology Press, MIT/John Wiley).

1957 *A Proposal: Key to an Effective Foreign Policy*, with Max F. Millikan (New York: Harper).

1960 *The Making of Modern America, 1776–1940: An Essay on Three Themes* (monograph, available in mimeograph, Center for International Studies, MIT, Cambridge, Mass.)

The Stages of Economic Growth: A Non-Communist Manifesto (Cambridge University Press) second edition, 1971.

The United States in the World Arena (New York: Harper & Row) second edition, 1969.

1963 *The Economics of Take-off into Sustained Growth* (edited) (London: Macmillan; New York: St Martin's Press).

1964 *View from the Seventh Floor* (New York: Harper & Row).

1971 *Politics and the Stages of Growth* (Cambridge University Press).

1972 *The Diffusion of Power* (New York: Macmillan).

1975 *How It All Began: Origins of the Modern Economy* (New York: McGraw-Hill).

1978 *The World Economy: History and Prospect* (Austin: University of Texas Press; London: Macmillan).
Getting from Here to There (New York: McGraw-Hill; London: Macmillan).
1980 *Why the Poor Get Richer and the Rich Slow Down: Essays in the Marshallian Long Period* (Austin: University of Texas Press; London: Macmillan).
1981 *British Trade Fluctuations, 1868–1896: A Chronicle and a Commentary*, Ph.D. dissertation, Yale University, 1940 (New York: Arno Press).
Pre-Invasion Bombing Strategy: General Eisenhower's Decision of March 25, 1944 (Austin: University of Texas Press; Farnborough: Gower).
The Division of Europe after World War II: 1946 (Austin: University of Texas Press; Farnborough: Gower).
1982 *Europe after Stalin: Eisenhower's Three Decisions of March 11, 1953* (Austin: University of Texas Press).

ARTICLES, REVIEWS

1938 'Investment and the Great Depression', *Economic History Review*, 8, 136–8.
1939 'Investment and Real Wages, 1873–86', *Economic History Review*, 9, 144–59.
1940 'How Money Works', Public Affairs pamphlet, with Arther D. Gayer.
'James Harvey Rogers as an Economist', in *James Harvey Rogers, 1886–1939: In Memoriam* (Stamford, Conn.: Overbrook Press).
'Explanations of the "Great Depression" 1873–96: An Historian's View of Modern Monetary Theory', *Economic History* (Supplement of *The Economic Journal*), 4, 356–70.
1941 'Business Cycles, Harvests, and Politics: 1790–1850', *Journal of Economic History*, 1, 206–21.
1942 'Adjustments and Maladjustments After the Napoleonic Wars', *American Economic Review Supplement*, 32, 13–23.
1943 'Bagehot and the Trade Cycle', in *The Economist, 1843–1943* (Oxford University Press).
1946 'The American Diplomatic Revolution', an inaugural lecture before the University of Oxford on 12 November 1946.
1947 'The Political Basis for U.S. Foreign Policy', *Lloyds Bank Review*, October 1947, pp. 39–40.
1950 'Government and Private Enterprise in European Recovery', *Tasks of Economic History*, Supplement X, pp. 105–13.
'The United Nations' Report on Full Employment', *Economic Journal*, 60, 323–50, review.
1951 'Some Notes on Mr. Hicks and History', *American Economic Review*, 41, 316–24.
'The Historical Analysis of the Terms of Trade', *Economic History Review*, 4, 53–76.
'Two Analyses of Britain's Transition', review of Keith Hutchison, *The Decline and Fall of British Capitalism* and Robert A. Brady, *Crisis in Britain: Plans and Achievements of the Labour Government*, *Journal of Economic History*, 11, 55–9.
1953 *'A Note on "The Diffusion of Ideologies"'*, *Confluence*, 2, 31–42.
Review of Sir John Clapham, *A Concise Economic History of Britain, From Earliest Times to A.D. 1750*, *American Economic Review*.

'Notes on a New Approach to U.S. Economic Foreign Policy', *World Politics*, 5, 302–12.

'Toward a General Theory of Action', *World Politics*, 5, 530–54. Review of Talcott Parsons and Edward A. Shils (eds), *Toward a General Theory of Action*.

1954 'Factors in a British Trade Cycle', *Journal of Economic History*, 14, 266–70, review of R. C. O. Matthews, *A Study in Trade-Cycle History, Economic Fluctuations in Great Britain, 1833–42*.

1955 'Marx Was a City Boy, or Why Communism May Fail', *Harper's Magazine*, February 1955.

Review of *History of Peterborough, New Hampshire*, George Abbot Morison, Book One – *Narrative*, Etta M. Smith, Book Two – *Genealogies*.

'Russia and China Under Communism', *World Politics*, 7, 513–31.

'Trends in the Allocation of Resources in Secular Growth', in Leon H. Dupriez (ed.), *Economic Progress* (Louvain: Institut de Recherches Economiques et Sociales).

'Some General Reflections on Capital Formation and Economic Growth', in *Capital Formation and Economic Growth*, National Bureau of Economic Research (Princeton University Press).

1956 'The Take-off into Self-Sustained Growth', *Economic Journal*, 66, 25–48.

1957 'The Fallacy of the Fertile Gondolas', *Harvard Alumni Bulletin*, 25 May 1957.

'Ideas and Reality', *Confluence*, 6, 199–214.

'The Interrelation of Theory and Economic History', *Journal of Economic History*, 17, 509–23.

1958 'Foreign Aid: Next Phase', with Max F. Millikan, *Foreign Affairs*, 36, 418–36.

'The American National Style', *Daedalus*, 87, 110–14.

'The National Style', in Elting E. Morison (ed.), *The American Style: Essays in Value and Performance* (New York: Harper).

1959 'Débats et Combats. Histoire et Sciences Sociales: La Longue Durée', *Annales*, October–December 1959, pp. 710–18.

'The Stages of Economic Growth', *Economic History Review*, 11, 1–16.

'The Stages of Economic Growth and the Problems of Peaceful Coexistence', Lecture at the Institute of World Economy and International Relations, Academy of Sciences of the USSR, Moscow, May 25, 1959, published in *Fortune*.

1960 'The Problem of Achieving and Maintaining a High Rate of Economic Growth: A Historian's View', *American Economic Review*, 50, 106–18.

'Industrialization and Economic Growth', in *Proceedings* of First International Conference of Economic History, Stockholm (Paris: Mouton).

'The Dynamics of American Society', in *Postwar Economic Trends in the United States* (New York: Harper).

'Economics for the Nuclear Age', *Harvard Business Review*, 38, 41–9.

1962 'Some Lessons of History for Africa', in American Society of African Culture (ed.), *Pan-Africanism Reconsidered* (Berkeley and Los Angeles: University of California Press).

1963 'The Third Round', *Foreign Affairs*, 42, 1–10.

1964 'The Challenge of Democracy in Developing Nations', *Department of State Bulletin*, 50, 251–60.

'The Problems of Nuclear Arms', H. V. Hodson (ed.), *The Atlantic Future* (London: Longmans).

'The Planning of Foreign Policy', in E. A. Johnson (ed.), *The Dimensions of Diplomacy* (Baltimore: Johns Hopkins Press).

1965 'The Chapter That Keynes Never Wrote', *Department of State Bulletin*, 52, 454–9.

1966 'The Sharing of the Good Life', *Department of State Bulletin*, May 23, 1966.

1967 'The Great Transition: Tasks of the First and Second Post-War Generations' (Leeds University Press).

1969 'The Anglo-American Situation', in *The American Oxonian*, 56, 105–10.

1970 'The Past Quarter-Century as Economic History and the Tasks of International Economic Organization', *Journal of Economic History*, 30, 150–87.

'The Irrelevance of the Relevant', *The Addendum*, 1, 1–8.

1971 'An Historian Looks at History: 1970', *Southwestern Historical Quarterly*, 74, 385–92.

1972 Review of Ronald D. Brunner and Garry D. Brewer, *Organised Complexity: Empirical Theories of Political Development* (New York: Free Press), in *Political Science Quarterly*, 87, 280–2.

'Stages of Enterprise: The Business of America', in Daniel J. Boorstin (ed.), *American Civilization* (London: Thames and Hudson).

1973 'The Role of the President in a World of Diffusing Power', School for Advanced International Studies, 17, 19–34.

'The Politics of Arms Control or How to Make Nuclear Weapons Wither Away', in William R. Kintner and Robert L. Pfaltzgraff, Jr. (eds), *SALT: Implications for Arms Control in the 1970's* (Pittsburgh Press).

1975 'The Developing World in the Fifth Kondratieff Upswing', *The Annals*, 420, 111–24.

'Is the American Style Viable', *The Educational Forum*, 40, 457–68.

1976 'The Bankruptcy of Neo-Keynesian Economics', *Intermountain Economic Review*, 7, 1–12.

'A Rejoinder', *Intermountain Economic Review*, 7, 61–4.

'The Case for Sectoral Planning', in *National Economic Planning*, (Washington, D.C.: Chamber of Commerce of the United States).

1977 'A National Policy Towards Regional Change', *New England Economic Indicators*, May 1977, pp. 5–11.

'How Close is a Planned Economy?' *The Wharton Magazine*, 2, 32–7. A conversation with Walt W. Rostow and Paul A. Samuelson.

1978 'Food as the Foundation of Civilization', in Gary H. Koerselman and Kay E. Dull (eds), *Food and Social Policy, I* (Ames, Iowa: Iowa State University Press).

'Energy and Full Employment', in Charles J. Hitch (ed.), *Energy Conservation and Economic Growth* (Boulder, Colorado: Westview Press).

'Growth Rates at Different Levels of Income and Stage of Growth: Reflections on Why the Poor Get Richer and the Rich Slow Down', in *Research in Economic History: An Annual Compilation of Research*, 3 (Greenwich, Conn.: JAI Press.).

'The South: Regional Development and National Responsibility', in *Texas Business Review*, 52, 141–4.

1979 'A Fresh Start for the Americas', *Americas*, 31, 39–44.

'The Economic Power of the United States', in Donald W. Harward (ed.), *Power: Its Nature, Its Use, and Its Limits* (Cambridge, Mass.: Schenkman).

'A Simple Model of the Kondratieff Cycle', in Paul Uselding (ed.), *Research in Economic History: A Research Annual* (Greenwich, Conn.: JAI Press) 4, 1–36.

1980 'Energy and the Fate of the Nation', *Chemical Times and Trends*, 3, 25–8.

'Energy Target for the United States: A Net Export Position by 1990', *ORBIS*, 24, 3, 459–89.

Index